Fools, Frauds and Firebrands

T0191283

Also by Roger Scruton

Non fiction

Fiction

Fools, Frauds and Firebrands

Thinkers of the New Left

Roger Scruton

BLOOMSBURY CONTINUUM
LONDON • OXFORD • NEW YORK • NEW DELHI • SYDNEY

BLOOMSBURY CONTINUUM
Bloomsbury Publishing Plc
50 Bedford Square, London, WC1B 3DP, UK
29 Earlsfort Terrace, Dublin 2, Ireland

BLOOMSBURY, BLOOMSBURY CONTINUUM and the Diana logo are
trademarks of Bloomsbury Publishing Plc

First published 2015
Paperback edition, 2016
New edition, 2019

A catalogue record for this book is available from the British Library

Library of Congress Cataloguing-in-Publication data has been applied for

ISBN: PB: 978-1-4729-6521-9; ePDF: 978-1-4081-8734-0; ePUB: 978-1-4081-8735-7

6 8 10 9 7

Typeset by Integra Software Services Pvt. Ltd.
Printed and bound in the U.S.A. by Berryville Graphics Inc., Berryville, Virginia

To find out more about our authors and books visit www.bloomsbury.com
and sign up for our newsletters

CONTENTS

INTRODUCTION

n a previous book published in 1985 as *Thinkers of the New Left*, I brought together a series of articles from *The Salisbury Review*. I have reworked the original articles, cutting out writers like R. D. Laing and Rudolf Bahro who have nothing to say to us today, and including substantial new material devoted to developments that are increasingly influential – for example the stunning 'nonsense machine' invented by Lacan, Deleuze and Guattari, the scorched-earth attack on our 'colonial' inheritance by Edward Said, and the recent revival of 'the communist hypothesis' by Badiou and Žižek.

My previous book was published at the height of Margaret Thatcher's reign of terror, at a time when I was still teaching in a university, and known among British left-wing intellectuals as a prominent opponent of their cause, which was the cause of decent people everywhere. The book was therefore greeted with derision and outrage, reviewers falling over each other for the chance to spit on the corpse. Its publication was the beginning of the end for my university career, the reviewers raising serious doubts about my intellectual competence as well as my moral character. This sudden loss of status led to attacks on all my writings, whether or not they touched on politics.

One academic philosopher wrote to Longman, the original publisher, saying, 'I may tell you with dismay that many colleagues here [i.e. in Oxford] feel that the Longman imprint – a respected one – has been tarnished by association with Scruton's work.' He went on in a menacing manner, expressing the hope that 'the negative reactions generated by this particular publishing venture may make Longman think more carefully about its policy in the future'. One of Longman's best-selling educational writers threatened to take his products elsewhere if the book stayed in print and, sure enough, the remaining copies of *Thinkers of the New Left* were soon withdrawn from the bookshops and transferred to my garden shed.

I have naturally been reluctant to return to the scene of such a disaster. Gradually, however, in the wake of 1989, a measure of hesitation has entered the left-wing vision. It is now common to accept that not everything said, thought or done in the name of socialism has been intellectually respectable or morally right. I was perhaps more than normally alert to this possibility on account of my involvement, at the time of writing, with the underground networks in communist Europe. That involvement had brought me face to face with destruction, and it was obvious to most people who troubled to expose themselves to this destruction that leftist ways of thinking were the ultimate cause of it. *Thinkers of the New Left* appeared in samizdat editions in Polish and Czech, and was subsequently translated into Chinese, Korean and Portuguese. Gradually, and especially after 1989, it became easier for me to express my vision, and I have allowed my publisher, Robin Baird-Smith, to persuade me that a new book might bring relief to students compelled to chew on the glutinous prose of Deleuze, to treat seriously the mad incantations of Žižek, or to believe that there is more to Habermas's theory of communicative action than his inability to communicate it.

The reader will understand from the above paragraphs that this is not a word-mincing book. I would describe it rather as a provocation. However, I make every effort to explain what is good in the authors I review as well as what is bad. My hope is that the result can be read with profit by people of all political persuasions.

In preparing this book for the press I have been greatly helped by comments and criticisms from Mark Dooley, Sebastian Gardner, Robert Grant and Wilfrid Hodges, all of whom are innocent of the crimes committed in the following pages.

Scrutopia, January 2015

1 WHAT IS LEFT?

The modern use of the term 'left' derives from the French Estates General of 1789, when the nobility sat on the king's right, and the 'third estate' on his left. It might have been the other way round. Indeed, it *was* the other way round for everyone but the king. However, the terms 'left' and 'right' remain with us, and are now applied to factions and opinions within every political order. The resulting picture, of political opinions spread in a single dimension, can be fully understood only locally, and only in conditions of contested and adversarial government. Moreover, even where it captures the outlines of a political process, the picture can hardly do justice to the theories influencing that process, which form the climate of political opinion. Why, therefore, use the word 'left' to describe the writers considered in this book? Why use a single term to cover anarchists like Foucault, Marxist dogmatists like Althusser, exuberant nihilists like Žižek and American-style liberals like Dworkin and Rorty?

The reason is twofold: first the thinkers I discuss have identified themselves by that very term. Second, they illustrate an enduring outlook on the world, and one that has been a permanent feature of Western civilization at least since the Enlightenment, nourished by the elaborate social and political theories that I shall have occasion to discuss in what follows. Many of my subjects have been associated with the New Left, which rose to prominence during the 1960s and 70s. Others form part of the broad ground of post-war political thinking, according to which the state is or ought to be in charge of society and empowered to distribute its goods.

Thinkers of the New Left was published before the collapse of the Soviet Union, before the emergence of the European Union as an imperial power and before the transformation of China into an aggressive exponent of gangland capitalism. Thinkers on the left have naturally had to accommodate those developments. The collapse of communism in Eastern Europe and the weakness of socialist economies elsewhere gave a brief credibility to the economic policies of the 'new right', and even the British Labour Party climbed on to the bandwagon, dropping Clause IV (the commitment to state ownership) from its constitution and accepting that industry is no longer the direct responsibility of government.

For a while it even looked as though there might be an apology forthcoming, from those who had devoted their intellectual and political efforts to whitewashing the Soviet Union or praising the 'people's republics' of China and Vietnam. But the moment of doubt was short-lived. Within a decade the left establishment was back in the driving seat, with Noam Chomsky and Howard Zinn renewing their intemperate denunciations of America, the European left regrouped against 'neo-liberalism', as though this had been the trouble all along, Dworkin and Habermas collecting prestigious prizes for their barely readable but impeccably orthodox books, and the veteran communist Eric Hobsbawm rewarded for a lifetime of unswerving loyalty to the Soviet Union by his appointment as 'Companion of Honour' to the Queen.

True, the enemy was no longer described as before: the Marxist template did not easily fit the new conditions, and it seemed a trifle foolish to champion the cause of the working class, when its last members were joining the ranks of the unemployable or the self-employed. But then came the financial crisis, with people all around the world thrown into comparative poverty while the seeming culprits – the bankers, the financiers, and the speculators – escaped with their bonuses intact. As a result, books critical of market economics began to enjoy a new popularity, whether reminding us that real goods are not exchangeable (Michael Sandel: *What Money Can't Buy*) or arguing that markets, in current conditions, cause a massive transfer of wealth from the poorest to the richest (Joseph Stiglitz: *The Price of Inequality*, and Thomas Piketty: *Capital in the Twenty-first Century*). And from the ever-fertile source of Marxist humanism thinkers extracted new arguments to describe the moral and spiritual degradation of humanity in the condition of free exchange (Gilles Lipovetsky and Jean Serroy, *L'esthétisation du monde: vivre à l'âge du capitalisme artiste*; Naomi Klein, *No Logo*; Philip Roscoe, *I Spend, Therefore I Am*).

Thinkers and writers on the left therefore soon returned to equilibrium, assured the world that they had never really been taken in by communist propaganda, and renewed their attacks on Western civilization and its 'neo-liberal' economics as the principal threat to humanity in a globalized world. 'Right-wing' has remained as much a term of abuse today as it was before the fall of the Berlin Wall, and the attitudes described in this book have adapted themselves to the new conditions with very little moderation of their oppositional zeal. This curious fact is one of many puzzles that I consider in what follows.

The left-wing position was already clearly defined at the time when the distinction between left and right was invented. Leftists believe, with the Jacobins of the French Revolution, that the goods of this world are unjustly distributed, and that the fault lies not in human nature but in usurpations practised by a dominant class. They define themselves in opposition to established power, the champions of a new order that will rectify the ancient grievance of the oppressed.

Two attributes of the new order justify the pursuit of it: liberation and 'social justice'. These correspond roughly to the liberty and equality advocated at the French Revolution, but only roughly. The liberation advocated by left-wing movements today does not mean simply freedom from political oppression or the right to go about one's business undisturbed. It means emancipation from the 'structures': from the institutions, customs and conventions that shaped the 'bourgeois' order, and which established a shared system of norms and values at the heart of Western society. Even those left-wingers who eschew the libertarianism of the 1960s regard liberty as a form of *release* from social constraints. Much of their literature is devoted to deconstructing such institutions as the family, the school, the law and the nation state through which the inheritance of Western civilization has been passed down to us. This literature, seen at its most fertile in the writings of Foucault, represents as 'structures of domination' what others see merely as the instruments of civil order.

Liberation of the victim is a restless cause, since new victims always appear over the horizon as the last ones escape into the void. The liberation of women from male oppression, of animals from human abuse, of homosexuals and transsexuals from 'homophobia', even of Muslims from 'Islamophobia' – all these have been absorbed into the more recent leftist agendas, to be enshrined in laws and committees overseen by a censorious officialdom. Gradually the old norms of social order have been marginalized, or even penalized as violations of 'human rights'. Indeed, the cause of 'liberation' has seen the proliferation of more laws than were ever invented to suppress it – just think of what is now ordained in the cause of 'non-discrimination'.

Likewise the goal of 'social justice' is no longer equality before the law, or the equal claim to the rights of citizenship, as these were advocated at the Enlightenment. The goal is a comprehensive rearrangement of society, so that privileges, hierarchies, and even the unequal distribution of goods are either overcome or challenged. The more radical egalitarianism of the nineteenth-century Marxists and anarchists, who sought for the abolition of private property, perhaps no longer has widespread appeal. But behind the goal of 'social justice' there marches another and more dogged egalitarian mentality, which believes that inequality in whatever sphere – property, leisure, legal privilege, social rank, educational opportunities, or whatever else we might wish for ourselves and our children – is unjust until proven otherwise. In every sphere in which the social position of individuals might be compared, equality is the default position.

Built into the mild-mannered prose of John Rawls that assumption might pass unnoticed. In Dworkin's more agitated calls for 'respect as an equal', as opposed to 'equal respect', it might cause people to wonder where the argument is going. But the most important point to notice is that it is an argument that allows *nothing to stand in its way*. No existing custom, institution, law or hierarchy; no tradition, distinction, rule or piety can trump equality, if it cannot provide itself with independent credentials. Everything that does not conform to the egalitarian goal must be pulled down and built again, and the mere fact that some custom or institution has been handed down and accepted is no argument in its favour. In this way 'social justice' becomes a barely concealed demand for the 'clean sweep' of history that revolutionaries have always attempted.

The two goals of liberation and social justice are not obviously compatible, any more than were the liberty and equality advocated at the French Revolution. If liberation involves the liberation of individual potential, how do we stop the ambitious, the energetic, the intelligent, the good-looking and the strong from getting ahead, and what should we allow ourselves by way of constraining them? Best not to confront that impossible question. Best to summon the old resentments rather than to examine what would follow from expressing them. By declaring war on traditional hierarchies and institutions in the name of its two ideals, therefore, the left is able to obscure the conflict between them. Moreover, 'social justice' is a goal so overwhelmingly important, so unquestionably superior to the established interests that stand against it, as to purify every action done in its name.

It is important to take note of this purifying potential. Many people on the left are sceptical towards utopian impulses; at the same time, having allied themselves beneath a moralizing banner, they inevitably find themselves galvanized, inspired and eventually governed by the most fervent members of their sect. For politics on the left is politics with a *goal*: your place within the alliance is judged by the lengths you are prepared to go to on behalf of 'social justice', however defined. Conservatism – at least, conservatism in the British tradition – is a politics of custom, compromise and settled indecision. For the conservative, political association should be seen in the same way as friendship: it has no overriding purpose, but changes from day to day, in accordance with the unforeseeable logic of a conversation. Extremists within the conservative alliance, therefore, are isolated, eccentric and even dangerous. Far from being more deeply committed partners in a common enterprise, they are separated by their very purposefulness from those whom they seek to lead.[1]

Marx dismissed the various socialisms current in his day as 'utopian', contrasting 'utopian socialism' with his own 'scientific socialism' that promised 'full communism' as its predictable outcome. The 'historical inevitability' of this condition relieved Marx of the necessity to describe it. The 'science' consists in the 'laws of historical motion' set out in *Das Kapital* and elsewhere, according to which economic development brings about successive changes in the economic infrastructure of society, enabling us to predict that private property will one day disappear. After a period of socialist guardianship – a 'dictatorship of the proletariat' – the state will 'wither away', there will be neither law nor the need for it, and everything will be owned in common. There will be no division of labour and each person will live out the full range of his needs and desires, 'hunting in the morning, fishing in the afternoon, tending cattle in the evening and engaging in literary criticism after dinner', as we are told in *The German Ideology*.

To say that this is 'scientific' rather than utopian is, in retrospect, little more than a joke. Marx's remark about hunting, fishing, hobby farming and lit. crit. is the only attempt he makes to describe what life will be like without private property – and if you ask who gives you the gun or the fishing rod, who organizes the pack of hounds, who maintains the coverts and the waterways, who disposes of the milk and the calves and

---

[1] The argument here is spelled out at length in my book, *How to be a Conservative*, London, Bloomsbury, 2014. See also Chapter 10 below.

who publishes the lit. crit., such questions will be dismissed as 'beside the point', and as matters to be settled by a future that is none of your business. And as to whether the immense amount of organization required for these leisure activities of the universal upper class will be possible, in a condition in which there is no law, no property, and therefore no chain of command, such questions are too trivial to be noticed. Or rather, they are too serious to be considered, and therefore go unnoticed. For it requires but the slightest critical address, to recognize that Marx's 'full communism' embodies a contradiction: it is a state in which all the benefits of legal order are still present, even though there is no law; in which all the products of social cooperation are still in existence, even though nobody enjoys the property rights which hitherto have provided the sole motive for producing them.

The contradictory nature of the socialist utopias is one explanation of the violence involved in the attempt to impose them: it takes infinite force to make people do what is impossible. And the memory of the utopias has weighed heavily on both the New Left thinkers of the 1960s, and on the American left liberals who adopted their agenda. It is no longer possible to take refuge in the airy speculations that contented Marx. Real thinking is needed if we are to believe that history either tends or ought to tend in a socialist direction. Hence the emergence of socialist historians, who systematically downplay the atrocities committed in the name of socialism, and blame the disasters on the 'reactionary' forces that impeded socialism's advance. Rather than attempting to define the goals of liberation and equality, thinkers of the New Left instead created a mythopoeic narrative of the modern world, in which the wars and genocides were attributed to those who have resisted the righteous 'struggle' for social justice. History was rewritten as a conflict between good and evil, between the forces of light and the forces of darkness. And, however nuanced and embellished by its many brilliant exponents, this Manichean vision remains with us, enshrined in the school curriculum and in the media.

The moral asymmetry, which attributes to the left a monopoly of moral virtue, and uses 'right' always as a term of abuse, accompanies a logical asymmetry, namely, an assumption that the onus of proof lies always on the other side. Nor can this onus be discharged. Thus in the 1970s and early 1980s, when the theories of Marx were being recycled as the true account of the sufferings of humanity under 'capitalist' regimes, it was rare to find any mention in the left-wing journals of the criticisms that

Marx's writings had encountered during the previous century. Marx's theory of history had been put in question by Maitland, Weber and Sombart;[2] his labour theory of value by Böhm-Bawerk, Mises, and many more;[3] his theories of false consciousness, alienation and class struggle by a whole range of thinkers, from Mallock and Sombart to Popper, Hayek and Aron.[4] Not all those critics could be placed on the right of the political spectrum, nor had they all been hostile to the idea of 'social justice'. Yet none of them, so far as I could discover when I came to write this book, had been answered by the New Left with anything more than a sneer.

That said, we must recognize that the Marxist spectacles are no longer on the left-wing nose. Why they were removed, and by whom, it is hard to say. But for whatever cause, left-wing politics has discarded the revolutionary paradigm advanced by the New Left, in favour of bureaucratic routines and the institutionalization of the welfare culture. The two goals of liberation and social justice remain in place: but they are promoted by legislation, committees and government commissions empowered to root out the sources of discrimination. Liberation and social justice have been bureaucratized. In looking back at the left intellectuals in the decades before the collapse of the Soviet Union, therefore, I am observing a culture that now survives largely in its academic redoubts, feeding from the jargon-ridden prose that it amassed in university libraries, in the days when universities were part of the anti-capitalist 'struggle'.

But note that word. It belongs to an enclosed vocabulary, one that entered the language with Marxism and which was gradually simplified and regimented in the years when socialists were occupying the intellectual high ground. From its earliest days the communist movement had fought over language, and esteemed the theories of Marx partly because they provided convenient labels with which to brand both friend

---

[2] F. W. Maitland, *The Constitutional History of England*, London, 1908; W. Sombart, *Der Moderne Kapitalismus*, Berlin, 1902, 1916, 1927, and *Socialism and the Social Movement*, tr. M. Epstein, London, 1909; Max Weber, *Economy and Society*, tr. E. Fischoff et al., ed. Guenther Roth and Claus Wittich, vol. 1, New York, 1968.
[3] Eugen von Böhm-Bawerk, *Karl Marx and the Close of his System*, Clifton, NJ, 1949; Ludwig von Mises, *Socialism*, 2nd edn, New Haven, 1953.
[4] W. H. Mallock, *A Critical examination of Socialism*, London, 1909; W. Sombart, op. cit.; Karl Popper, *The Open Society and its Enemies*, 5th edn, London, 1966; F. A. Hayek, *The Road to Serfdom*, London, 1945; Raymond Aron, *Main Currents of Sociological Thought*, vol. 1, tr. Richard Howard and Helen Weaver, London, 1968.

and enemy and to dramatize the conflict between them. And this habit proved contagious, so that all subsequent leftist movements were to some extent tainted by it. Indeed, the transformation of the language of politics has been the principal legacy of the Left, and it is one aim of this book to rescue that language from socialist Newspeak.

We owe the term 'Newspeak' to George Orwell's chilling portrait of a fictitious totalitarian state. But the capture of language by the left is far older, beginning with the French Revolution and its slogans. When it took the turn that fascinated Orwell it was with the Socialist International and the eager engagement of the Russian intelligentsia. Those who emerged triumphant from the Second International in 1889 had been granted a vision of a transformed world. This Gnostic revelation was so clear that no argument was necessary, and no argument possible, that would provide it with a justifying proof. All that mattered was to distinguish those who shared the vision from those who dissented. And the most dangerous were those who dissented by so small a margin that they threatened to mingle their energies with yours, and so to pollute the pure stream of action.

From the beginning, therefore, labels were required that would stigmatize the enemies within and justify their expulsion: they were revisionists, deviationists, infantile leftists, utopian socialists, social fascists, and so on. The division between Menshevik and Bolshevik following the Second Congress of the Russian Social Democratic Labour Party in 1904 epitomized this process: those peculiar fabricated words, which were themselves crystallized lies, since the Mensheviks (minority) in fact composed the majority, were thereafter graven in the language of politics and in the motives of the communist elite.

The success of those labels in marginalizing and condemning the opponent fortified the communist conviction that you could change reality by changing words. You could create a proletarian culture, just by inventing the word 'proletcult'. You could bring about the downfall of the free economy, simply by shouting 'crisis of capitalism' every time the subject arose. You could combine the absolute power of the Communist Party with the free consent of the people, by announcing communist rule as 'democratic centralism' and describing the countries where it was imposed as 'people's democracies'. Newspeak reassembles the political landscape, dividing it in unfamiliar ways, and creating the impression that, like the anatomist's description of the human body, it reveals the hidden frame on which the superficial unities are hung. In that way it makes it easy to dismiss as illusions the realities by which we live.

Newspeak occurs whenever the primary purpose of language – which is to describe reality – is replaced by the rival purpose of asserting power over it. The fundamental speech-act is only superficially represented by the assertoric grammar. Newspeak sentences sound like assertions, but their underlying logic is that of the spell. They conjure the triumph of words over things, the futility of rational argument, and also the danger of resistance. As a result Newspeak developed its own special syntax, which – while closely related to the syntax deployed in ordinary descriptions – carefully avoids any encounter with reality or any exposure to the logic of rational argument. Françoise Thom has argued this in her brilliant study *La langue de bois*.[5] The purpose of communist Newspeak, in Thom's ironical words, has been 'to protect ideology from the malicious attacks of real things'.

Human individuals are the most important of those real things, the obstacles that all revolutionary systems must overcome, and which all ideologies must destroy. Their attachment to particulars and contingencies; their embarrassing tendency to reject what has been devised for their betterment; their freedom of choice and the rights and duties through which they exercise it – all these are obstacles to the conscientious revolutionaries, as they strive to implement their five-year plan. Hence the need to phrase political choice in such a way that individuals have no part in it. Newspeak prefers to speak of forces, classes and the march of history, and regards the actions of Great Men as acceptable subjects for discussion only because Great Men, like Napoleon, Lenin and Hitler, are really the expression of abstract forces, such as imperialism, revolutionary socialism and fascism.[6] The 'isms' that govern political change work *through* people, but not *from* them.

Connected with the relentless use of abstractions is the feature that Thom describes as 'pan-dynamism'. The world of Newspeak is a world of abstract forces, in which individuals are merely local embodiments of the 'isms' that are revealed in them. Hence it is a world without action. But it is not a world without movement. On the contrary, everything is in constant motion, swept onwards by the forces of progress, or impeded by the forces of reaction. There is no equilibrium, no stasis and no rest in the

---

[5] Françoise Thom, *La langue de bois*, Paris, 1984, tr. C. Janson, *Newspeak*, London, 1985.
[6] See the famous letter from Engels to Borgius, translated Sidney Hook, *New International* 1 (3) (September–October 1934), pp. 81–5.

world of Newspeak. All stillness is a deception, the quietus of a volcano that could erupt at any time. Peace never appears in Newspeak as a condition of rest and normality. It is always something to 'fight for', and 'Fight for Peace!', 'Struggle for Peace!' took their place among the official slogans of the Communist Party.

From the same source comes the penchant for 'irreversible' changes. Since everything is in motion and the 'struggle' between the forces of progress and the forces of reaction is always and everywhere, it is important that the triumph of ideology over reality be constantly recorded and endorsed. Hence progressive forces always achieve 'irreversible changes', while reactionary forces are wrong-footed by their contradictory and merely 'nostalgic' attempts to defend a doomed social order.

Many words with respectable origins end up as Newspeak, used to denounce, exhort and condemn without regard for observable realities. Of no word has this been more true than the term 'capitalism', when used to condemn free economies as forms of slavery and exploitation. We can disagree with the central argument put forward by Marx in *Das Kapital*, while accepting that there is such a thing as economic capital. And we might describe an economy in which substantial capital is in the hands of private individuals as capitalist, meaning that term as a neutral description that may or may not, in due course, form part of an explanatory theory. But that is not how the term is used in such phrases as 'the crisis of capitalism', 'capitalist exploitation', 'capitalist ideology', and so on, where it functions again as a spell, the equivalent in economic theory of Khrushchev's great scream from the rostrum of the United Nations: 'We will bury you!' By describing free economies with this term, we cast the spell that extinguishes them. The reality of the free economy disappears behind the description, to be replaced by a strange baroque edifice, constantly falling to the ground in a dream-sequence of ruin.

The concepts that arise in normal dialogue arise from the need to compromise, to reach agreements, to establish peaceful coordination with people who do not share our projects or our affections, but who are as much in need of space as we are. Such concepts have little or nothing to do with the schemes and plans of the revolutionary left, since they permit those who use them to change course, to drop one goal and pick up another, to amend their ways and to show the kind of flexibility on which lasting peace always, in the end, depends.

Hence, although I, the intellectual in my garret, can contemplate with satisfaction and a clear conscience the 'liquidation of the bourgeoisie', when I enter the shop downstairs I must speak another language. Only in the most distant sense is this woman behind the counter a member of the bourgeoisie. If I choose nevertheless so to see her it is because I am conjuring with the word 'bourgeois' – I am trying to gain power over this person through labelling her. In confronting the shopkeeper as a human being I must renounce this presumptuous bid for power, and accord to her a voice of her own. My language must make room for her voice, and that means it must be shaped to permit the resolution of conflict, the forging of agreement, including the agreement to differ. I make remarks about the weather, grumble about politics, 'pass the time of day' – and my language has the effect of softening reality, of making it pliable and serviceable. Newspeak, which denies reality, also hardens it, by turning it into something alien and resistant, a thing to be 'struggled with' and triumphed over.

I may have come down from my garret with a plan in view, intending the first move towards the liquidation of the bourgeoisie about which I had read in my Marxist textbook. But this plan will not survive the first exchange of words with my chosen victim, and the attempt to impose it or to speak the language that announces it will have the same effect as the wind in Aesop's fable, competing with the sun to remove the coat of a traveller. Ordinary language warms and softens; Newspeak freezes and hardens. And ordinary discourse generates out of its own resources the concepts that Newspeak forbids: fair/unfair; just/unjust; right/duty; honest/dishonest; legal/illegal; yours/mine. Such distinctions, which belong to the free exchange of feelings, opinions and goods, also, when freely expressed and acted upon, create a society in which order is spontaneous and not planned, and in which the unequal distribution of assets arises 'by an invisible hand'.

Newspeak does not merely impose a plan; it also eliminates the discourse through which human beings can live without one. If justice is referred to in Newspeak, it is not the justice of individual dealings, but 'social justice', the kind of 'justice' imposed by a plan, which invariably involves depriving individuals of things that they have acquired by fair dealing in the market. In the opinion of almost all the thinkers whom I discuss in what follows, government is the art of seizing and then redistributing the things to which all citizens are supposedly entitled. It is not the expression of a pre-existing social order shaped by our free agreements and our natural disposition to hold ourselves and our neighbours to account. It is the creator and manager of a social order framed according to an idea of 'social justice' and imposed on the people by a series of top-down decrees.

Intellectuals are naturally attracted by the idea of a planned society, in the belief that they will be in charge of it. As a result they tend to lose sight of the fact that real social discourse is part of day-to-day problem solving and the minute search for agreement. Real social discourse veers away from 'irreversible changes', regards all arrangements as adjustable, and allows a voice to those whose agreement it needs. From just the same source stems the English common law and the parliamentary institutions that have embodied the sovereignty of the British people.

Repeatedly in what follows we will encounter the Newspeak of left-leaning thinkers. Where conservatives and old-fashioned liberals speak of authority, government and institutions, those on the left refer to power and domination. Laws and offices play only a marginal part in the left-wing vision of political life, while classes, powers and the forms of control are invoked as the root phenomena of the civil order, together with the 'ideology' that mystifies those things and rescues them from judgement. Newspeak represents the political process as a constant 'struggle' concealed by fictions of legitimacy and allegiance. Peel away the ideology, and the 'truth' of politics is revealed. The truth is power, and the hope of deposing it.

Hence almost nothing of political life as we know it finds a place in the thinking of those whom I describe in these pages. Institutions like Parliament and the common law courts; spiritual callings associated with churches, chapels, synagogues and mosques; schools and professional bodies; private charities, clubs, and societies; Scouts, Guides and village tournaments; football teams, brass bands and orchestras; choirs, theatre-groups and philately groups – in short all the ways in which people associate, and create from their consensual intermingling the patterns of authority and obedience through which they live, all the 'little platoons' of Burke and Tocqueville – are missing from the leftist worldview or, if present (as they are present in Gramsci and E. P. Thompson, for example), both sentimentalized and politicized, so as to become part of the 'struggle' of the working class.

We should not be surprised that, when the communists seized power in Eastern Europe, their first task was to decapitate the little platoons – so that Kádár, when Minister of the Interior in the 1948 government in

Hungary, managed to destroy five thousand in a single year. Newspeak, which sees the world in terms of power and struggle, encourages the view that all associations not controlled by the righteous leaders are a danger to the state. And by acting on this view you make it true. When the seminar, the troop or the choir can meet only with the permission of the Party, the Party automatically becomes their enemy.

In this way, it seems to me, it is not an accident that the triumph of leftist ways of thinking has so often led to totalitarian government. The pursuit of abstract social justice goes hand in hand with the view that power struggles and relations of domination express the truth of our social condition, and that the consensual customs, inherited institutions and systems of law that have brought peace to real communities are merely the disguises worn by power. The goal is to seize that power, and to use it to liberate the oppressed, distributing all the assets of society according to the just requirements of the plan.

Intellectuals who think that way are already ruling out the possibility of compromise. Their totalitarian language does not set out a path of negotiation but instead divides human beings into innocent and guilty groups. Behind the impassioned rhetoric of the *Communist Manifesto*, behind the pseudo-science of Marx's labour theory of value, and behind the class analysis of human history, lies a single emotional source – resentment of those who control things. This resentment is both rationalized and amplified by the proof that property owners form a 'class'. According to the theory, the 'bourgeois' class has a shared moral identity, a shared and systematic access to the levers of power, and a shared body of privileges. Moreover all those good things are acquired and retained through the 'exploitation' of the proletariat, which has nothing to part with except its labour, and which will therefore always be cheated of its just deserts.

That theory has been effective not merely because it serves the function of amplifying and legitimizing resentment, but also because it is able to expose its rivals as 'mere ideology'. Here, I believe, is the most cunning feature of Marxism: that it has been able to pass itself off as a science. Having hit on the distinction between ideology and science, Marx set out to prove that his own ideology was *in itself* a science. Moreover, Marx's alleged science undermined the beliefs of his opponents. The theories of the rule of law, the separation of powers, the right of property, and so on, as these had been expounded by 'bourgeois' thinkers like Montesquieu and Hegel, were shown, by the Marxian class analysis, to be not truth-seeking but power-seeking devices: ways of hanging on to the privileges conferred by the bourgeois order. By exposing this ideology as a self-serving pretence the class-theory vindicated its own claims to scientific objectivity.

There is a kind of theological cunning in this aspect of Marxist thought, a cunning that we find also in Foucault's conception of the *episteme*, which is an updated version of Marx's theory of ideology. Since the class-theory is a genuine science, bourgeois political thought is ideology. And since the class-theory exposes bourgeois thought as ideology, it must be science. We have entered the magic circle of a creation myth. Moreover, by dressing up the theory in scientific language Marx has endowed it with the character of a badge of initiation. Not everybody can speak this language. A scientific theory defines the elite that can understand and apply it. It offers proof of the elite's enlightened knowledge and therefore of its title to govern. It is this feature that justifies the charge made by Eric Voegelin, Alain Besançon and others, that Marxism is a kind of Gnosticism, a title to 'government through knowledge'.[7]

Looked at with the superman superciliousness of Nietzsche, resentment may seem like the bitter dregs of the 'slave morality', the impoverished loss of spirit that comes about when people take more pleasure in bringing others down than in raising themselves up. But that is the wrong way to look at it. Resentment is not a good thing to feel, either for its subject or its object. But the business of society is to conduct our social life so that resentment does not occur: to live by mutual aid and fellowship, not so as to be all alike and inoffensively mediocre, but so as to gain others' cooperation in our small successes. Living in this way we create the channels through which resentment drains away of its own accord: channels like custom, gift, hospitality, shared worship, penitence, forgiveness and the common law, all of which are instantly stopped up when the totalitarians come to power. Resentment is to the body politic what pain is to the body: it is bad to feel it, but good to be capable of feeling it, since without the ability to feel it we will not survive. Hence we should not resent the fact that we resent, but accept it, as a part of the human condition, something to be managed along with all our other joys and afflictions. However, resentment can be transformed into a governing emotion and a social cause, and thereby gain release from the constraints that normally contain it. This happens

---

[7] See Eric Voegelin, *Science, Politics and Gnosticism*, Washington, 1968; Alain Besançon, *The Intellectual Origins of Leninism*, tr. Sarah Matthews, Oxford, 1981.

when resentment loses the specificity of its target, and becomes directed to society as a whole. That, it seems to me, is what happens when left-wing movements take over. In such cases resentment ceases to be a response to another's unmerited success and becomes instead an existential posture: the posture of the one whom the world has betrayed. Such a person does not seek to negotiate within existing structures, but to gain total power, so as to abolish the structures themselves. He will set himself against all forms of mediation, compromise and debate, and against the legal and moral norms that give a voice to the dissenter and sovereignty to the ordinary person. He will set about destroying the enemy, whom he will conceive in collective terms, as the class, group or race that hitherto controlled the world and which must now in turn be controlled. And all institutions that grant protection to that class or a voice in the political process will be targets for his destructive rage.

That posture is, in my view, the core of a serious social disorder. Our civilization has lived through this disorder, not once or twice but half a dozen times since the Reformation. In considering the thinkers whom I discuss in this book we will, I believe, understand this disorder in a new way – not merely as a misplaced religion or a form of Gnosticism, as other commentators have seen it, but also as a repudiation of what we, the inheritors of Western civilization, have received as our historical bequest. I call to mind the words of Goethe's Mephistopheles, when called upon to explain himself: *Ich bin der Geist der stets verneint* – I am the spirit who always denies, the one who reduces Something to Nothing, and who thereby undoes the work of creation.

This essential negativity can be perceived in many of the writers whom I discuss. Theirs is an oppositional voice, a cry against the actual on behalf of the unknowable. The generation of the 1960s was not disposed to ask the fundamental question how social justice and liberation could be reconciled. It wished only for the theories, however opaque and unintelligible, that would authorize its opposition to the existing order.[8] It had identified the rewards of intellectual life through an imagined unity between the intellectuals and the working class, and had sought for a language that would expose and delegitimize the 'powers' that maintained the 'bourgeois' order in being. Newspeak was essential to its programme, reducing what others saw as authority,

---

[8] See Peter Collier and David Horowitz, *Destructive Generation: Second Thoughts about the Sixties*, New York, Simon & Schuster, 1989.

legality and legitimacy to power, struggle and domination. And when, in the works of Lacan, Deleuze and Althusser, the nonsense machine began to crank out its impenetrable sentences, of which nothing could be understood except that they all had 'capitalism' as their target, it looked as though Nothing had at last found its voice. Henceforth the bourgeois order would be vaporized and mankind would march victorious into the Void.

2 RESENTMENT IN BRITAIN: HOBSBAWM AND THOMPSON

I t is a remarkable feature of the English reading public that it is always ready to treat historians as leaders in the world of ideas. As the newly formed Labour Party took shape as a political force in the early twentieth century, the popular histories of H. G. Wells, the Webbs and their fellow Fabians made socialism synonymous with 'progress'. The rewriting of history with the socialist message buried deep within it thereafter became a kind of orthodoxy on the left, with R. H. Tawney's *Religion and the Rise of Capitalism* of 1926 becoming a seminal text for a whole generation of British intellectuals. For Tawney the Labour movement stood side by side with the Protestant churches against the 'acquisitive society' that he had criticized in an earlier book of that title. It was a famous historian, Arnold Toynbee, who gave his name to Toynbee Hall, home of the Workers Educational Association (WEA), where Tawney resided along with his friend William Beveridge, who was to be one of the architects of the Welfare State. Labour history and the WEA were thereafter inextricably mixed, and it became almost a dogma on the British intellectual left that you joined forces with the workers by teaching them history.

Among the historians whose work laid the foundations for the New Left in Britain two in particular stand out, both for the brilliance of their writing and for the far-reaching impact of their commitments. Eric Hobsbawm and E. P. Thompson were nurtured by the communist movement that swept so many into its embrace before and during the Second World War. And both were active in supporting the peace movement in the years when this was the key aim of Soviet foreign policy. But while Hobsbawm was an establishment figure and a respected member of the academy, Thompson was never comfortable in an academic environment, and left the University of Warwick in protest at its commercialization in 1971. He prided himself as a freelance intellectual in the mould of Karl Marx. His writings appeared in reviews and pamphlets, and his magnum opus – *The Making of the English Working Class* – lay well outside the framework of academic social history as that was conceived in 1963, when the work was published.

Hobsbawm has been much criticized, less for his communist sympathies than for his dogged loyalty to the Party throughout the exposure of its crimes, abandoning his membership only when he had no choice, the Communist Party of Great Britain having finally dissolved itself in embarrassment in 1990. Thompson, by contrast, had left the Party in 1956, in response to the Soviet invasion of Hungary, which the Communist Party of Great Britain refused to condemn, Hobsbawm affirming (in the *Daily Worker*, 9 November 1956) that he approved of what was happening in Hungary, though 'with a heavy heart'. Until his death in 2012 Hobsbawm continued to extend his heavy-hearted approval to atrocities that other former communists reviewed with growing outrage, and this has cast a certain shadow over his reputation. But his case also illustrates just how far you can go in collaborating with crime, when the crime is committed on the left. Crimes committed on the right receive no such absolution; and this tells us something important about left-wing movements, which seem to have the capacity assumed by religions, both to authorize crime and to wash the conscience of those who connive at it.

It is indeed in religious terms that we should understand the fascination that communism exerted over young intellectuals between the wars. The Cambridge spies – Philby, Burgess, Maclean and Blunt – betrayed many people to their deaths and, by revealing the identities of those East European patriots who were organizing resistance to the Nazis in the hope of a democratic, rather than a communist, future, they ensured that Stalin would be able to 'liquidate' the most important opponents of his planned advance into Eastern Europe.

This caused no apparent remorse to the spies, who were animated by a compulsive repudiation of their country and its institutions. They belonged to an elite whose members had lost confidence in their right to inherited privilege, and who had made a religion from negating the values instilled by the society into which they were born. They were hungry for the philosophy that would vindicate their destructive fixation, and the Communist Party provided it, offering not only doctrine and commitment, but membership, authority and obedience – the very things that, in their inherited form, the spies were determined to reject.

Clandestine organizations create a band of visiting angels, who will move among ordinary people crowned by a halo that is observable only to themselves. But this Freemasonry of the elect was not the only source of the Communist Party's appeal. Its doctrine promised both a radiant future and a path of heroic 'struggle' on the way to it. European society had all but destroyed itself in the First World War, from which ordinary people emerged with only losses and no compensating gains. To young intellectuals disillusioned with the ensuing reality, Utopia had become a precious asset. It was the one thing to be trusted, precisely because it contained nothing real. It demanded sacrifice and commitment; it filled life with meaning, by providing a formula that rewrote every negative as a positive, every destructive act as an act of creation. Utopia issued instructions, implacable, secret but authoritative instructions that ordered you to betray everything and everybody that stood in its way – which meant everything and everybody. The thrill of all this was irresistible to people who were taking revenge on a world that they had refused to inherit.

It was not only in Britain that the Communist Party exerted its malignant influence. In a vivid and disturbing book Czesław Miłosz has described the Satanic power of communism over his generation of Polish intellectuals, closing their minds to all countervailing arguments and extinguishing, one by one, the loyalties by which their fellow citizens lived – loyalties to family, Church, country and the legal order.[1] The writers, artists and musicians of France and Germany also fell under the spell. The Communist Party appealed not because of its concrete policies or any believable programme of action within the existing order. It appealed because it addressed the *inner* disorder of the intellectual class, in a world where there was nothing real to believe in.

The Party's ability to turn the negative to the positive, and repudiation to redemption, offered precisely the psychic therapy of which those who had lost all religious faith and all civic affection stood in need. Their negative condition was well expressed, on behalf of the French intellectuals, by André Breton, in his second Surrealist Manifesto of 1930:

Everything remains to be done, every means must be worth trying, in order to lay waste the ideas of family, country, religion ... [Surrealists] intend to savour fully the profound sorrow, so well acted, with which the bourgeois public ... greets the steadfast and unyielding need they

---

[1] *The Captive Mind*, 1953, tr. Jane Zielonko, Harmondsworth, Penguin Modern Classics, 2001.

display to laugh like savages in the presence of the French flag, to vomit their disgust in the face of every priest, and to level at the breed of 'basic duties' the long-range weapon of sexual cynicism.

Childish though that seems in retrospect, it is also a transparent appeal for help. Breton is calling for a system of belief that would offer a new order and a new form of membership – one that would turn all those negatives around, and rewrite them in the language of self-affirmation.

Hobsbawm had more excuse than most of the Communist Party's new recruits. Born in Alexandria to Jewish parents, orphaned in childhood, and living in Berlin with the relatives who had adopted him, he suffered the trauma of Hitler's rise to power in his most vulnerable years. Escaping in the nick of time with his adoptive family to England he found himself uprooted, traumatized, with a mind wiped clean of all inherited loyalties and yet hungry for something that would give sense to the intellectual life to which he was so perfectly adapted and which would also recruit him in the war against fascism. He attached himself to the communist cause with unswerving devotion, and studied the ways in which he could advance that cause through scholarship.

It is impossible to know, and probably unwise to enquire, how much intellectual communists of Hobsbawm's generation were involved in the subversive activities that we now associate with the circle around Philby, Burgess and Maclean. Suspicions have been raised concerning the historian of the English civil war, Christopher Hill, a Foreign Office official during the crucial last two years of the war, when Stalin was dependent on his London spies to facilitate the takeover of Eastern Europe. Hill, subsequently Master of Balliol, was a member of the Communist Party Historians Group in Oxford after the war, alongside Hobsbawm, Thompson and Raphael Samuel. In 1952 he and Samuel founded the influential journal *Past and Present*, devoted to the Marxist reading of history. Associated with this work was the radical sociologist Ralph Miliband, who came as a refugee from Belgium in 1940, and whose Polish father had fought in the Soviet army against his own country in the Polish–Soviet war of 1920 – the war in which Lenin tried, but failed, to establish the bridge that would unite the communist movements in Russia and Germany.

Miliband was an active contributor to the *New Reasoner*, established by E. P. Thompson and others in 1958. This joined with the *Universities and Left Review* to become the *New Left Review* in 1960 (see Chapter 7 below). His sympathies were with the international socialist movement, but he was never, to my knowledge, a member of the Communist Party, even if inclined to the revolutionary, rather than the parliamentary 'road to socialism'. His disappointment with the Labour Party, which he joined in 1951, finds vitriolic expression in his book *Capitalist Democracy in Britain*, published in 1982. In that work Miliband argues that the Labour Party, through endorsing the institutions of British politics, had effectively silenced the voice of the working class, and so helped to contain the 'pressure from below' that had elsewhere erupted in revolution. At the same time he grudgingly acknowledged that the ability of British institutions to contain protests from below explains the unparalleled peace that the British people have enjoyed since the end of the seventeenth century. Substitute the words 'respond to' for the word 'contain' and that sentence would be the first step in a right-wing riposte to Miliband's skewed reading of our national history.

Whatever the extent of their involvement in communist politics, those writers are distinguished from the Cambridge spies and the fellow travellers by one fact above all, which is their intellectual seriousness. They saw communism as an attempt to put the philosophy of Karl Marx into practice, and accepted Marxism as the first and only attempt to elevate the study of history to the status of a science. Their interest for us today is inseparable from their desire to rewrite history in Marxist terms, and in doing so to use historical understanding as an instrument of social policy.

No reader of Hobsbawm's historical works can fail to be engaged by them. Their breadth of knowledge is matched by the elegance of their prose, and it is a testimony to Hobsbawm's talents, as a scholar and a man of letters, that he was elected to Fellowship by both the British Academy and the Royal Society of Literature. His four-volume history of the emergence of the modern world – *The Age of Revolution 1789–1848*, *The Age of Capital 1848–1875*, *The Age of Empire, 1875–1914*, and *The Age of Extremes, 1914–1991* – is a remarkable work of synthesis, seriously misleading only in the fourth volume, where the attempt to whitewash the communist experiment and to lay the blame for all ills at the door of 'capitalism' has an aspect that is partly sinister, partly quaint. Hobsbawm's account of the Industrial Revolution and its imperial outreach – *Industry and Empire: From 1750 to the Present Day* – has won a well-deserved place as a school textbook on the subject, reprinted almost every year since its first publication in 1968. Reflecting on the method adopted in those books Hobsbawm wrote that 'no serious discussion of history is possible which doesn't refer back to Marx or, more exactly, which does not start where he starts. And that means, basically...a materialist conception of history.'[2] And it is from this claim that any evaluation of Hobsbawm's contribution to the intellectual life should begin.

Marx's 'materialist' theory of history was a response to Hegel, who had seen the evolution of human societies as driven by the consciousness of their members, as this is expressed in religion, morality, law and culture. Not so, Marx famously wrote. It is 'not consciousness that determines life, but life that determines consciousness' (*The German Ideology*). Life is not a conscious process occurring in the realm of ideas, but a 'material' reality, rooted in the needs of the organism. And the basis of social life is likewise material, involving the production, distribution and exchange of goods. Economic activity is the 'base' on which the 'superstructure' of society rests. Those 'mental' or 'spiritual' factors that are so often singled out as the agents of historical change – religious movements, legal innovations, the self-understanding and culture of local communities, even the institutions that form the identity of a nation state – are to be understood as by-products of material production. Human societies evolve because productive forces grow, necessitating constant revolutions in property relations, from slavery to feudalism to capitalism and beyond. The social superstructure changes in response to the needs and opportunities of production, in something like the way species adapt to evolutionary pressure. And the consciousness of a society, in religion, culture and law, is the outcome of this process, driven, in the last analysis, by the laws of economic growth.

How to make sense of this is a fascinating question to which only one modern thinker has, to my knowledge, given a plausible answer – and that is G. A. Cohen, in *Karl Marx's Theory of History: A Defence*.[3] But the idea can be grasped in outline through a few examples. Consider the changes in English land law during the course of the nineteenth century. These empowered life-tenants to sell their estates free from encumbrances, so permitting the use of the land for mining and industrial production. That is an example of economic forces bringing about a far-reaching change in property relations and a transfer of power and initiative from the landed aristocracy to the rising middle class. Consider the rise of the

---

[2] 'What Can History Tell us about Contemporary Society', in *On History*, London, Abacus, 1998, p. 42.
[3] Princeton, NJ, Princeton University Press, 1979.

novel as an art form during the second half of the eighteenth century. This addressed the self-image of the emerging society, entrenching ideas of liberty and individual responsibility in the life-plans of the property-owning class. That shows the emergence of a new artistic form in response to fundamental changes in the economic order. Consider the various electoral reforms during the nineteenth century. These served to consolidate the power of the new property-owning classes, and to ensure that legislation would protect their interests. That shows political institutions changing in response to economic need.

In all such examples we see the demand of productive forces for the institutions and the culture that will facilitate their expansion. The expansion of the productive forces is the *basic* fact, the one that explains all the social changes that are brought about in response to it. Institutions and cultural forms exist because they offer their support to economic relations, in the way that the roof on a house supports the walls on which it stands. And the economic relations exist because they enable productive forces to grow in response to technological and demographic change.

However, it is one thing to claim that institutions come into being because they are functional, but another, and trivial, thing to claim that they disappear because they are dysfunctional. Thus when the law of inheritance impeded the development of natural resources in England it became economically dysfunctional. As a result there was pressure to change the law. But it does not follow that the original law came into being because it was economically functional. It might have been – indeed it was – a response to demands of family and dynastic ambition. Furthermore, social institutions can be economically dysfunctional and still persist, on account of other functions that they perform, or merely because of the affection that maintains them in being as 'ours'. Thus the policy of the Tokugawa Shogunate, which isolated Japan from much of the world between 1641 and 1853, was economically dysfunctional, preventing the explosion of international trade that subsequently led to the great wealth of the country. But it was functional in other ways, endowing Japan with a period of extended peace that has few parallels in the history of any nation, and encouraging the development of the refined Shinto culture that made such consoling room for the dead.

So what exactly does the Marxist theory of history amount to? There is an indisputable web of connections between social and economic life; but which is cause and which effect cannot be determined, since there are no experiments that could put the matter to the test. In practice, therefore,

Marxist history is less an explanation than a shift of emphasis. Where others might study law, religion, art and family life, Marxists concentrate on the 'material' realities, which means the production of food, houses, machinery, furniture and means of transport. If you are sufficiently selective, you can give the impression that the production of material goods is the real motor of social change, since without them, after all, no other goods can exist. While this is a useful stimulus in the search for salient facts, it falls well short of a causal explanation, and is quite misleading as an account of modern history, in which legal and political innovation has been as often the cause of economic change as the effect of it.

More interesting for Marxist historians of Hobsbawm's generation has been the idea of class. And, as we shall see in discussing Perry Anderson (Chapter 7), such historians emphasize periods of upheaval and rebellion, hoping to find evidence of a 'class struggle' that fuels the social and political turmoil. In this connection Marx distinguished 'the class in itself' from 'the class for itself'. In a capitalist system the proletariat consists of all those who have nothing to exchange save their labour power. Objectively speaking the members of the proletariat form a class because they have shared economic interests, in particular the interest in breaking free from 'wage slavery' and obtaining control over the means of production. The bourgeoisie form a class for the same reason – namely their shared interest in retaining control over the means of production. From those competing interests arises the 'class struggle', which is a contest in the world of material forces, of which the participants themselves may not be fully aware.

People do not merely *have* economic interests. They are sometimes conscious of them. And in becoming conscious they develop elaborate stories of their entitlement and of the justice or injustice of their situation. When this happens, and when the consciousness of shared economic interests is itself also shared, the 'class for itself' comes into being. And this, for Marx, is the first step towards revolution.

All that is both poetic and exciting. But is it true? And if it is true, does it point to a new way of doing history? Hobsbawm, Thompson, Hill, Samuel and Miliband thought that the answer to both those questions is 'yes'. As a result they set out to rewrite the history of the British people as a history of 'class struggle'. The result is a constant emphasis on the material goods and social advantages of the rising middle class, and on the impoverishment and degradation of the workers. Here is a typical summary from Hobsbawm, dealing with the reign of George IV. It follows a prolonged sneer directed at the rural aristocracy with their hunting, shooting and public schools:

> Equally placid and prosperous were the lives of the numerous parasites of rural aristocratic society, high and low – that rural and small-town work of functionaries of and suppliers to the nobility and gentry, and the traditional, somnolent, corrupt and, as the Industrial Revolution proceeded, increasingly reactionary professions. The Church and the English universities slumbered on, cushioned by their incomes, their privileges and abuses, and their relations among the peerage, their corruption attacked with greater consistency in theory than in practice. The lawyers, and what passed for a civil service, were unreformed and unregenerate...[4]

No doubt there is truth in that. But it is framed in the language of class war, and in terms that do not concede a place for any defence either of the people described or of the system that contained them. Those 'parasites' might equally have been described as merchants and tradesmen, and the 'reactionary' professions as the teachers, doctors and agents who, for all their faults, ensured that social capital was passed on and improved throughout the nineteenth century. As in every period, there must have been a few good people among them, including many averse to corruption. Hobsbawm concedes that corruption in the Church was being vigorously criticized; but he dismisses the criticism as more consistent 'in theory than in practice'. As for the lawyers and the civil servants, they are not entitled to a hearing. Even the extraordinary social mobility of nineteenth-century Britain, which enabled Sir Robert Peel, father of the Prime Minister, to rise in a lifetime from yeoman farmer to titled captain of industry, is wrapped in the same vindictive language, as though it were a fault of the class system that it could extend a welcome to those who made their way in it.

The description of the new working class is loaded the other way. Its traditional world, and the old 'moral economy', as E. P. Thompson was to describe it, had been destroyed by the Industrial Revolution. Confined in the new sprawling cities, reminded at every point of their 'exclusion from human society', condemned to work for the market rate, as defined by liberal economists, which was the lowest rate at which labour would

---

[4] *Industry and Empire*, Harmondsworth, Penguin, 1969, p. 81.

exchange for money, the workers were saved from starvation, when unemployed, by a Poor Law 'not so much intended to help the unfortunate as to stigmatize the self-confessed failures of society'.[5]

This was in fact the time of the Friendly Societies and Building Societies, which were creating the opportunities for working people to become home-owners and members of the new middle class. It was the time of the Mechanics Institutes, established by charitable members of the middle class to offer education to those in full-time employment. It was the time of the working men's libraries, of the colliery bands and of the Factory Acts which one by one destroyed the worst of the abuses that the industrial process made possible. But all those things are dismissed by Hobsbawm, for whom they are not gestures of kindness but simply ways of prolonging the exploitation.

In this way Hobsbawm is able to describe the – admittedly far from painless – process whereby the Industrial Revolution was accommodated by our social and political institutions as one of 'class struggle', albeit a struggle loaded at every point against the working class. And where the facts run directly counter to the Marxist story he explicitly tries to evade them. Thus Marx famously predicted that wages would fall under capitalism, as the workers are forced to accept an ever-harder bargain in order to enjoy their 'wage slavery', which was all that was on offer. Research has refuted this prediction, and shown that wages and living standards were, with a few hiccups, steadily rising throughout the Industrial Revolution.[6] Rather than accept this, and rewrite his history accordingly, Hobsbawm puts the whole issue in brackets, as though to prevent it from contaminating the purity of his beliefs:

> Whether [their material poverty] actually increased or not has been hotly debated among historians, but the very fact that the question can be put already supplies a gloomy answer: nobody seriously argues that conditions deteriorate in periods when they plainly do not, such as the 1950s.[7]

In other words, it is enough for the historian to consider what has been argued: no need to go one stage further and arrive at the truth.

---

[5] Ibid., p. 88.
[6] Peter H. Lindert and Jeffrey G. Williamson, 'English Workers' Living Standard During the Industrial Revolution: A New Look', *Economic History Review* 36 (1983): 1–25.
[7] Ibid., p. 91.

Facts are more interesting and memorable when part of a drama, and if history is to play a part in politics the drama has to be the drama of modern life. But to claim that the result is new, scientific and theory-based in the way that the old narratives of national achievement and institutional reform were not is surely quite unjustified. Marxist history means rewriting history with class at the top of the agenda. And it involves demonizing the upper class and romanticizing the lower.

Hobsbawm's rewriting of history according to the Marxist template of 'class struggle' involves debunking those sources of loyalty that tie ordinary people not to their class (as the Marxist doctrine requires) but to their nation and its traditions. Class is an attractive idea for left-wing historians because it denotes a thing that divides us. By seeing society in class terms we are programmed to find antagonism at the heart of all the institutions through which people have attempted to limit it. Nation, law, faith, tradition, sovereignty – these ideas by contrast denote things that unite us. It is in terms of them that we attempt to articulate the fundamental togetherness that mitigates social rivalries, whether of class, status or economic role. Hence it has been a vital project on the left, to which Hobsbawm made his own distinctive contribution, to show that these things are in some way illusory, standing for nothing durable or fundamental in the social order. To put the point in Marxist terms, the concept of class belongs to science, that of the nation to ideology. The idea of the nation and its traditions belongs to the mask drawn across the social world by the bourgeois need to misperceive it.

Hence, in *Nations and Nationalism since 1780* Hobsbawm sets out to show that nations are not the natural things they claim to be but inventions, designed to fabricate a specious loyalty to this or that prevailing political system. In *The Invention of Tradition* – a collection edited by Hobsbawm and Terence Ranger[8] – a variety of authors argue that many social traditions, ceremonies and badges of ethnic identity are recent creations, encouraging people to imagine an immemorial past from which they descend and which endows their social membership with a specious form of permanence. Those two books belong to a growing library of studies devoted to 'the invention of the past', including such classics as Benedict Anderson's *Imagined Communities: Reflections on the Origins and Spread of Nationalism*, 1983, and Ernest Gellner's *Nations and Nationalism*, 1983.

---

[8] Eric Hobsbawm and Terence Ranger, *The Invention of Tradition*, Cambridge, CUP, 1992.

This literature has established beyond reasonable doubt that, when people become conscious of their past, and lay claim to it as a collective possession, they do not think as empirical historians and social statisticians think. They think as prophets, poets and mythmakers think, projecting back on to their forebears the present sense of their identity, in order to lay claim to the past as *theirs*. But what follows from this? Exactly the same process can be witnessed in the historiographical writings of Hobsbawm, Thompson and Samuel, in which what is projected on to the past is not the present consciousness of nationhood but the present experience of class. There is, in the New Left's attacks on the nation and national identity, a failure to take its own intellectual inheritance seriously. Marx distinguished the class in itself from the class for itself, precisely because he believed that the class structure of modern societies existed long before people became aware of it. What Hobsbawm's account of the Industrial Revolution illustrates is the way in which a modern 'class consciousness' can be read back into the conditions that preceded it, and so create the sense of belonging to a long tradition of 'struggle', which unites the present professor with the mounds of the industrial dead and in that way glorifies his labours.

Likewise we should distinguish the nation in itself from the nation for itself. Of course the latter is a recent invention, the expression of a consciousness that develops over time and in response to present emergencies. In no way does this show national loyalty to be somehow more of a fiction than the class solidarity that appeals to writers like Hobsbawm. In Shakespeare's history plays we see an early version of the national consciousness that was to flower during the Napoleonic wars and later to unite the British people in the fight against Nazi Germany.[9] When challenged by the rise of Nazism this 'nation for itself' proved far more effective than the international solidarity of the proletariat, which showed itself, by contrast, to be a mere dream of the intellectuals.

It is easy to dismiss traditions as invented when the examples chosen are those discussed by the authors gathered together by Hobsbawm and Ranger. Scottish country dancing and the highland kilt; the Lord Mayor's procession and the Ceremony of Nine Lessons and Carols; the uniforms and customs of the county regiments – all such things are of course the

---

[9] Though of course in Shakespeare's time the national consciousness had England as its focus: the 'British' identity had yet to be clearly formulated. See Linda Colley, *Britons: Forging the Nation 1707–1837*, London, 1992.

product of the imagination. But the imagination also provides us with symbols of a deep and lasting reality; and those particular examples of 'tradition for itself' are of little significance when set beside the 'tradition in itself' that conservatives wish to enhance and preserve.

Consider the example that, properly understood, leaves the Marxist theory of history in ruins: the common law of the English-speaking people. Not only has this been in existence for a thousand years, with precedents from the twelfth century still authoritative in our twenty-first-century courts. It has developed according to an internal logic of its own, maintaining continuity in the midst of change and welding English society together through all national and international emergencies. It has shown itself to be the motor of history and the initiator of economic change, and in no respect can it be relegated to the epiphenomenal 'superstructure' that the Marxists believe to be without autonomous causal power. The great works of Coke, Dicey and Maitland to my mind leave no doubt in this matter, and of course you won't find them mentioned in the leftist literature. For they leave almost nothing standing of the edifice built by Marx.[10]

The common law is only one example of an enduring tradition that lives *in* itself whether or not also *for* itself. Other examples include the liturgy of the Catholic communions, diatonic tonality in music, the symphony orchestra and the brass band, the pas de Basque in formation dances, the two-piece suit and tie,[11] the offices of Parliament, the crown, the knife and fork, sauce béarnaise, greetings such as Grüß Gott and sabah an-noor, grace before meals, manners, honour in peace and in war. Some of those traditions are trivial; some are absolutely foundational to the community in which they occur; and all are dynamic, changing over time in response to the changed circumstances of those attached to them, so as to hold communities together in the face of internal and external threat. Study those things, notice how many of them are absent from or disparaged in the works of the leftist historians, and you will begin to wonder whether Marxism has made any great contribution to our understanding of historical development.

Before leaving the works of Hobsbawm it is worth pausing to consider his account of the Russian Revolution.[12] Hobsbawm does not describe

---

[10] Sir Edward Coke, *Institutes of the Lawes of England*, 1628–1644; A. V. Dicey, *Introduction to the Study of the Law of the Constitution*, 1889; F. W. Maitland, *The Constitutional History of England*, 1919.
[11] See Anne Hollander, *Sex and Suits*, New York, Knopf, 1994.
[12] *The Age of Extremes*, pp. 56–84.

Lenin's policies in detail, but summarizes them in Marxist Newspeak. Thus he writes that Lenin acted on behalf of 'the masses', in the face of ruthless opposition from the 'bourgeoisie': 'Contrary to the Cold War mythology, which saw Lenin essentially as an organizer of coups, the only real asset he and the Bolsheviks had was the ability to recognize what the masses wanted…' (p. 61), and 'if a revolutionary party did not seize power when the moment and the masses called for it, how did it differ from a non-revolutionary one?' (p. 63). Hobsbawm brushes away the question of who the 'masses' were, and whether they really called for the violence that the Party was about to impose on them. He quotes Lenin's own sinister Newspeak with approval: 'Who – he said so often enough – could imagine that the victory of socialism "can come about…except by the complete destruction of the Russian and European bourgeoisie"?' And without pausing to consider what that 'complete destruction' amounted to, Hobsbawm dismisses all objections to Lenin's methods as though no question had ever been raised about them:

> Who could afford to consider the possible long-term consequences for the revolution of decisions which had to be taken *now*, or else there would be an end to the revolution and no further consequences to consider? One by one the necessary steps were taken… (p. 64)

Whatever the Bolsheviks did was achieved by 'the necessarily ruthless and disciplined army of human emancipation' (p. 72), and on those grounds Hobsbawm is able to pass over all that Lenin *actually* did on his way to the 'complete destruction' of the bourgeoisie.

And what a strange form this 'emancipation' took! Because Marxist history does not bother with things like law and judicial process, Hobsbawm sees no need to mention Lenin's decree of 21 November 1917, which abrogated the courts, the bar and the legal profession, and left the people without the only protection that they had ever had from arbitrary intimidation and arrest. After all, it is only the bourgeoisie, who were in any case on their way to 'complete destruction', who would have recourse to law courts. Lenin's founding of the Cheka, precursor of the KGB, and his empowering it to use all the terrorist methods required in order to express the will of the 'masses' against that of mere people, is of course not mentioned. Nor is the famine of 1921, the first of three man-made famines in early Soviet history, used by Lenin in order to impose the will of the 'masses' on those recalcitrant Ukrainian peasants who had yet to accept that description of themselves. Reading these pages of *The Age of Extremes* I found myself astonished that the book had not been dismissed as a scandal of the same order as David Irving's whitewash of the Holocaust. But once again I was forced to acknowledge that crimes committed on the left are not really crimes, and in any case those who excuse them or pass over them in silence always have the best of motives for doing so.

That brings me to E. P. Thompson. If Thompson remains important for us today it is because he was acutely aware of the problems posed by the Marxist theory of class, and of the fast and loose ways in which the 'in itself' and the 'for itself' have been muddled. For Thompson it is the class *for* itself that matters. On the original Marxist theory, according to which a class is defined by a position in the relations of production, and by an economic function that unites all those who fill it, the English working class ought to have existed from the time of the first capitalist production in medieval England.[13] Thompson affirms that, on the contrary, nothing then existed that could be usefully compared to the 'working class' of the nineteenth century. Elsewhere he castigates those Marxist historians who, anxious to give credence to the schematic history of the *Communist Manifesto*, try to persuade us that the economy of France before the ('bourgeois') Revolution was 'feudal'. All such ideas, Thompson believed, show a fixation on simple categories at the expense of the complexity of historical phenomena.

It is difficult to disagree. Nevertheless, Thompson remained convinced that the Marxist theory of class struggle is illuminating, and that it can be applied in modified form to the history of England. In *The Making of the English Working Class* he argues that no simple 'materialist' idea of class is adequate: 'class is defined by men as they live their own history, and, in the end, this is its only definition'. In other words the class in itself comes into being with the class for itself, and the old Marxist idea that class precedes class-consciousness is without force. How otherwise can we give sense to the idea that classes are always engaged in a 'struggle'? Roberto Michels expressed the point succinctly: 'It is not the simple *existence* of oppressive conditions, but it is the *recognition of these conditions by the oppressed*, which in the course of history has constituted the prime factor of class struggles'.[14] That raises the question – which was crucial for the New Left

---

[13] In other words, from the Middle Ages. See Alan MacFarlane, *The Culture of Capitalism*, London, 1987, and *The Origins of English Individualism*, London, 1978.

[14] Roberto Michels, *Political Parties*, tr. E. and C. Paul, London, 1915, p. 248.

generally – whether people can really be oppressed without thinking that they are.

The English working class, Thompson argues, was the product of many things, not merely of the economic conditions of industrial manufacture, but also of the non-conformist religion that provided to all people the language with which to express their new attachments; of the movement for parliamentary and electoral reform; of the associations within the manufacturing towns; of a thousand other particulars that helped to forge an identity and a resolve that would articulate the needs and grievances of the industrial workforce. This idea of class, as formed by the interaction between 'material' circumstances and the consciousness of them, is surely more persuasive than that adopted by Hobsbawm. In Thompson's application it presents a picture of the working class that no one need dissent from: as a collection of people distinguished in part by the wage-labour through which they earned their living, but also implicated in established social customs, political institutions, religious beliefs and moral values, all of which united them to the national tradition that they shared with their fellow citizens.

It is difficult to use that idea to advance the Marxist analysis of society, according to which the proletariat emerges as a new and international force, without local ties or national identity, and with no interest in preserving the established political order. Thompson's 'revisionist' interpretation of English history shows how much our political traditions have been able to adapt to altered circumstances, and to give institutional expression to grievances that are thereby conciliated and overcome. A working class shaped by non-conformist values, anxious for representation in Parliament, which consciously identifies itself with the seventeenth-century parliamentarians and through the works of Bunyan, can scarcely be described as one side of a Marxist 'class struggle', the sworn enemy of all established order and all institutions that have bestowed legitimacy on the powers that be. But Thompson insists that his interpretation attributes to the working class the historic role that the leftist myth has assigned to it. He writes: 'Such men met Utilitarianism in their daily lives, and they sought to throw it back, not blindly, but with intelligence and moral passion. They fought, not the machine, but the exploitative and oppressive relationships intrinsic to industrial capitalism.'[15]

---

[15] *The Making of the English Working Class*, London, 1963, Penguin edn, 1968, p. 915.

The men in question were the members of the English Working Class, as Thompson describes it. But note the peculiar vagueness of that (concluding) observation, which has retreated from concrete reality into Marxist Newspeak. What *were* they fighting? A mere 'ism' – Utilitarianism? But how do you fight a philosophical doctrine, and with what weapons available to the industrial working class? Or were they fighting exploitation and, if so, how is exploitation here defined? Did the workers believe oppressive relationships to be 'intrinsic' to industrial capitalism, and what hangs on the words 'industrial' and 'capitalism'? Would 'industrial communism', for example, be just as bad?

Thompson returns no clear answer to such questions; the implication that the working class was bound together by its opposition to capitalism is brought in by sleight of hand. Certainly the workers reacted for the most part negatively to the factories and to the conditions that prevailed in them. But the private ownership of those factories – which is all that 'capitalism' means in this context – was surely irrelevant to their deeper concern. What troubled them were the conditions under which they had to work in order to earn their wages; and they would have been just as troubled if the factories had been owned by the state, or by cooperatives, or by anyone else who claimed that his hands were tied. What they really wanted was *a better deal*; and by degrees they came to understand that they would acquire that deal only by increasing their own bargaining power. The answer did not lie in public ownership of the factories, but in unionization of the workforce. As subsequent history made clear, unions advance the interests of their members only where wages are the market price of labour: in other words, only in a free ('capitalist') economy.

The point takes us back to Hobsbawm, and the Marxist theory of class. Thompson's analysis of the English working class finishes by describing this class as a collective agent, which does things, opposes things, fights things, and which may succeed or fail. Elsewhere ('The Peculiarities of the English', in *The Poverty of Theory*) Thompson expresses a healthy scepticism towards this anthropomorphic vision of historical processes, which has persisted through so much Marxist theory of the 'class struggle'. But to use this 'metaphor', as Thompson describes it, is still to imply things that may not be true. History certainly does contain collective agents, which act as a 'we' and with a sense of common purpose. It is an important conservative thesis that classes are not among them.

What is it, then, that brings people most effectively together as a 'we', that enables them to combine their forces in a sense of common destiny and shared interest? As Thompson makes clear, it is precisely those features that are not part of the 'material' conditions that are here of greatest significance: language, religion, custom, association and traditions of political order – in short, all those forces that absorb competing individuals into the shared identity of a nation. To identify the working class as an agent, even if 'metaphorically', is to ignore the true significance of national consciousness as a genuine agent of change.

The sentimentalizing of the proletariat has been an integral part of Labour historiography, and Thompson was by no means immune to it. He saw himself as part of a great work of emancipation, which would unite him with the workers in a bond of grateful affection. This work, which had attracted him to the Communist Party, later required him to stand against the machinations of international capitalism, long after his recognition that the Soviet Union is not the natural ally for someone who seeks to be the friend of the working class. In *The Poverty of Theory* he wrote:

> [Marx] appears to propose, not an angelic nature, but men who within the context of certain institutions and culture can conceptualise in terms of 'our' rather than 'my' or 'their'. I was a participating witness, in 1947, in the euphoric aftermath of a revolutionary transition, of exactly such a transformation in attitudes. Young Yugoslav peasants, students and workers, constructing with high morale their own railway, undoubtedly had this affirmative concept of *nasha* ('our'), although this *nasha* – as may have proved fortunate for Yugoslavia – was in part the *nasha* of socialist consciousness, and in part the *nasha* of the nation.[16]

This adroit smuggling in of the *nasha* of socialist conscience, when the only real evidence is that people were working together as they do when liberated from foreign occupation, is evidence of Thompson's emotional need.

It is easy to agree that, 'within the context of certain institutions and culture', people think in terms of 'our' rather than 'my' or 'their': the recognition of this truth is what unites conservatives and nationalists

---

[16] 'The Peculiarities of the English', in *The Poverty of Theory*, p. 67.

against the 'socialist consciousness' that was at that moment being taught to the Yugoslavs. For as we now know, the Yugoslavs were being hoodwinked. The whole process of reconstruction was being manipulated by Marshal Tito, the Croat whom Stalin had backed to take over, once he had seen to the death of the patriots whose names and locations he had obtained from Philby and Blunt at the Foreign Office.

The country put together by Tito created neither the 'our' of socialist consciousness, if there is such a thing, nor that of the nation. When the real '*nasha*' of the Serbs, the Croats, the Slovenians and the Montenegrins was at last to assert itself, it was against each other, and in heartfelt rejection of the monstrous order that Stalin and Tito had imposed on them. The reference to a '*nasha* of socialist consciousness' is nothing more than a sentimentalization, reminiscent of the heroic worker who stares sternly into the future from the lurid poster on the wall. I doubt that there is any native speaker of a Slavonic language of the post-war generation who could now hear such a phrase without suppressing a bitter smile.

This is not to imply that Thompson's historiography is mere propaganda. Far from it. Like Hobsbawm he had a beautiful investigative mind, attuned to empirical facts and with a masterly capacity to assemble them. He eloquently and powerfully asserted the obligation of every historian to discard his tidy theories when they conflict with the evidence. And he vigorously denounced the burgeoning charlatanism of the New Left, exemplified at its most grotesque in Althusser (see Chapter 6 below). It was partly for this reason that he was ousted by Perry Anderson from the *New Left Review* and cast out into the cold, where mere 'empiricists' were rumoured to survive on meagre scraps of information, without the benefit of those 'grand theories' that were now taking over. Every reader of *The Poverty of Theory* must feel grateful for a left-wing thinker who is determined to think within the bounds of common sense and intellectual honesty.

At the same time, a simplifying self-deception haunts the pages of the volume in which that essay appears. This self-deception is nowhere more manifest than in the lamentations over workers who reveal the true source of the 'institutional and cultural' bond that unites them:

In the action of the dockers on the Victoria and Albert docks, who threatened to refuse to service all ships which were not decorated in honour of Mafeking's relief – those same dockers upon whose support

Tom Mann had sought to found a proletarian internationalism – we can already see the overwhelming defeats ahead.[17]

In other words the workers, who should be expressing their true nature in the cause of 'proletarian internationalism', were betrayed into old-fashioned patriotism by the ideology of the bourgeoisie. Would they have been cured, I wonder, by a dash of *nasha*?

Thompson's self-deception is manifest, too, in his open letter to Kołakowski, in which a veteran communist, who had believed in and seen through the Marxist creed as applied in Eastern Europe, is berated for his 'apostasy':

> My feelings have even a more personal tone. I feel, when I turn over your pages in *Encounter*, a sense of personal injury and betrayal. My feelings are no affair of yours: you must do what you think is right. But they explain why I write, not an article or polemic, but this open letter.[18]

Only someone who has pitched the stakes too high, who has identified himself with a doctrine without sufficient warrant for his belief in it, could adopt that injured tone. In this letter, and in the later articles on disarmament,[19] we witness the *need* that animated Thompson's writing: the need to believe in socialism, as the philosophy of the proletariat, and in the proletariat itself, as the innocent patient and heroic agent of modern history.

This need to believe has taken surprising forms. Perhaps none is more remarkable than the refusal to consider the evidence that writers like Kołakowski put before us: the evidence that the communist tyranny derived its nature precisely from the same posturing sentimentality about the workers, and the same simplifying denigration of 'capitalism' and all that might seem to be implied by it, that have inspired Thompson's writings. Thompson believed in the power of ideas. But he refused to recognize the consequences of the ideas that were dearest to him.

Thompson's uncritical attitude to his own sermonizing was of a piece with his attitude to Marxism. For in the last analysis it was Marxism that made it possible to invent the past. Human beings appear in

---

17 Ibid., p. 98.
18 'An Open Letter to Leszek Kołakowski', in ibid., p. 160.
19 Collected as *Zero Option*, London, 1982, and *The Heavy Dancers*, London, 1984.

the Marxist history only as 'forces', 'classes' and 'isms'. Legal, moral and spiritual institutions have only a marginal place or are brought into the discussion only when they can be easily seen in terms of the abstractions that speak through them. The dead categories, imposed on the living matter of history, reduce everything to formulae and stereotypes. Thompson describes a past that is overlaid with the grid of his own emotions.

The Marxist marginalization of institutions, law and the moral life was not confined to the New Left historians in Britain. The French *annales* historians, who preferred social statistics to grand narratives, the 'domination' theory of Foucault, Gramsci's account of revolutionary *praxis* and the Frankfurt School attack on the 'instrumentalization' of the social world, all had the effect of downgrading institutions and putting fictitious mechanisms in the place of them. Only in one part of the world have recent thinkers on the left seen the operation and reform of the law as the principal subject-matter of politics, and that is the United States of America. Thanks to the American Constitution, and the long tradition of critical thinking inspired by it, American leftism has more often than not taken the form of legal and constitutional argument, interspersed with reflections on justice that are mercifully free from the class resentments that speak in the works of the European left. Hence, even though they argue for an ever-increasing role for the state in the lives of ordinary people, Americans on the left are described not as socialists but as liberals, as though it were freedom, rather than equality, that they promise. In the chapter that follows I shall explore what this has in recent years amounted to.

3 DISDAIN IN AMERICA: GALBRAITH AND DWORKIN

The triumph of the United States Constitution was to make private property, individual liberty and the rule of law immovable features, not only of the political landscape in America but also of American political science. Almost all left-leaning American philosophy in recent times has been founded in those classical liberal preconceptions, and very little of it has challenged the fundamental institutions of 'bourgeois' society, as the Marxists conceive this. Instead it has directed attention to the pathology of the free society – to 'consumerism', 'conspicuous consumption', the world of 'mass society' and mass advertisement. From Veblen to Galbraith what has distressed the American critics of the free economy is not private property – which is the cornerstone of their own independence – but the private property of others. In recent times it is the spectacle of property in the hands of ordinary, gross, uneducated people that has troubled the domestic critics of American capitalism.

Far from seeing this 'consumerism' as the necessary result of democracy, the left has tried to show that consumerism is not democracy but a pathological form of it. Property is, in America, too palpable, too physical a fact, and while one may deceive oneself about the hearts and minds of the common people it is impossible to remain deceived about the trash that they scatter about their yards. To the visitor from the East Coast cities, the suburban sprawl of Texas is an appalling affront to civilization: through property, advertising and the media the ordinary American puts himself on display, and thereby undermines the illusion of equality. He is plainly of another species from the liberal who stands up for him, and this is a hard truth that must nevertheless be swallowed.

A solution to the dilemma that recommended itself during the 1960s to such thinkers as Baran, Sweezy and Galbraith was to regard the squalor of modern America as the product of a 'system' of established power.[1] It is not popular demand, but political purpose, that fosters the consumer culture. Capitalists and politicians shamelessly encourage the people to expand their appetites, despite the overwhelming arguments for curbing them. In fighting against the consumer culture, therefore, liberals are not disparaging ordinary Americans but striking a blow against the powers that oppress them.

The European Marxist, looking back at the miseries of the early Industrial Revolution in England, is very likely to be tempted by the vision of Hobsbawm and Thompson, who saw 'class struggle' in every social upheaval. But, apart from a brief period during the Depression, the Marxist vision has never had wide acceptance on the American left. America lacks the multiple barriers to social advancement that have existed in Europe; it has abundant space, abundant resources, abundant will and opportunity; in particular it has a political structure inimical to the creation of long-standing hereditary elites. The result is that 'classes', such as they are, remain fluid, temporary, without apparent moral attributes.[2]

There is a kind of theology involved in the discourse of 'class struggle'. Cosmic forces clash in the workplace and on the streets of the great industrial cities of England, and these forces must be concentrated into opposing phalanxes like the warring angels in Milton's *Paradise Lost*. For this to happen the working man must identify his boss as an antagonist, whose interests are in every particular opposed to his own; and the intellectual must stand side by side with the worker in pursuit of the justice that both are struggling for.

That story has little purchase in America, where both employer and employee are climbing the ladder of success, differing only in their relative advancement. Hence the intellectual opponents of the American culture of hard work and upward mobility do not enjoy the 'solidarity of the intellectuals and the proletariat' that has been such a powerful force in shaping the agenda of European socialism. They must address themselves directly to the powers that be. They have achieved this through the creation of a 'counter-establishment', with a social authority that trumps the mere money of the capitalist class. That is how we should read the *New York Review of Books*, whose disdainful overview of the American cultural wilderness has been such a powerful force in shaping

---

[1] See especially P. A. Baran and P. M. Sweezy, *Monopoly Capital*, London and New York, 1966.
[2] See W. Sombart, *Why Has There Been No Socialism in America?*, London, 1906.

the oppositional stance of university teachers and journalists since the 1960s: its message is that they have the money, but *we* have the brains.

In the same spirit America has produced an impressive tradition of sarcastic economists, learned and witty commentators on the great hive of production that pays so generously for their scorn. Thorstein Veblen began the tradition with a classic study – *Theory of the Leisure Class* (1899) – in which he praised the utility of the vices peculiar to those at the upper end of the social scale. His irony was in the same vein as Mandeville's in *The Fable of the Bees*, but there was a novel twist. The 'conspicuous consumption' of Veblen's 'leisure class' is useful precisely for the perpetuation of the leisure class, by recycling the profits gleaned from others' labour. Not that Veblen envisaged an alternative, or at any rate, classless scheme of things. Too sceptical to embrace such a solution and remorselessly scathing of the intellectual fraud, as he saw it, of Marxism, he remained aloof from the American reality, mutedly chuckling at the symbiotic perfection with which the organism held itself together.

It is no small praise of J. K. Galbraith to say that he was, at his best, as witty and engaging as Veblen. What he lacked in sociological insight he made up for in audacity and, like his great predecessor, he constantly enlarged his perspective, through the deliberate pursuit of controversy. His theory was global, in the wide-ranging manner of 'political economy' as this had been conceived by Smith, Ricardo and Mill. Like Veblen he was not an orthodox man of the left. Nevertheless his conclusions, and the arguments adduced in their favour, were of great importance in the formulation of the left-wing position during the 1960s. By then Galbraith (although born and raised in Canada) had been appointed United States ambassador to India by President Kennedy. He went on to serve as economic advisor to the governments of India, Pakistan and Sri Lanka. He was appointed BBC Reith Lecturer in 1966, and by the time he died, aged 98, in 2006, he had received fifty honorary degrees from universities around the world. He could fairly be described as the most established critic of the establishment ever to have enjoyed its acclaim, closely rivalled in this status only by Edward Said and Ronald Dworkin.

Galbraith believed that traditional economic theory, with its emphasis on competitive markets, cannot be applied to the dynamics of the 'new industrial state', an expression that he coined to denote both the 'capitalist economies' of the West and the 'socialist economies' of the Soviet empire. Moreover, he argued, the traditional emphasis on production, as the criterion of social, economic and political success, is no better than ideology, a convenient belief that oils the wheels of the new kind of state while poisoning the sources of contentment.

Galbraith offered an analysis of the entire socio-economic system of industrial production, taking into account a host of facts that he claimed had been previously ignored: 'oligopoly', 'countervailing power', centralized decision making and the steady decline both in the profit motive and in the effectiveness of competition. There emerges from this analysis – spread over several important books – a slowly focusing image of industrial society as an impersonal system, controlled by a 'technostructure' with a vested interest in production. The legitimacy of this system depends on the propagation of political myths – in particular the 'Cold War' myth, whereby the arms race and the consequent over-production of technology, with its incidental effect on the production of everything else, is firmly embedded in the political process. These myths are themselves by-products of deep structural changes within the underlying economies of the 'capitalist' world, which have moved progressively away from the entrepreneurial paradigm assumed by Marx, Marshall, Böhm-Bawerk and Samuelson.[3] Increasingly, Galbraith argues, the 'market' has been superseded as the fundamental determinant of prices and production. As the capacity develops to control and manipulate demand, industry breaks free from its limiting influence. The consumer is reduced from sovereign to subject, and firms begin to obey a self-generating process of planning that spreads throughout the industrial system and which has no other purpose than its own expansion.

In modern economies, Galbraith argues, ownership and control are almost entirely separated: those who make decisions on behalf of a firm are less and less those who enjoy the profits, nor need they be personally liable for the consequences of what they do. Terms of employment are fixed by the impersonal forces that work through the firm and which determine the various rewards of its members – workforce, management and directors. Nothing in principle prevents the rewards offered to the worker from surpassing those earned by the manager. In these and other ways the cherished idea of capitalist 'exploitation' meets its nemesis, and so does the Marxist conception of class. There are indeed two classes in the modern free economy: the employees and the unemployed. Neither has a monopoly of power over the other, since the political process

---

[3] Alfred Marshall, *Principles of Economics*, 1890; Eugen von Böhm-Bawerk, *Karl Marx and the Close of his System*, 1896; Paul Samuelson, *Foundations of Economic Analysis*, 1947, 1983.

provides each with a defence against coercion, and between the two classes there is maximum social mobility.

The resulting economy illustrates what Galbraith calls 'countervailing power'. To understand the structure of profit and reward, he argues, we must look neither to ownership nor to control, but to the interaction of the power of producers with the 'countervailing' powers that stake their claims in the product and negotiate for a share of it. These powers are not market forces but, on the contrary, forces that inherently distort the configuration of the market. Two in particular are politically significant: the trade unions, which negotiate the price of labour, and the oligopolic buyers, who negotiate the price of the product. Even if the powers exercised by these two forces are unequal, they establish prices by agreement and not by force. Whether or not the result is a system of 'just rewards' cannot be settled in the abstract, and certainly not by those Marxist theories that regard all relations in a capitalist society as concealed forms of coercion.

Serious-minded socialists, confronted by Galbraith's argument, would be forced to re-examine their promised alternative to the capitalist system. It becomes extremely questionable that centralized control of a system that has already emancipated itself from the control of the capitalist would alter the real position of the worker. Socialist plans merely perpetuate the given system of control, while increasing the anonymity and unaccountability of its exercise. Hence 'socialism', Galbraith writes, 'has come to mean government by socialists who have learned that socialism, as anciently understood, is impractical'.[4] Furthermore, the socialist vision is dependent, for its cogency, on a form of capitalism that no longer exists: it depends on the image of the ruthless entrepreneur, motivated by profit alone, who employs only those who are compelled by need to take his wages. Socialism has defined itself against that image, and hence 'the misfortune of democratic socialism has been the misfortune of the capitalist. When the latter could no longer control, democratic socialism was no longer an alternative.'[5]

Such arguments are of course over-simple. Nevertheless, if Galbraith's vision of the modern capitalist economy is even partly true, the socialist critique is no longer relevant. And since Galbraith's vision is essentially

---

[4] *The New Industrial State*, rev. edn, London, 1972, p. 101.
[5] Ibid., p. 104.

that of Max Weber, the socialist critique has been irrelevant for quite a long time.[6] But Galbraith adds an extended critique of his own, and one with a rhetorical force that matches the force of traditional socialism. He sets out to destroy the image of the capitalist economy as a self-equilibrating mechanism, structured by 'market forces'.

Countervailing power, he argues, of the kind exemplified by the trade unions, the oligopolies and the new 'technostructures' within the corporation, is self-generating, while the power of competition is not. Hence, in the long run, the 'capitalist' economy will be taken over by powers with an inherent tendency to grow, and will be voided of the competition that would discipline them in the public interest.[7] Planning takes precedence over interaction, and planning ceases to content itself with the short-term response of the market. The 'technostructure' that sustains the modern corporation becomes increasingly ambitious, forms links with other firms, with government and with every organization that could serve to extend its power. By a variety of devices the corporation evades liability to its directors and shareholders,[8] and embarks upon the autonomous pursuit of its own aggrandizement. Neither the profit of the enterprise, nor the pecuniary incentives of the executive, count for much in determining the direction of decision making:

> ... the reality is that the executive's present level of income allows for identification (with the firm's goals) and adaptation (of the firm's goals to his own). These are the operative motivations. They are also the only personally reputable ones: the executive cannot afford to have it thought that his commitment to the goals of the corporation is less than complete or that he is at all indifferent to his opportunity to shape these goals. To suggest that he subordinates these latter motives to his response to pay would be to confess that he is an inferior executive.[9]

The quotation illustrates Galbraith's principal intellectual device. A psychological observation, expressed in ironical tones, is used to support an economic theory of immense and far-reaching consequences. If true, it follows that a standard assumption – that firms tend to maximize

---

[6] *Economy and Society* (1922), ed. Guenther Roth and Claus Wittich, Berkeley, University of California Press, 1978.
[7] *American Capitalism: The Concept of Countervailing Power*, Cambridge, MA, p. 104.
[8] *The New Industrial State*, op. cit., pp. 81ff.
[9] Ibid., p. 139.

profit – is false, and that a received theory of the market economy is invalid. According to Galbraith firms tend to maximize not profit but power. Moreover, they do this not in competition with other firms but in league with them, for the power is not that of the individual enterprise but that of the 'technostructure' common to them all.

It is fair to say that economic opinion has not been persuaded that Galbraith is right.[10] What is more significant than the ultimate truth-value of his conclusions, however, is the quality of the evidence adduced in their favour: no statistics, no detailed analysis of the modern firm or its specific instances, no examination of the structure of decision making, no real comparison between the private corporation and the state monopoly and no theory of the legal personality of the corporations in a modern state. We are offered nothing more than social psychology, expressed in the ironical idiom of Veblen, and nurtured on the professor's constitutional disdain for the empty life of the executive.

From the same attitude comes Galbraith's cajoling of a 'conventional wisdom' whose tenets he either caricatures or leaves undefined. It is this 'conventional wisdom' that Galbraith berates in his most famous book – *The Affluent Society* (1958, rev. edn 1969) – for its emphasis on free competition, open markets and such indisputably important virtues as the 'balanced budget'. 'Conventional wisdom' is painted as the main instrument of social control, comparable to the official ideology of a communist state:

> In the communist countries, stability of ideas and social purpose is achieved by formal adherence to an officially proclaimed doctrine. Deviation is stigmatised as 'incorrect'. In our society, a similar stability is enforced far more informally by the conventional wisdom.[11]

It is hard to tell how serious Galbraith is in such pronouncements. Nevertheless, an important feature should be noticed, since it heralds the main thrust and influence of later work: communist ideology, he says, stigmatizes deviation as 'incorrect', while our 'conventional wisdom' *enforces* stability.

---

[10] See, e.g., Elizabeth Brunner, 'Industrial Analysis Revisited', in Harry Townsend, *Price Theory: Selected Readings*, 2nd edn, Penguin, 1980, and references therein. It should be said that one *corollary* of Galbraith's theory – that firms sometimes (and perhaps increasingly often) tend to pursue *satisficing* rather than *maximizing* solutions, is fairly widely supported. See R. Nelson and S. Winter, *An Evolutionary Theory of Economic Change*, Cambridge, MA, 1982.

[11] *The Affluent Society*, rev edn, London, 1969, p. 17.

Thus, by a sleight of hand, the 'capitalist system' is made to look as oppressive as its communist counterpart. The fact that millions had paid with their lives for their 'deviation' and others continued to suffer imprisonment, harassment and loss of every conceivable social advantage for the slightest 'error', seems altogether to have eluded Galbraith's observation. At the same time, his own freedom, not only to express his 'unconventional' (in fact fairly conventional Keynesian) views, but also to rise to the highest positions of intellectual influence and power as a result of them, is carefully hidden behind the little word 'enforced'.

The Affluent Society comprises Galbraith's main attack on the ethos of production which, he argues, has 'come to be a goal of pre-eminent importance in our lives', although 'not a goal which we pursue either comprehensively or even very thoughtfully'.[12] The thoughtless pursuit of production is responsible for the chaos and squalor of modern capitalist societies, in which public services are sacrificed to a super-abundance of consumer goods. More importantly, this pursuit has brought about a dangerous attempt to guarantee a constant increase in demand. The idea that demand will always increase to match supply is a discredited tenet of classical economics, refuted by the theory of diminishing marginal utility. But, in the face of the 'threat' posed by this theory, 'conventional wisdom' has shown itself to be brilliantly resourceful: 'the diminishing urgency of wants was not admitted'.[13] Instead the assumption was made that goods are an important and even an urgent thing to provide, and therefore that we *ought* to produce them, so that a moral imperative takes over from our diminishing appetites. Thus the wants supplied by consumer goods are raised to a higher category, where the law of diminishing marginal utility no longer applies. Though a person can have enough wine, water or petrol, honour and achievement are always in short supply.

Galbraith proceeds to his celebrated description of the consumer society, in which human desires are no longer the controlling motive of production but the principal items of manufacture. The constant flow of goods is sustained by the deliberate creation of desires – through advertising, through the constant variegation of products, through the vast propaganda machine that tells us we are dishonoured by our failure to consume:

---

[12] Ibid., pp. 131–2.
[13] Ibid., p. 141.

As a society becomes increasingly affluent, wants are increasingly created by the process by which they are satisfied... Wants thus come to depend on output. In technical terms, it can no longer be assumed that welfare is greater at an all-round higher level of production than at a lower one. It may be the same. The higher level of production has, merely, a higher level of want creation necessitating a higher level of want satisfaction.[14]

This is an updating of a thesis that goes back to the Old Testament – the thesis that man, in his fallen condition, is subject to the tyranny of appetite, because his appetites are not truly his, but imposed on him, magicked into him, by others, and notably by the idols and fetishes of the marketplace.

This story turns the proof of our freedom – namely, that we can obtain what we want – into the proof of our enslavement, since our wants are not really ours. Something like it underlies Veblen's sarcasm about 'conspicuous consumption' and the attack on advertising in Vance Packard's highly influential book, *The Hidden Persuaders*.[15] The story is a haunting presence in Marx's theories of alienation and commodity fetishism. We shall encounter another and highly influential version of it in Chapter 5, when considering the Frankfurt School and its criticism of cultural capitalism. And it has been recently polished and refreshed for the use of postmodern consumers in a brilliant book by Gilles Lipovetsky and Jean Serroy.[16] But its antiquity also suggests its futility as a source of modern complaints. The search for a policy to overcome original sin is not a coherent political project. And if the problem before us is that human beings can be manipulated, and want to be manipulated, what is the benefit in replacing one style of manipulation by another?

In order to combat public squalor, Galbraith argues, we must spend more on public services and more on education, welfare and centralized planning. We should also tax production, so countering the urge that breeds the present mischief, and at the same time financing the public services that are proposed as its cure.[17] But of course a tax on production can finance public services only if the level of production is high, and as

---

[14] Ibid., p. 152.
[15] Vance Packard, *The Hidden Persuaders*, New York, 1957.
[16] Gilles Lipovetsky and Jean Serroy, *L'esthétisation du monde: Vivre à l'âge du capitalisme artiste*, Paris, Gallimard, 2012.
[17] *The Affluent Society*, p. 278.

for the rest of Galbraith's solution, only detailed comparative judgements could conceivably give any grounds for it – judgements of a kind that Galbraith has no interest in making, and which would certainly show his 'solution' to be a fantasy.

Such is typical of Galbraith's approach. Too much in love with his sardonic psychology to displace it from the central position that it occupies in his thoughts, he is at the same time acutely aware that no mere psychologist is likely to gain the politician's ear. Only the academic economist can wield real power over the system that he irritates, for only he seems to have a physician's knowledge of its diseases. Hence Galbraith, like Marx, disguises psychology as economics and offers his preposterous political recommendations as though they had all the authority of a Hayek or a Keynes.

In this way, despite his dismissive attitude towards socialism, Galbraith is able to vault into the territory that socialism has made its own. He begins to see the entire political organism of America in economic terms, as a 'system' whose every limb and sinew moves in response to the imperatives of business. The central, crippling myth of Marxism lays hold of his imagination and becomes the foundation of a profoundly oppositional standpoint. Law, politics, culture and institutions take second place to a crudely described 'economic system', whose impersonal imperatives supposedly govern all of social life. This vision has provided the theoretical basis for one of the most important tenets of the New Left in America: the theory that the 'capitalist' state is as much a system of control as the communist state, since it is a servant of the corporations, and the necessary completion of a planning process that originates in the technostructure of the oligopolic firm.[18]

The technostructure in turn comes to identify with the state,[19] and acquires the same centralized, impersonal movement towards a complete and all-comprehending plan. American production therefore generates (in the words that were President Eisenhower's parting gift to Soviet propaganda) an 'industrial-military complex' and, along with it, a 'weapons culture' through which to legitimize the vast expenditure on defence. The principal instrument in this legitimizing process is the 'Cold War myth', whereby the continuous expansion of the economy is justified through military imperatives. This 'war without fighting' neatly obviates

---

[18] *The New Industrial State*, pp. 256–7.
[19] Ibid., p. 311.

the danger that fighting will stop'[20] and therefore justifies constant technological advance and with it the endless variegation of production and the unceasing renewal of the will to consume.

Galbraith's description of the American 'system', maintained in being by a 'Cold War myth', enabled him to level at America the very same criticisms that were at the time being made of the Soviet Union. He acknowledges that 'no-one may minimise the difference made by the First Amendment'.[21] But he goes on to add that the systems of economic management are strictly comparable. Both are subject to 'the imperatives of planning', which means in both cases 'setting aside the market mechanism in favour of the control of prices and individual economic behaviour'.[22] The passing reference to the First Amendment serves merely to marginalize the political difference, and to turn attention to the economic resemblance, which is, for Galbraith, the *deep* truth about both America and its Soviet rival. As Galbraith elaborates this fantasy, it becomes clear that the resemblances between the Soviet Union and the USA that he regards as *deep* are precisely the most shallow, while what he regards as so shallow that it is barely noticeable – the presence or absence of free speech, constitutional government and the rule of law – is what is deepest in both arrangements.

Galbraith's criticisms of the American system predictably earned him a secure position within it. But his appointment as ambassador to India in 1961 imposed a certain measure of realism on his vision, and he was momentarily aware of the truth that a century of Marxist thinking had contrived to deny: that it is not the economic system of a nation that determines its character but its political institutions. He saw too that a political order that confers honours on its critics is of a radically different kind from one that does them to death in labour camps.

In the course of his office Galbraith delivered lectures at various Indian universities on the theme of economic development, giving support to the now discredited thesis that foreign aid is a necessary preliminary to the 'take-off' of third-world economies. At the same time he acknowledged the truth which – thanks to the work of such writers as P. T. Bauer, Elie Kedourie and, more recently, Dambisa Moyo[23] – has since

---

[20] Ibid., p. 332.
[21] *The New Industrial State*, p. 334.
[22] Ibid.
[23] P. T. Bauer, *Dissent on Development*, London, 1971; Elie Kedourie. *The Crossman Confessions and Other Essays*, London, 1984; Dambisa Moyo, *Dead Aid*, London, 2009.

become widely recognized, namely that foreign aid is ineffective without foreign institutions, and in particular without a rule of law, security of contract and the parliamentary processes brought to the third world by the European imperialists (some of them at least) and subsequently threatened with destruction.[24]

These lectures therefore give the lie to the myth that flourishes in Galbraith's 'economic' discourse – the myth of the corporation as a sinister, expansive, uncontrollable monster whose impersonal purposes govern our lives and satisfactions. He recognizes the real difference between the corporation in a capitalist economy and the 'collective' of the Soviet system, namely, that the first is a genuine person in law, the second a kind of oppressive fiction.[25] The communist collective, whether factory, farm, union or branch of the Party, was protected from the real consequences of its actions, enjoyed extensive and unspoken immunity from legal redress and could not be brought to task by any of its inferiors.

This touches on one of the achievements of European civilization and of the Roman law from which it arose. Powers in the Western constitutional state are identified, wherever possible, as juridical persons, and so subordinated to the rule of law. The personal corporation can be accused of, and therefore ruined by, its own insolent actions, and for this reason Galbraith rightly urged us to protect it.[26] It was precisely the impersonality of the communist institutions that made them unaccountable, ensuring that nothing could control or limit them save coercion, and also that the coercion must be applied to them *from outside*. That is the real truth of the Cold War: that personal government, faced with an expansionist but wholly impersonal power, could not protect itself through negotiation and diplomacy but only through a strategy of deterrence.

Galbraith justified himself as the necessary critic of the business community. As he once put it: 'Those who afflict the comfortable serve equally with those who comfort the afflicted.'[27] But who is truly comfortable in the modern American establishment: the businessman or his academic critic, the productive heart of the system or the parasite fed by its labour?

Of none of the critics of the American settlement is that question more pertinently asked than of Ronald Dworkin. Born in Massachusetts

---

[24] *Economic Development*, Cambridge, MA, 1964, p. 42.
[25] Ibid., p. 95.
[26] Ibid., p. 98.
[27] *American Capitalism*, p. 52.

in 1931, Dworkin moved from legal practice into the academy in 1962, becoming Hohfeld Professor of Jurisprudence at Yale in 1968. In 1969 he moved to Oxford as Professor of Jurisprudence, combining that position with a professorship in New York University from 1976 until his death in 2012. Like Galbraith he collected honorary doctorates by the score, along with prestigious prizes of the kind that the left establishment confers upon its members. And through his polemical writings in the *New York Review of Books* Dworkin exerted a far-reaching influence over public understanding of the American legal inheritance, and therefore over the direction of American politics.

Dworkin was not, as Galbraith was, a witty satirist. He did not laugh at his real or imagined conservative opponents, but bathed them in a continuous flood of scorn. He cherished the image of himself as the fertile and devastating critic of a conservative legal inheritance that had no intellectual arguments of its own. But his best work, which dates from his early years in the academy, tends towards the opposite conclusions from those that he willed upon it. In this work Dworkin presents a theory of the judicial process which, far from undermining the assumptions of conservative jurisprudence, provides a novel way of grounding them.

From Bentham and Austin to Kelsen and Hart, academic jurisprudence has been dominated by some form of 'legal positivism',[28] whose main tenets are identified by Dworkin thus: first, law is distinguished from social standards by its conformity to some 'master rule' – such as the rule that what is prescribed by the Queen in Parliament is law. Second, all difficulties and indeterminacies in the law are resolved by 'judicial discretion', and not by the discovery of genuine answers to independent legal questions. Finally, a legal obligation exists when, and only when, an established rule of law imposes it.

Those three tenets together define the idea of law as a system of command, answering to no internal constraint besides that of consistency, and issued by a supreme and sovereign authority with the purpose of regulating social behaviour. Adjudication is a matter of ascertaining, first the law, second the facts, and third the application of the one to the other. That idea is mistaken, Dworkin argues, as are all three of the tenets from which it derives. A 'master rule' is neither necessary nor sufficient for

---

[28] See Jeremy Bentham, *Introduction to the Principles of Morals and Legislation*, London, 1789; H. Kelsen, *General Theory of Law and State*, Chicago, 1945; H. L. A. Hart, *The Concept of Law*, Oxford, 1961.

a system of law. It is not necessary, since law may arise, as did our own system of common law, entirely from judicial reasoning, which takes note primarily of judicial precedents and their 'gravitational force'. Nor is it sufficient, since a supreme legislature can make law only if there are courts to apply it, and judges in these courts must employ 'principles' which are not derivable from the master rule.

Principles, Dworkin argues, are less mutable than rules, and more fundamental to the character of the legal system. Without them adjudication would be either impossible or full of unacceptable gaps. The existence of these principles is proved by 'hard cases', in which a judge must determine the rights and liabilities of parties without the benefit of any law that explicitly defines them. The adjudication of such a case is not an exercise of 'discretion' but an attempt to determine the real and independently existing rights and duties of the parties – so, at least, judges must think, if they are to exercise their judicial powers. Judges cannot think of themselves as inventing the rights and duties that they define; nor can they imagine that they are exercising some 'discretion' that they do not need in the normal conduct of their office. They must call on principles that have a different authority from that of the rules issued by the legislature. Those principles (such as that no one may profit from his own wrong) are permanent features of the judicial process, invoked in the application of law even to central and unproblematic cases.

Such considerations serve to show, Dworkin believes, that the theories of the 'master rule' and of 'judicial discretion' are myths. Furthermore, the inescapable fact of hard cases serves to refute the third tenet of legal positivism, that all legal obligation is created by a pre-existing and pre-established legal rule. In hard cases law is not so much applied as discovered. And this process of discovery is responsible for the structure both of common law and of equity. It is, therefore, the foundation upon which the English and American systems have been built.

One might add that no system of edicts can amount to law until applied by impartial courts, and in accordance with recognized procedures of adjudication. Processes of reasoning that are inseparable from passing judgement – the hearing of both sides, the impartial perspective, the public accountability for the verdict – will therefore be an essential component of every true legal system, whether or not included, as in English administrative law, as 'principles of natural justice'.

We may interpret Dworkin's argument as defending a procedural view of justice. According to this view, law requires adjudication; adjudication requires a principled attitude towards the particular case; the principled attitude views judgment not as a decision but as a discovery; finally, discovery invites the agreement of others and responds to the 'gravitation' of other judgments, with which it aims to harmonize. According to that appealing picture (integral to many conservative visions of political order), law is the 'common pursuit of true judgment', in which perennial human disputes are resolved by principles that arise naturally and inevitably in the mind of those who take an impartial view of them.

Dworkin does not draw that conclusion, and this for an important reason. He wants his reader to take him not as a spokesman for 'natural justice', but as someone who is giving the true interpretation of the American Constitution – the interpretation that has been obscured by conservative obfuscation. Hence he writes that

> Our constitution rests on a particular moral theory, namely, that men have moral rights against the state. The difficult clauses of the Bill of Rights, like the due process and equal protection clauses, must be understood as appealing to moral concepts rather than laying down particular conceptions; therefore a court that undertakes the burden of applying those clauses fully as law must be an activist court, in the sense that it must be prepared to frame and answer questions of political morality.[29]

In other words, the American Constitution authorizes the Supreme Court to take an 'activist' approach, so as freely to reject legislation that does not conform to the 'political morality' of its members. For Dworkin there was nothing unconstitutional in the decision of that court in *Roe v. Wade*, the 1973 case that permitted abortion throughout the Union, in defiance of the elected legislatures of most of the States. It was not necessary to examine the details of Justice Blackmun's contorted decision, which depended upon finding a 'right of privacy' in the US Constitution, despite the fact that the document mentions nothing of the kind, and which arbitrarily declared that the unborn have no constitutional rights. It was sufficient that the 'political morality' of the court saw nothing wrong with abortion, and something wrong with forbidding it.

In almost all Dworkin's writings you will find this special pleading for judicial activism, provided that the activists are political liberals.

---

[29] *Taking Rights Seriously*, London, 1976, p. 147.

While purporting to give a general theory of law, Dworkin's real interest is one of advocacy, on behalf of a political position towards which, in the conservative view of things, the law is at most neutral, and in some respects deeply opposed. He returns always to the Constitution, as though it is *this* that is the decisive ground for legal decisions; for the American Constitution has spawned four hundred or more thick volumes of case law, and can be read as sacred texts are read, through the spectacles of a thousand theologians.

However, Dworkin's self-assumed status as 'priest of the Constitution' was a thin disguise. His examples are drawn, in his early articles, largely from cases in English civil law (such as *Spartan Steel and Alloys Ltd. v. Martin*[30]), or American cases that apply principles derived from English precedents (such as *Henningsen v. Bloomfield Motors Inc.*[31]). It cannot be right, therefore, to conclude that the judicial process, as Dworkin describes it, is an offshoot of the United States Constitution. His arguments in fact derive from a position that one might call 'procedural naturalism', and which underlies the conservative defence of common-law justice. According to this position law arises spontaneously from the attempt to reach an agreed conclusion among impartial judges, in those matters where one party is held to have wronged another. Independent and impartial judges don't just summon their judgments from the air, even if they have no legal rule to guide them. They are guided along the path of practical reason, which obliges them to acknowledge established precedents and either to distinguish them or to apply them.

The resulting system of common law does not depend upon legislation either for its content as a conflict-resolving device, or for its form as a system of imperatives. Nor does it depend upon a written constitution, or anything that remotely resembles the 'political morality' that Dworkin discerns in the United States Constitution. It embodies the solutions that have arisen over time to the conflicts that result from our attempt to live together in societies. It offers remedies to injured parties, and thereby helps to maintain the equilibrium of the social order. To put it another way, the common law is not the expression of a revisionist 'political morality', nor is it the application of principles embodied in a constitution. It is the application of principles inherent in the very idea of impartial justice, and which are tacitly assumed in all our consensual transactions.

---

[30] [1973] 1 QB 27.
[31] 32 N.J. 358, 161 A.2d 69 (N.J., 1960).

That conservative vision of the law was defended in other terms by Adam Smith in his lectures on jurisprudence.[32] And it has been interestingly revived in our time by Hayek, a writer who is ignored entirely by Dworkin. Hayek's argument for common-law justice dominates Volume I of *Law, Legislation and Liberty*. 'To modern man,' Hayek argues, 'the belief that all law governing human action is the product of legislation appears so obvious that the contention that law is older than law-making has almost the character of a paradox. Yet there can be no doubt that law existed for ages before it occurred to man that he could make or alter it.'[33] People cannot form a society and then give themselves laws, as Rousseau had imagined. For the existence of law is presupposed in the very project of living in society – or at least, in a society of strangers. Law is real, though tacit, long before it is written down, and it is for the judge to discover the law, by examining social conflicts and laying bare the shared assumptions that permit their resolution. Law in its natural condition is therefore to be construed on the model of the common law of England, which preceded the legislative powers of Parliament, and which for many centuries looked upon Parliament not as a legislative body but as another court of law, whose function was to resolve the questions that could not be answered from a study of existing precedents.

Hayek points out that written law and sovereign legislation are late-comers to human society, and that both open the way to abuses which, in the common law, are usually self-correcting.[34] The distinction between law and legislation has been tacitly recognized in many European languages – *diritto* versus *legge*, *droit* versus *loi*, *Recht* versus *Gesetz*, *právo* versus *zákon* and so on. Interestingly enough, it has no such clear marker in English, even though English law is nearly unique in preserving common-law procedure. The legislator sees law as a human artefact, created for a purpose, and may endeavour to use law not merely to rectify injustices but also to bring about a new social order, in conformity with some 'political morality' – which is essentially how Dworkin sees the American Constitution. For him law is not a summary of the rights, duties

---

[32] Adam Smith, *Lectures on Jurisprudence*, Glasgow Edition of the Works of Adam Smith, 1976, reissued Liberty Press, 2005.
[33] *Law, Legislation and Liberty*, one-volume edition, London, 1982, p. 73.
[34] Ancient writers on the whole concurred with Hayek's view of law. According to Demosthenes, 'every law (*nomos*) is a discovery and a gift of the gods' (*Antiphon* I, iii, 27), a view maintained by Plato in *The Laws*, by the Greek tragedians, and many other ancient sources. See the discussion in Rémi Brague, *La loi de Dieu: histoire philosophique d'une alliance*, Paris, 2005.

and procedures implicit in common-law government, but a blueprint for the new liberal society.

There is nothing to prevent the radical legislator from passing laws that fly in the face of justice, by granting privileges, confiscating assets and extinguishing deserts in the interests of some personal or political agenda. One sign of this is the adoption of 'social justice' as the goal of law, rather than natural justice as a procedural constraint. For Hayek, by contrast, the goal of the common law is not social engineering but justice in the proper sense of the term, namely the punishment or rectification of unjust actions. The judge, examining the specific case, attempts to find the rule that will settle it. According to Hayek, such a rule is part of a network of rules, all of which are implicitly counted upon by those who engage in free transactions. Judges rightly think of themselves as discovering the law, for the reason that there would be no case to judge, had the existence of the relevant law not been implicit in the conduct of the parties.

In the English system it is certainly true that the law is discovered, rather than invented, by the judge.[35] It is true too that the law is formulated as a rule – the rule in *Rylands v. Fletcher*, for example, which tells us that 'the person who for his own purposes brings on his lands and collects and keeps there anything likely to do mischief if it escapes, must keep it in at his peril, and, if he does not do so, is prima facie answerable for all the damage which is the natural consequence of its escape'.[36] But it is also true that a judge may find for one of the parties, without formulating explicitly the rule that justifies his judgment: it may be a matter of controversy what the *ratio decidendi* is, of a case that all agree to have been rightly decided. This interesting fact provides further support for the idea that the law exists prior to its judicial determination, and that the belief that this is so both guides the judge and limits his ambitions. You cannot use the common-law procedures to change the nature of society, to redistribute property that has been acquired without fraud or coercion, to violate ordinary understandings or to upset long-standing expectations and natural relations of trust. For the common law is the working out of the rules already implicit in those things. It is a network woven by an invisible hand.

True laws – 'abstract rules', as Hayek calls them – are therefore not part of a plan of action, but arise from the enterprise of social cooperation over time. They are the parameters within which the cooperation of strangers to their

---

[35] I have argued for this position in *England: An Elegy*, London, 2000, Ch. 6.
[36] [1868] UKHL 1.

mutual advantage becomes possible. As with the market the benefit that they confer is in part epistemic. By following these rules we equip ourselves with practical knowledge that will be especially useful when venturing forth into the unforeseeable – namely, knowledge of how to conduct ourselves towards others, so as to secure their cooperation in advancing our aims.

Just as prices in a market condense into themselves information that is otherwise dispersed throughout contemporary society, so do laws condense information that is dispersed over a society's past.[37] From this thought it is a small step to reconstructing Burke's celebrated defence of custom, tradition and 'prejudice' against the 'rationalism' of the French Revolutionaries. To put Burke's point in a modern idiom: the knowledge that we need in the unforeseeable circumstances of human life is neither derived from nor contained in the experience of a single person, nor can it be deduced *a priori* from universal laws. This knowledge is bequeathed to us by customs, institutions and habits of thought that have shaped themselves over generations, through the trials and errors of people many of whom have perished in the course of acquiring it. Such is the knowledge contained in the common law, which is a social bequest that could never be adequately replaced by a doctrine, a plan or a constitution, however entrenched that constitution may be in a vision of individual rights.

If we believe, with Smith and Hayek, that law lies deeper in the psyche than legislation, that it is not concerned with imposing a plan, or a 'political morality' independent of the natural justice that dictates its procedures, we will understand why socialist revolutions begin by abrogating the rule of law, and why judicial independence is a rare feature in states that wish to conscript civil society to a top-down agenda. Yet Dworkin, who wishes to take advantage of the deep truths contained in the common law, also has an ideological purpose, and constantly strains to graft it on to a system of law that is inherently resistant to it. The common law is concerned to do justice in the individual case, not to pursue some far-reaching reform of the manners, morals and customs of the community as a whole. It is a quiet and vigilant presence in the lives of ordinary people. It does not seek to be invoked, but on the contrary, steps in reluctantly, when called upon to rectify a wrong. This is so far

---

[37] Of course the processes involved are different in either case. Prices are informative partly because those who over-price or under-price their goods are quickly driven from the market; the common law is informative because judgments that create conflicts are gradually overruled, and judgments that reinforce the implied social order gradually assume the status of precedents.

from the vision of Dworkin that it is surprising that he does not look elsewhere for his conception of law. But he argues as an advocate, rather than a philosopher: any argument that trips up his opponent is useful, provided Dworkin can use it to move towards his goal.

The goal is clear: to vindicate the liberal causes of the day. At the time of Dworkin's most important work, *Taking Rights Seriously*, these causes arose largely from the Civil Rights movement and from opposition to the Vietnam War. Hence they included civil disobedience and reverse discrimination. Sexual liberation was important too and, as the agenda moved on, Dworkin was to add feminism, the advocacy of 'abortion rights' and even (to the dismay of many feminists) pornography to his agenda. Briefly, if conservatives were against it, he was for it. He provided intellectual fireworks, patrician disdain, and cosmopolitan mockery in a prolonged copious flourish. And he assumed that it was never he but always his opponent who bore the onus of proof. For Dworkin, as for the writers for the *New York Review of Books* generally, the left-liberal position was so obviously right that it was for the conservative to refute it. It was for the conservative to show that there is a consensus of moral conviction against pornography, to show that his opposition to gay rights (in whatever form these might be currently promoted) was something more than 'prejudice', to show that segregation is within the spirit of the Constitution, or that the refusal to salute the flag or to serve in the army is not.[38]

This bludgeoning of the conservative conscience is taken to considerable extremes. Thus Dworkin writes: 'since rights are at stake, the issue is...whether tolerance would destroy the community or threaten it with great harm, and it seems to me simply mindless to suppose that the evidence makes that probable or even conceivable.'[39] For a conservative it is a matter of common sense that constant liberalization, constant remaking of law in the image of the elite lifestyles of New York, may eventually threaten the community with harm. The view is dismissed out of hand. It is *mindless* to suppose that the evidence makes it probable; mindless even to suppose that it makes it *conceivable*. This is a remarkable judgement. Anthropologists have demonstrated many times that the imposition of urban manners on sub-Saharan society destroys its cohesion. But it is apparently mindless even to *conceive* that the transfer of New York manners to rural Georgia might have a comparable effect.

---

[38] Examples from *Taking Rights Seriously*.
[39] Ibid., p. 196.

In the essay 'Taking Rights Seriously', which contains the core of Dworkin's thinking, he discusses the famous 'Chicago Seven Trial'. In this trial certain leftist militants were accused of conspiring to cross state lines with the intention of causing a riot. It was clear to Dworkin that the Chicago Seven were protected by their constitutional right to free speech. Here is what he had to say to those who do not agree with him:

> It may be said that the anti-riot law leaves [them] free to express [their] principles in a non-provocative way. But that misses the point of the connection between expression and dignity. A man cannot express himself freely when he cannot match his rhetoric to his outrage, or when he must trim his sails to protect values he counts as nothing next to those he is trying to vindicate. It is true that some political dissenters speak in ways that shock the majority, but it is arrogant of the majority to suppose that the orthodox methods of expression are the proper ways to speak, for this is a denial of equal concern and respect. If the point of the right is to protect the dignity of dissenters, then we must make judgements about appropriate speech with the personalities of the dissenters in mind, not the personality of the 'silent' majority for whom the anti-riot law is no restraint at all.[40]

Dworkin's argument implies that the right to speech exists in order to 'protect' the dignity of dissenters. It is remarkable for its covert conclusion: the more 'silent', and the more law-abiding your activities, the less you may protest against the provocative utterances of those who don't care a fig for your values. The voice of dissent is the voice of the hero; it is for *his* sake that the constitution was designed. The essay advances in that way to the conclusion that 'any government's harsh treatment of civil disobedience, or campaign against vocal protest, may be thought to count against its sincerity'. In other words, a truly sincere government, having passed a law, will be lenient towards those who disobey it.

But of course, he doesn't really mean it. Imagine that the Chicago Seven had been right-wing militants, stirring up disaffection in a cause abhorrent to Dworkin – anti-abortion, say, or anti-immigration. You can be sure that they would not have been offered rights consonant with the degree of their indignation, nor would their 'dignity' have merited anything better than imprisonment.

---

[40] Ibid., p. 201.

In the essay on 'civil disobedience' Dworkin deals in a peremptory manner with conservatives who argue that we should punish those who encourage disobedience to the law. 'It might have been argued', he writes, 'that if those who counsel draft resistance are free from persecution, the number of those who resist induction will increase; but not, I think, much beyond the number of those who would resist in any event.'[41] He is writing of the Vietnam war, arguing that here 'conscience is deeply involved', and that 'it is hard to believe that many who counselled resistance (to the draft) did so on any other grounds'. The implication is that this conscience – because it has lent itself, however absolutely, however unthinkingly, to a left-leaning cause – deserves the protection of the law. More: it may even defy the law, since 'if the issue is one touching fundamental personal or political rights, and it is arguable that the Supreme Court has made a mistake, a man is within his social rights in refusing to accept that decision as conclusive.'[42]

In other words, the liberal conscience can rest satisfied with a mere opinion as to what the law might have been or ought to be. The conservative conscience, however, is never entitled to an equal indulgence, but must always labour under an immovable burden of proof. Thus civil disobedience in the cause of segregation is automatically without the credentials of civil disobedience in a liberal cause. 'If we take no action against the man who blocks the school house door...we violate the moral rights, confirmed by law, of the [black] schoolgirl he blocks. The responsibility of leniency cannot go this far.'[43] Dworkin's opponent is not to comfort himself with the view that the law is, in this respect, 'arguably' mistaken. It is *sufficient* that blacks have a moral right 'as individuals' not to be segregated. Of course, every conscript also has a right, as an individual, to the presence of his fellows in the ranks beside him. But that right, we are given to understand, is 'less fundamental'. Besides, no one can really respect the personality that motivates the segregationist's sense of his rights, since 'except in very rare cases a white student prefers the company of other whites because he has racist social and political convictions, or because he has contempt for blacks as a group'.[44]

The last remark – itself a careless dismissal of a whole group of Americans on grounds that could easily be characterized as racist –

---

[41] Ibid., p. 219.
[42] Ibid., p. 215.
[43] Ibid., p. 210.
[44] Ibid., p. 236.

serves as the premise to a discussion of reverse discrimination. This was, at the time, a leading liberal cause, and Dworkin was especially wily in the defence of it. A practice in which individuals from some historically 'disfavoured group' are admitted to an advantage from which others with better qualifications are excluded clearly poses a challenge to the idea that there are universal human rights, which belong to each person as an individual. And Dworkin admits that 'racial criteria are not necessarily the right standards for deciding which applicants should be accepted by law schools',[45] and it is comforting to those who find racism distasteful to read that racial criteria, in such a case, are not *necessarily* right. But the syntax already suggests where Dworkin's argument – or rather, his barrister's brief – is aiming. He goes on as follows:

> ... neither are intellectual criteria, nor indeed any other set of criteria. The fairness – and constitutionality – of any admissions program must be tested in the same way. It is justified if it serves a proper policy that respects the right of all members of the community to be treated as equals, but not otherwise.[46]

How could this be so? Dworkin has two reasons for this. The first resides in a general distinction he makes between 'equal treatment' and 'treatment as an equal', believing that the Constitution is aiming to ensure the latter, regardless of the 'equal protection' clause. Thus I treat John and Mary equally when, in considering them for a job, I consider only their qualifications and the likelihood that they will each do the job well. But that might not be enough if I am to treat them as equals. To reach that more exacting standard I must consider the extent to which women have been discriminated against, and therefore the extent to which it has required, from Mary, a greater effort to reach the stage of being considered for the job than it has required from John. In that case, to treat the two *as equals* might require me to compensate for Mary's unfair disadvantages, by giving her precedence over John.

That is one argument, which of course immediately transfers the concept of a right from the individual to the group, so that individuals are no longer considered merely as individuals when it comes to assessing their rights, but also as members of groups, some of which might be

---

[45] Ibid., p. 239.
[46] Ibid.

burdened with an immovable handicap, notably white males. But Dworkin has another argument too. In the case under consideration, he maintains, there are *no* relevant rights. There is no such thing as a right to be considered for a place in law school on the basis of intellectual merit. Hence, if rights are still to provide our guiding principle, we must shift attention from the individual case to the overall policy. Does the policy *serve* the cause of rights, or does it *obstruct* that cause?

By virtue of these two arguments variously applied and suitably adapted to the opponent's attempts to meet them, Dworkin is able to get rid of the annoying obstacle of individual rights, and return everything to the 'moral theory' contained, somewhere, somehow, in the Constitution. This theory advocates one overriding right, which is the right to be treated as an equal, a right that translates into a system of handicaps and privileges, distributed according to group membership rather than citizenship of the country or membership of the human race.

There is indeed some plausibility in the view that an individual has no right to be considered on his merits when applying for an educational benefit. But the reason is quite different from the one given by Dworkin. The benefit is a *gift*, and it is the right of the donor to bestow it as he will. If that were Dworkin's point, then he would be arguing within the great tradition of American liberalism, against the belief that we are entitled to coerce individuals in the interests of policy. But he has no hesitation in applying such coercion. In the given case the law school must certainly be constrained to offer its places as policy dictates. (It could not, for example, offer them to whites or males only.) But the policy is not the normal meritocratic one that seems to be implied in the Equal Protection Clause of the Constitution. For to apply that policy is to create social inequalities and 'we must take care', Dworkin argues, 'not to use the Equal Protection Clause to cheat ourselves of equality'. We must not allow our preoccupation with individual rights to obstruct policies that will (according to Dworkin at least) generate greater equality, and more effective rights, in the long run.

The example is extremely interesting. For it shows the ease with which the liberal may deprive his opponent of his only defence. The liberal says, in effect, 'I recognize no argument except individual rights, and the policies needed to secure them.' And when the conservative seeks to defend his rights, the liberal pulls the rug from beneath him, saying 'these are *not* rights'. The conservative argues that, if a privilege is to be granted, either it is a gift, in which case the donor can determine how it is to be distributed, or it is an entitlement, in which case the default position, laid down by the Constitution, is one of 'equal treatment'. It is, of course, a further, and judicial question, what equal treatment amounts to in the given case. But the assumption is that it means conferring on to each person the rights guaranteed by the Constitution, neither more nor less.

Elsewhere Dworkin ridicules the feeling that concessions to the individual and his 'rights' may sometimes be overridden by a policy designed to secure social and political stability. He argues, against certain standard utilitarian moves, that no issue of mere policy can override an individual's claim to just treatment. 'We must not', he writes, 'confuse strategy with justice, nor facts of political life with principles of political morality.'[47] Or at least, not when criticizing Lord Devlin's argument in favour of embodying elements of traditional sexual morality in the law, or when pouring scorn on 'popular indignation, intolerance and disgust' (not to be confused, we are told, with 'moral conviction'). The strategy which champions the underdog may ride roughshod over any rights the conservative names, for if the conservative names them, you can be sure they are not 'rights', just as you can be sure that, when the conservative seeks to prevent something, it is not from moral conviction, which is what liberals have, but from sentiments of 'indignation, intolerance and disgust'.

Of course, there are deep and difficult questions of political philosophy at issue here. Dworkin may very well be right in his supposition that the benefits that the conservative wishes to defend are not genuine rights. But which rights *are* genuine, and on what grounds? To refer in a vague way to the American Constitution and the alleged 'moral theory' on which it was founded is not to answer that question, especially when the cases cited in illustration were decided in the English courts. Dworkin is adamant that he is arguing from principles, not rescindable laws; but when the discussion enters the higher realm of philosophy we need to know how those principles are justified. And this is a question from which he flees.

In a subsequent book, *Law's Empire*, Dworkin elaborates a new strategy for winning arguments, and this is to view law *hermeneutically*, as in every particular 'open to interpretation', and therefore always open to interpretation in the liberal's favour.[48] An interpretation, Dworkin argues, is an attempt to give the *best* reading of some human artefact – the reading that shows it to be most suited to its final aim. On this view a

---

[47] Ibid., p. 253.
[48] *Law's Empire*, Cambridge, MA, Harvard University Press, 1988.

critical interpretation of a work of art is an attempt to give the reading that accords to it the greatest aesthetic value. What the 'best' interpretation consists in depends upon the activity discussed. Obviously the law is not a pursuit of aesthetic value. Of what, then? One answer would be justice. But it is not, or not obviously, the answer that Dworkin gives – once again, faced with the challenge to come clean he retreats into shadowy by-ways. Sometimes he emphasizes the role of law in 'guiding and constraining the power of government' – in other words, in safeguarding individual rights. Sometimes he writes of its function in resolving conflicts, as in much of the civil law. In more theoretical passages he describes law as constrained by an ideal of integrity, and in the end this seems to be his preferred theory, albeit an obscure one.

This search for the 'best' reading of the law is carried out at many levels: in the law courts (when judges interpret the law, when they adjudicate hard cases, and when they try to reconcile their decisions with the relevant precedents); in the reflections of jurists (when they rationalize or criticize the decisions of the courts); in the arguments of legal philosophers (when they search for first principles).

For Dworkin law should be seen not as a command, nor as a convention, nor as a prediction, nor as a mere instrument of policy. Law is rather (according to his mood) an expression of civil, or moral, or constitutional rights; a realization of a 'political morality'; an embodiment of the 'associative obligations' of the community over which it is exercised. If he shifts so rapidly and confidently between those various idioms, it is partly because he has a theory (which looms large but faint in his stylistic twilight), according to which those functions of the law coincide.

Here and there he expresses the theory in quasi-religious terms. 'Our' law, he argues, is a 'protestant' activity. In saying this he makes no mention of the fact that the common law has been with us throughout the days of highest Popery, enjoying the explicit sanction of the Church's Canon Law. He is concerned again to take up the causes of *Taking Rights Seriously*, and to describe law as a weapon in the hands of the protestor. 'We', he suggests, in belonging to the peculiar legal tradition that is 'ours', subscribe to a highly individualistic morality, which emphasizes the rights of the individual against the authority of the sovereign power, and which is through and through 'political' in its force and application. This condition of 'political morality' defines the community to which 'we' all suppose ourselves to belong. Faced with an opponent who believes that 'we' are not all readers of the *New York Review of Books* Dworkin is, as we have seen, reluctant to concede that individual rights can trump embedded liberal policies. Nevertheless, he wishes to argue that the law aims to uphold the rights and responsibilities that are recognized within a 'community', and thereby to ensure the identity of that community through time – just as each individual ensures his identity through time by taking responsibility for his past and future actions.

In a highly charged and misleading analogy Dworkin compares the law to a 'chain novel' – a novel continued by many authors, with the shared aim of producing a single and integrated work of art. In following a precedent a judge is engaged in an act that both interprets what went before, and also changes the context of interpretation. The constraint is that he should endeavour to embody and to continue the 'integrity' of the law – in other words, to uphold the rights and responsibilities that have been enshrined in the law by the community. The 'integrity' of the law is, in the end, the same phenomenon as the personality of the community that it serves.

Having summarized the theory as I understand it I shall express it in my own words. Law, as 'we' know it, is not a body of rules but a tradition, and its significance lies not in its results but in its 'meaning' – in that which we recuperate through interpretation. The law also expresses a corporate personality, which is that of the community in its political aspect. The law enshrines rights, responsibilities and – let me add, though Dworkin characteristically doesn't – duties, and carries them forward from generation to generation.

The process of adjudication requires specific institutions – for example judicial independence and an authoritative record of past decisions. But it depends even more on a certain 'public spirit', generated by the shared allegiance of the people. This allegiance is neither contractual nor universal, but the recognition of the common destiny that binds people together in a nation state.

If I remark that such a theory of law has already been defended in the name of political conservatism, it is not in order to discount any claim to originality on Dworkin's part – for his way of arriving at these conclusions is marked at every point by a distinctive and exuberant intellect. It is rather to draw attention to Dworkin's isolation from all traditions of thought outside the fields of Anglo-American jurisprudence and analytical philosophy. He would have spared his readers much trouble had he realized the extent to which his conclusions had been anticipated by Smith, Burke, Hegel and de Maistre. And while this would have meant renouncing one of his favourite postures – that of the enlightened liberal, who has yet to be convinced that there is such a thing as intellectual conservatism – it would have forced him to confront the enormous disharmony that exists between his defence of 'our' legal tradition, and his combative advocacy of the causes (such as reverse discrimination) which are currently undermining it.

Dworkin's 'we' includes all Anglophone liberals, but perhaps not all Americans outside the coastal cities. His examples, as I noted above, are taken from English and American law, and are discussed in the light of the common-law principles of precedent and *stare decisis* (though without reference to the important distinction between common law and equity). Most of the world is governed by systems of law that, ostensibly at least, do *not* obey those principles. Many European countries have legal systems based on the *Code Napoléon*, in which the doctrine of precedent is officially repudiated (at least in the form adopted by the English courts). Nevertheless those countries are governed by law, and by a system of appeals designed to protect individual rights (though perhaps not the same rights as are buried within the common law).

And here, I think, is where we see the profound weakness of Dworkin's way of arguing. It is the way of the barrister, snatching whatever useful trick is to hand, but not the way of the philosopher, with an eye for universal truth. Dworkin never once mentions the *Code Napoléon*, nor the many similar codified systems that have grown up in imitation of it. Nor does he mention Roman Law, even though that law contains interesting devices whereby hard cases can be reconciled with underlying principle. Nor does he mention Canon Law – the foundation of European criminal justice systems – let alone Islamic Law, in which there is genuine interpretation and judicial independence, even though 'what the law says' has been spoken for all time through the Prophet. And of course, Dworkin omits all mention of Communist Law – the systems of 'socialist legality' installed by Stalin, which had no authoritative precedents, no properly maintained legal record and no judicial independence. And why does Dworkin never mention International Law, the most controversial of all claimants to the title? Are these all deviant cases?

Had Dworkin considered at least some of the rival systems, he would have been forced to conclude that 'we' are a smaller group than he imagines, and that there is a need for a theory that is wider in scope, richer in concepts, and less dependent on a one-sided diet of examples than the theory that he has given us. But that also shows that Dworkin's theory of 'interpretation' is not so much a true philosophy of law as an instrument of advocacy, with which to confiscate the American Constitution from its conservative devotees. Outside the context of his lifelong barrister's brief it is impossible to say how the theory should be applied, or what it really amounts to.

A conservative, faced with the task of developing a theory of law that is something more than advocacy, would be unhappy with a concept of interpretation that is tied to a specific historical context, and which seems expressly designed to validate the 'political morality' of Ronald Dworkin. He would, I believe, begin his theory from a concept that has no part to play in Dworkin's account, the concept of sovereignty. Sovereignty means the legitimate power to command obedience. For those, like Hobbes, Hegel and de Maistre, who have looked into the abyss, it is the *sine qua non* of legal order, the condition from which peaceful and consensual relations begin. Neither terrorism, nor its institutional form in totalitarian government, cast their shadow across Dworkin's empire. Dworkinian man is a creature already securely governed by law, and safely protected by clever jurists from its more unwelcome commands. His 'political morality' consists almost entirely of rights and claims, and makes little room for the ideas of duty and obedience. When it comes to fighting for his country he can rely on the escape clause of civil disobedience. When conservatives attempt to impose their oppressive morality in matters of sex, marriage and abortion he can easily discover a right to whatever it is he wants to do, 'interpreted' into the Constitution by obliging liberal judges.

But what, in the end, does 'interpretation' amount to? To say that the purpose of interpreting an activity is to give the 'best' version of it is to say very little. We do not say what football is by arguing that the purpose of football is to play football well. We need a more concrete, and also more nuanced theory of what the 'best' consists in. Dworkin, like Hans-Georg Gadamer (to whom he refers in the crucial passage), makes much of the example of language.[49] And it is of course true that language provides our central example of interpretation. But what is the 'best' interpretation of another's utterance? Not necessarily the interpretation that renders it true, or useful, or compatible with whatever else the other person says or believes. It is the interpretation that tells us what the utterance means.

---

[49] Hans-Georg Gadamer, modern expositor of 'hermeneutics', whose *Truth and Method* – 1960, tr. various, London, Sheed and Ward, 1979 – contains a vague but influential plea for the priority of interpretation over explanation in the human sciences.

Literary critics are used to the idea that 'what a text means' is not the same thing as 'what the author *says* it means'. All the discussions around the intentional fallacy and the 'death of the author' have, however, passed Dworkin by, and he leaves us with an idea of 'the best' interpretation that is entirely improvised around his preferred conclusions. It is impossible to derive from his argument any theory as to what goes on when, for example, a judge tries to get round an unjust or oppressive law by invoking principles of equity. Indeed the whole tradition embodied by our court of Chancery goes unmentioned in Dworkin's argument. And he never tells us what happens when judges apply a law because they *must* and not because it harmonizes with other aspects of the legal system – as when forced to override contractual agreements in the interests of social legislation.

I suspect that a real scholar, troubled by the idea of interpretation, would have taken time off from his favourite causes to look at the concept of *ijtihād* in Islamic law. Until the triumph of the *Ash'arite* theologians in the tenth century of our era, and the destructive dogma that 'the gate of *ijtihād* is closed', jurists from the four accepted schools agreed that the law governing a particular case should be arrived at by interpretation of the Koran and the hadiths, according to certain principles that would harmonize the decision with the explicit statements issued through the mouth of the Prophet. Much scholarly work has been devoted to understanding exactly how the early Islamic jurists proceeded and it would have been interesting to read what Dworkin made of it – or of anything else outside the impetuous flourishes of his liberal advocacy. But you will look for such things in vain. It is uncertain to the very end of his argument what 'interpretation' is, or who is meant by his all-pervasive first-person plural. He ends with these words: 'that is what the law is for us; for the people we want to be and the community we aim to have'. To which the only coherent response is 'speak for yourself'.

In the characters of Galbraith and Dworkin we see the emergence in America of a belligerent liberal establishment. Both were brilliant men, with a command of circumstantial reasoning. Both had a cavalier approach to serious scholarship. Both poured scorn on the received ideas of American society, in order to open the way to defiance. And meanwhile both enjoyed the enormous rewards that were available to those who subverted the old culture of family, enterprise, God and the flag. Examine their arguments closely, however, and you find short cuts, rhetoric, and a contempt for opposing views. For all their cleverness they leave the real intellectual issues exactly where they found them.

4 LIBERATION IN FRANCE: SARTRE AND FOUCAULT

uring the last decade of the nineteenth century the Dreyfus case, in which a Jewish officer in the French army had been exiled on trumped-up charges of treason, raised the question of what it is to be French. What kind of allegiance is needed if the country is to defend itself? The question was posed in the wake of France's humiliation by Bismarck's armies, provoking a patriotism that came too late to save the day, and which was only half in being by the time of the next emergency in 1914.

Zola's famous article 'J'accuse', appearing in a daily newspaper, *L'Aurore*, in 1898, pointed a finger at the French government and political classes, holding them to be guilty of anti-Semitism. Patriotism, Zola argued, has nothing to do with race, but everything to do with citizenship. Zola's article brought to a head the conflict concerning the relation between Catholic orthodoxy and the status of the Jewish citizen. It also raised questions about the very nature of France, and of the loyalty to France on which the country had been unable to call in its hour of need.[1]

Throughout *À la recherche du temps perdu* Proust obsessively returns to the Dreyfus case, as though it were the sole intrusion from the world of public events into the inner realm of exquisite feeling and intemperate lust that was his ruling preoccupation. Proust associated the 'outsider' character of the Jew in high society with the life of the closet homosexual in a Catholic culture. Nowhere is the Dreyfus case more prominent, indeed, than in the pages of *Sodome et Gomorrhe* devoted to homosexual desire – pages that are also a subtle plea for toleration towards those whose inner identity is concealed from the rest of society and who are therefore consciously living on the edge.

---

[1] The questions remain as alive today as they ever were: see Alain Finkielkraut, *Le mécontemporain*, Paris, Gallimard, 1991.

Proust and Zola were urban patriots, for whom citizenship took precedence over religion and culture. Among the *dreyfusards* were Catholic writers who sought for a more rooted, less legalistic, kind of patriotism. They identified France with the countryside, its peasant way of life, its settled economy and the native forms of Catholic piety. Although sincere Catholics, they wished to give a more territorial character to their devotion, and to attach their faith to the landscape of France in something like the way that the Anglican faith had been stitched to the landscape of England by the Victorian novelists and poets. Jeanne d'Arc, the warrior maiden whose beautiful story predated the Revolution by three centuries and a half, became a symbol of their new form of patriotism, which was to be a consecration of the land and the people as well as a reassertion of Christian commitment.

The leading figure in the movement was Charles Péguy, founder and editor of the famous *Cahiers de la quinzaine*, in which many of the most important works of the first decade of French twentieth-century literature made their appearance – including Romain Rolland's *Jean Christophe* and works by Anatole France and Julien Benda. Péguy's *Mystère de la charité de Jeanne d'Arc* appeared in 1911, three years before his death in battle in 1914, and it was largely thanks to Péguy's influence and campaigning that Jeanne d'Arc was canonized by the Church in 1920. Péguy's synthesis of Catholicism and patriotism was highly influential on the philosopher Jacques Maritain and his wife Raïssa, and around them congregated an influential circle of writers and thinkers in the years after 1918, when the French were struggling to recover from the senseless slaughter of the First World War.[2]

This post-war *renouveau catholique* included painters (Georges Rouault), composers (Charles Tournemire and Francis Poulenc), and such writers as Paul Claudel, Jean Cocteau, Francis Jammes, Charles du Bos, Gabriel Marcel and François Mauriac.[3] Their efforts can be witnessed in an extraordinary publication entitled *Chroniques*, the first volume of which appeared in 1925, under the editorship of Claudel,

[2] See Raïssa Maritain, *We Have Been Friends Together*, tr. Julie Kernan, New York, Longmans, Green and Co., 1942, and *Adventures in Grace*, tr. Julie Kernan, New York, Longmans, Green and Co., 1945. The story of the Maritains and their 'gathering in' of intellectual sympathizers is told by Jean-Luc Barré, tr. Bernard E. Doering, *Jacques and Raïssa Maritain: Beggars for Heaven*, South Bend, University of Notre Dame Press, 2005.
[3] See the study by Stephen Schloesser, *Jazz Age Catholicism: Modernism in Postwar Paris, 1919–1933*, Toronto, 2005.

Cocteau, Jacob, Maritain and (strange to say) G. K. Chesterton – all at the time passionately Catholic. The cause of French nationalism entered a rocky period, however, when another, more secular, and indeed often frankly atheist, rival began to gain ascendancy. This was the belligerently royalist *Action Française* of Charles Maurras (a movement which he had founded with a journal of that title in 1898, and which had grown in strength in the first two decades of the twentieth century). Maurras was an anti-Semite who had joined enthusiastically in the condemnation of Captain Dreyfus, and who had a singularly violent streak, issuing death threats against prominent politicians that earned him a prison sentence.

The crisis of the Second World War, with the capitulation of the French and the establishment of the Vichy regime, meant that the whole idea of French nationalism was thereafter tainted with the crime of collaboration. Much of post-war French literature has been a reaction to this. Maurras, for example, was a collaborator with the Vichy regime, and was tried after the war for giving aid and encouragement to the enemy. His death sentence was commuted to life imprisonment, though other intellectual members of his movement were less fortunate. One of them, the fiercely anti-Semitic novelist Robert Brasillach, was shot, notwithstanding a plea to General de Gaulle for clemency signed by many of the most important writers of the day, including Paul Valéry and Jean Cocteau. Writers after the war divided into the innocent and the guilty, the innocent being often self-styled, and including many who had hastily cobbled together a fiction of membership in the Resistance. The more open collaborators such as Maurras, Brasillach and the novelist Drieu la Rochelle were turned upon by a population whose own innocence was in many cases a retrospective fabrication.[4]

Not surprisingly, therefore, much of French war literature is devoted to the intricacies of treason, committed by people often more willing to lay down their arms for their safety than to lay down their life for their friend. Recall Maupassant's famous story *Boule de Suif*, concerning the attempt by a party of respectable bourgeois to sacrifice a prostitute – the unique patriot among them – to a German officer's embraces. Or consider those two powerful novels from between the

---

[4] It has been claimed that there were as many as five million letters of denunciation sent to the authorities in Vichy France, or to the German occupiers elsewhere. See André Halimi, *La Délation sous l'Occupation*, Paris, Éditions Alain Moreau, 1983.

world wars, Louis-Ferdinand Céline's *Voyage au bout de la nuit*, and
Marcel Aymé's *La jument verte*, the first concerning the moral chaos of
the First World War, the second treachery between neighbours in the
Franco-Prussian conflict of 1870–71. In both we see a country riven by
suspicions, searching for a patriotism that so often seems to elude it,
and seemingly devoid of the spirit of sacrifice that animates (however
wistfully and with whatever degree of self-deception) English literature
from the First World War.

Illustrative of the trauma is the writer Drieu la Rochelle. He had
fought bravely in the First World War, being three times wounded and
obtaining the Croix de Guerre. He emerged from the experience as one
of the leading literary figures in inter-war Paris. But he had no taste for
the Catholic revival and for the next twenty years led a disordered life,
devoted to the seduction of women and the composition of bleak novels
in which women and their sexuality occupy centre-stage. He repudiated
the nationalist ideas that he believed to have brought about the Great War
and advocated a united Europe and a new internationalism as the only
way to achieve a peaceful future.

At first Drieu supported the communists, as the evident advocates of
the internationalist cause, and joined the Party, along with so many of his
contemporaries. When he left the Party and declared himself a fascist it
was not because he repudiated what he had once believed. For him the
international socialism that had drawn him to the Communist Party was
now best expressed by the rising fascist parties in Germany and Italy.
And he can hardly be blamed for thinking this, at a time when the Nazis
and the Communists had entered their secret alliance. There is a kind of
death wish, a disgust with life, that unites the internationalist politics and
seedy experience of a character like Drieu.[5] His eventual suicide, which
saved him from being tried for treason, was already implicit in the *ennui*
and *nostalgie de la boue* that fill the pages of *L'homme couvert de femmes*,
a novel that expresses, in its very title, the divorce between sex and love
that defined Drieu's experience. His life, like his art, was a record of
spiritual devastation, for which he searched in vain for a political remedy.

The efforts of Péguy, Maritain and their followers to link Catholicism
and nationalism in a close embrace were unacceptable, not only to people
like Drieu la Rochelle, but also to the ordinary left-leaning intellectuals.
Many of them were unbelievers – the national culture having already

---

[5] See Pol Vandromme, *Drieu la Rochelle*, Paris, Editions Universitaires, 1958.

been partly colonized by the Deism of Auguste Comte and the atheism of Zola, Proudhon and Georges Sorel. The influence of Marxism was felt throughout society, and following the Russian Revolution the French Communist Party began to grow rapidly, recruiting many of the leading intellectuals, including the novelist and poet Louis Aragon, the painter Pablo Picasso, and the leading surrealist, André Breton.

It could be argued that the resulting *trahison des clercs* was less damaging than that of the Cambridge spies and their circle, since less depended upon France than on England during the war and its aftermath. But the guilty consciences of the post-war French intellectuals can be clearly seen in their intensely hostile reactions to the *Livre noir du communisme* edited by the ex-Maoist Stéphane Courtois and published in 1997. This book gives the body-count of communist crimes, and describes the intellectuals' part in condoning and inspiring them. It also insists on the comparison (for Courtois a near-identity) between communism and Nazism.[6] For many French intellectuals who had turned to the Communist Party as a reaction to the horrors of Nazism, this comparison was not just offensive: it was treasonable. Yet the communists were in some measure responsible for the erosion of the will to fight the Nazis, being under indirect orders from Hitler during the crucial months of France's defeat. (It was thanks to the PCF that the munitions factories went on strike when Hitler – then the beneficiary of the Nazi–Soviet pact – marched into France.)

The beliefs, campaigns and self-image of the post-war generation of writers must be read against that painful background. And in almost all of them one influence stands out, which is that of Alexandre Kojève, a Russian exile whose lectures on Hegel at the *École Pratique des Hautes Études* during the 1930s were attended by many of the big names in post-war French literature – Bataille, Lacan, Sartre, de Beauvoir, Lévinas, Aron, Queneau, Merleau-Ponty and many more. While the Communist Party was busy putting the machinery of industry in the hands of the Unions and the socialist State, Kojève – who was a high-ranking French civil servant, and one of the architects of the European Union – was softening the intellectual class with the Hegelian dialectic, the foundation of the Marxist religion that had swept to power in his native Russia. Sources in the French security services have alleged that Kojève was a Soviet agent. But we have no independent evidence of this. After all, he declared to all

---

[6] Stéphane Courtois, ed., *Le livre noir du communisme*, Paris, Robert Laffont, 1997.

and sundry that he was a follower of Josef Stalin, and what Soviet agent would say such a thing?[7]

Kojève's lectures on Hegel were subsequently edited into a volume by Raymond Queneau, the witty author of *Zazie dans le métro*. They are devoted to expounding the argument of Hegel's *Phenomenology of Spirit*, and in particular the dialectic of freedom, according to which the human being becomes a free self-consciousness through the process of conflict with the Other. Two ideas seem to have jumped from Kojève's mouth into the minds of his audience, to reappear as leitmotivs in the post-war literature: the identity of freedom and self-consciousness, and the dialectic of subject and object. It is worth giving a brief summary of them, and of their place in the philosophy of Hegel, since they will crop up in many of my discussions in later chapters.

For Hegel the process whereby we come to full consciousness of ourselves as subjects, and the process whereby we 'realize' our freedom, are one and the same. I know myself through my free actions, and through acting freely I create the self that I know. Self-knowledge is not a solitary exercise of introspection. It is a *social* process, in which I encounter and wrestle with the 'Other', whose will, conflicting with mine, forces me to recognize the Other in myself. In a justly famous passage Hegel argues that there is, both in the life of the individual and in the larger history of mankind, a transition from the 'life and death struggle' of conflicting wills, to the relation of lordship and bondage, in which one side has submitted and the other prevailed, and from thence to the life of labour, in which the slave creates for himself the conditions of freedom. The process continues until slavery gives way from its own inner dynamic to citizenship, legality and mutual agreement.[8]

Hegel drew conservative conclusions from his argument, and indeed provided some of the fundamental concepts of the right-wing view of things that I shall defend in the final chapter. But what impressed Kojève's audience of spiritually hungry atheists in the 1930s was the vision that lay dormant within Hegel's pages: the vision of radical freedom and the self-created individual. It dawned on them that, by exploring the self and its freedom, it was possible to re-enchant their disenchanted world, and to place the human subject once again at the centre of things. Moreover, they were granted a vision of the Fall, with which to explain their alienation.

---

[7] I am reminded of Max Frisch's play, *The Fire-Raisers*, ostensibly inspired by the communist takeover in Eastern Europe after 1945.
[8] Hegel, *The Phenomenology of Spirit*, Chapter 4.

The Fall was the Other, the Subject made Object, the thing against which freedom defines itself and with which it is locked in conflict.

Self and Other, Subject and Object, Freedom and Alienation – the opposites accumulated and spread like wildfire through the parched brains of Kojève's devotees, to reappear transmuted in the post-war literature, when a new wave of guilt and repudiation had engulfed their destroyed homeland. For Simone de Beauvoir the dialectic of self and other explained for the first time the subjection of women – the '*altérité*' to which women are condemned by the established way of representing them. To Georges Bataille the fascination of the subject with the object became the core component in eroticism, the way in which the world of things is infected with our freedom. For Lacan the Hegelian dialectic was recast as the story of the 'mirror stage' of the psyche, the moment in which the subject sees himself as object, and so becomes Other to himself. And so on for all the writers and thinkers who sat at Kojève's feet and learned from him to step back from Marx into Hegel, and to see that, whatever had gone wrong in the world, it was the Other who was to blame.

It is of course impossible to reduce a thinker as complex as Sartre to a single influence. Along with Kojève's Hegelianism Sartre was deeply immersed in the phenomenology of Husserl and its radical reworking in Martin Heidegger's strangely gripping philosophy of 'authenticity'. He studied for a year with Husserl in Germany, while preparing a thesis on imagination, and then taught in schools for most of the 1930s before being drafted into the French army, to be captured at Padoux in 1940. He was released, having pleaded ill-health on account of his weak eyesight, made his way back to Paris and took up teaching again at the Lycée Condorcet. He was active, but not dangerously so, in the Resistance, an experience that left a lasting impression on him, and his involvement with communist cadres in the immediate post-war period inspired his anti-communist play *Les mains sales*.

Sartre prospered under the occupation, was able to publish in 1943 his magnum opus, *L'être et le néant*, without censorship, and was co-founder in 1945 of the successful review *Les Temps modernes*, which he continued to edit for two decades. Having refused the Légion d'Honneur in 1945 he was unable to refuse the Nobel Prize for Literature in 1964 since the rules do not permit this. But he did not attend the award ceremony in Stockholm and gave away the prize-money to socialist causes. Sartre was never a member of the Communist Party, believing neither in parties nor in any other kind of institution. But *Les Temps modernes*, under his editorship, was unswerving in its support for communist campaigns. Moreover, his own political denunciations (typified by that directed against his former friend and co-editor Albert Camus in *Les Temps modernes*) were brutally Stalinist, just as his vision of the modern world was utopian and myopic: facts that approximate him so closely to the spirit of the French Communist Party as to make his self-proclaimed distance from it little more than a gesture. It was by way of ingratiating himself with the Party that he withdrew *Les mains sales* from the stage.

Sartre announced *Les Temps modernes* as a journal devoted to *la littérature engagée*. In no sense, however, does that phrase describe Sartre's earliest literary excursions – the brief study of the imagination published in 1936 and the novel *La nausée* of 1938, both reflections on the inner life and its separation from the world of action. It is fair to say that *La nausée* changed the course of French literature, by providing it with a new kind of narrative centre. The hero of *La nausée*, Roquentin, is filled with disgust at the world of things. He feels tainted by his incarnation, which unites him blatantly and irreversibly to a world that is other than himself. The experience of nausea occurs whenever existence loses its 'inoffensive air of an abstract category', and becomes instead 'the very stuff of things'. He sees then that 'what exists must exist to this point: to the point of mouldering, of bulging, of obscenity'. Here, for the first time fully in Sartre's work, we encounter his peculiar transformation of Kojève's version of the Other, the 'not-I' that stands immovably opposed to the 'I' of freedom and self-consciousness.

Roquentin's disgust – '*une éspèce d'écoeurement douceâtre*' – contrasts with his sense of his own inner freedom. Within him, he feels, there lies the capacity to repudiate the world, to refuse its overwhelmingness. His disgust therefore acquires a more specific focus, which is other people – and in particular those whom he considers to be 'bourgeois', whose faces blaze for him with an unjustifiable righteousness. The bourgeois is the Other incarnate, the omnipresent negation of the self. Roquentin contemplates the immersion of the bourgeoisie in the family and the state, their easy consolation in religion, in social gatherings and in roles – and his response is a fierce abnegation. The bourgeoisie are the epitome of bad faith, the living record of an abjured freedom, the testimony to the self betrayed. Whatever happens *he* will not so betray himself. And the story of his disgust is the story of his refusal to belong.

Roquentin was the first of many such literary creations – centres of consciousness who observe without belonging. Such is Meursault, the narrator of Camus's *L'Étranger* (1942), such too is the anonymous first-person narrator of Maurice Blanchot's *Au moment voulu* (1951), and such is the 'absent' narrator of Alain Robbe-Grillet's *La jalousie* (1957), the work that initiated the *nouveau roman*, in which nothing really happens and all feelings are implied. To the sceptical English reader all these suffering observers are so many withdrawn adolescents, who flatter themselves that their revulsion is a kind of holiness. Unfair, perhaps, but a way of acknowledging that there is another way entirely of seeing Roquentin, as a manifestation of the cardinal sin of pride, the sin of Milton's Satan, the sin that was Sartre's, and which he sought throughout his life to dignify with the highest theological titles.

In Roquentin Sartre began the task of creating his own salvation, from the premise of the self. And this is the task that he continued in his masterpiece, *Being and Nothingness* (1943), and in the famous lecture, 'Existentialism and Humanism', which he delivered in 1945. In an extraordinary combination of philosophical argument, psychological observation and lyrical evocation, Sartre sets out to describe the ordeal and the task of consciousness, in a world that has no meaning other than the meaning that I, through my freedom, can impress on it.

Medieval philosophers took from Aristotle the view that we answer the question 'what exists?' by identifying the essential natures of things. If this before me exists then it is something. If it is something, then there is something that it is. And the something that it is – a man, a dog, a stick, a pile of sand – is defined by an essence. Hence 'essence precedes existence': we know the world by understanding essences and looking for the things that exemplify them. But that way of seeing things, Sartre argues, depends upon an untenable metaphysics. There is no human nature, since there is no God to have a conception of it. Essences, as intellectual constructs, vanish with the mind that would conceive them. For us, therefore, our existence – our unconceptualized individuality, whose reality is freedom – is the sole premise of all inquiry, and the one sure point of observation on a world whose meaning has yet to be bestowed on it. The true premise of philosophy is 'existence precedes essence'. My existence is governed by no universal morality, and has no prefigured destiny such as might be contained in a vision of human nature. Man must make his own essence, and even his existence is, in a sense, an achievement: he exists fully only when he is what he purposes to be.

Consciousness is 'intentional': it posits an object in which it sees itself as in a mirror. As in Hegel's dialectic, object and subject arise together, in fundamental antagonism. Sartre expresses this antagonism in terms already borrowed from Hegel by Marx. The antagonism at the heart of being is that between the 'in-itself' and the 'for-itself' (the *en-soi* and the *pour-soi*). In setting itself up in relation to a fundamentally 'other' object, the self creates a separation in its world, a kind of crevasse. I myself occupy this crevasse: it is the realm of nothingness, *le néant*, which 'lies coiled in the heart of being, like a worm'.

Sartre unfolds an unforgettable portrait of the predicament in which we are placed by self-consciousness in the world of objects. For the religious worldview self-consciousness is a source of joy, proof of our apartness from nature, of our special relation to God and of our ultimate redemption, as we leap from the world into the arms of our creator. For Sartre self-consciousness is a kind of all-dominating nothingness, a source of anxiety: proof of our apartness, certainly, but also of our loneliness, which is a loneliness without redemption, since all the doors on our inner walls have been painted there by ourselves and none of them will open.

Moreover the self, the *pour-soi*, can never become an object of its own awareness. It is always the subject, the thing that knows, rather than the object known. I might turn my attention suddenly towards it, hoping to catch it unawares. But it flits out of sight before my gaze. To catch awareness unawares is exactly what is impossible. The experience of nothingness is therefore elusive as the ego is elusive: the self is nothing and nothing is the self. Occasionally, however – in expectation or in disappointment – we are aware of the sovereignty of nothingness and of the terrifying mutual dependence of nothingness and being. It is only a self-consciousness (a for-itself) that could bring this nothingness into the world. For the merely sentient organism the fracture has not opened between subject and object. With the fracture, however, comes the existential challenge. The question arises, 'How shall I fill this void that separates me from the world?' The anguish that floods the self in the wake of that question is the proof of freedom. There can be nothing more certain than my freedom, since nothing exists for me – nothing is *other* – until this fracture is opened, and my freedom exposed.

Anguish displays itself in the sense that objects are not properly distinct from each other, that they are inert, undifferentiated, awaiting separation. This is the origin of the peculiar metaphysical nausea of Roquentin, the primary object of which is the dissolution of the world. The world becomes slime – the *fango originale* of Boïto's and Verdi's *Iago*. Sartre concludes *Being and Nothingness* with an extended description of slime (*le visqueux*), evoking the queen of nightmares, who seems to rise from the trough of nothingness and confront me with an ultimate denial. Slime is a melting of objects, a 'moist and feminine sucking', something that 'lives obscurely under my fingers' and which 'I sense like a dizziness'. The slimy

> draws me to it as the bottom of a precipice might draw me...In one sense it is like the supreme docility of the possessed, the fidelity of a dog who *gives himself* even when one doesn't want him any longer, and in another sense there is underneath this docility a surreptitious appropriation of the possessor by the possessed.[9]

In slime we confront the absorption of the 'for-itself' by the 'in-itself': the world of objects coalesces around the subject and drags him under.

Slime is therefore an image of the 'self in danger': of a freedom lost to the 'fallen' world of objects. In reaction to this danger, into which freedom itself entices me, I may hide from myself, burying myself in some predetermined role, contorting myself to fit a costume that is already made for me, so crossing the chasm that divides me from objects only to become an object myself. This happens when I adopt a morality, a religion, a social role that has been devised by others and which provides a specious refuge from my own authenticity. The result is 'bad faith' – the crime of the good citizens upon whom Roquentin pours his vehement scorn. Slime repels me and attracts me, precisely because it is an image of the sweet sticky promise of bad faith.

The false simulation of the in-itself by the for-itself (of the object by the subject) is to be contrasted with the authentic individual gesture: the free act whereby the individual creates both himself and his world together, by casting the one into the other. Don't ask *how* this is done, since the process cannot be described. Its end-point is what matters, and this Sartre describes as commitment (*engagement*). But commitment to what?

There is no answer to that question that does not contradict the premise of authenticity. Any adoption of a system of values that is represented as objectively justified constitutes an attempt to bestow my freedom on the world of objects, and thereby to lose it. The desire for an objective moral order is an exhibition of bad faith, and a loss of the

---

[9] *Being and Nothingness*, tr. Hazel Barnes, London, Methuen, 1957, pp. 606–11.

freedom without which no morality of any kind would be conceivable. Sartre's own justification of a self-made morality is therefore inherently contradictory – a fact that in no way deters him from advancing it in the most passionate terms:

> I emerge alone and in dread in the face of the unique and first project which constitutes my being: all the barriers, all the railings, collapse, annihilated by the consciousness of my liberty; I have not, nor can I have, recourse to any value against the fact that it is I who maintain values in being; nothing can assure me against myself; cut off from the world and my essence by the nothing that I *am*, I have to realise the meaning of the world and my essence: I decide it, alone, unjustifiable, and without excuse.[10]

Political commitment is therefore a strange outcome of the cult of authenticity. To understand its necessity for Sartre we must see it in the context of his unremittingly jaundiced view of the 'objective' sources of value, all of which involve a kind of self-betrayal. It is as though he is looking for a metaphysical answer to the French surrender to the Nazis, in the form of an inner defiance of the jackbooted Other. His argument is rooted in the terms that Kojève took from Hegel. But unlike Hegel, whose philosophy was an affirmation of all that is, Sartre was the great denier, the Mephistopheles of Western philosophy, who believed that love, friendship, contract and the normal 'bourgeois' order are all shot through with contradiction.

Sartre introduces the notion of 'being for others' in order to describe the peculiar position in which I, as a self-conscious being, necessarily find myself. I am at once a free subject in my own eyes and a determined object in the eyes of others. When another self-conscious being looks at me, I know that he searches in me not for the object but also for the subject. The gaze of a self-conscious being therefore has a peculiar capacity to penetrate, to create a demand. This is the demand that I, as free subjectivity, reveal myself in the world. At the same time, my existence as a bodily object creates an opacity, an impenetrable barrier between my free subjectivity and the other who seeks to unite with it. This opacity is the origin of obscenity, and my recognition that my body stands to another as his does to me is the source of shame.

---

[10] *Existentialism and Humanism*, tr. Philip Mairet, London, 1948.

Those thoughts launch Sartre into his incomparable description of sexual desire. If I desire a woman, he argues, this is not simply a matter of lusting to gratify myself on her body. If it were just that, then any suitable object, even a simulacrum of a female body, would do just as well. My desire would then unite me with the world of objects, as I am united with it and dragged under by slime. I would experience the extinction of the 'for-itself' in the dark night of obscenity. In true desire what I want is the *other, herself*. But the other is only real in her freedom, and is falsely represented by every attempt to conceive her as an object. Hence desire seeks the freedom of the other, in order to appropriate it as its own.

The lover, who wishes to possess the body of the other only as, and only in so far as, she possesses it herself, is therefore tied by a contradiction. His desire fulfils itself only by compelling the other to identify with her body – to lose her for-itself in the in-itself of flesh. But then what is possessed is precisely not the freedom of the other, but only the husk of freedom – a freedom abjured. In a remarkable passage Sartre describes sadism and masochism as 'reefs upon which desire may founder'.[11] In sado-masochism one party attempts to force the other to identify with his suffering flesh, so as to possess him or her in the body through the very act of tormenting it. Again, however, the project comes to nothing: the freedom that is offered is abjured in the very offer. The sadist is reduced by his own action to a distant spectator of another's humiliation, separated from the freedom with which he seeks to unite himself by the obscene veil of tortured flesh.

The description of sexual desire expresses Sartre's most urgent observations, and is without compare in the philosophical literature. It is a description that Mephistopheles might have whispered into the ear of Faust, as he ruined the innocent Gretchen – both a paradigm of phenomenology, and a sincere expression of existential horror. For Sartre all relations with others are poisoned by the body – the spatio-temporal in-itself – that incarcerates our freedom. All loves, and ultimately all human relations, are founded on contradiction, as we strive both to be and not to be this thing that we are. Sartre was not arguing from his own experience. He was arguing *a priori*, that this is what desire must be, in the experience of a self-conscious subject.

Although Sartre was ugly, with a flaccid body and the face of a toad, he was highly successful with women, one of whom, Simone de Beauvoir,

---

[11] *Being and Nothingness*, op. cit., pp. 364–406.

remained his lifelong mentor and companion. Their free arrangement enabled her to watch his many seductions and to enjoy her own, often lesbian, affairs, thereby experiencing, both as participant and observer, the on-going proof that *pour-soi* can never unite with *pour-soi*, whatever the *en-soi* is up to or up. Commitment, as de Beauvoir discovered, cannot have another human as its object, but only – only what?

That is the unspoken question that haunts the devastated landscape of Sartre's prose. And Sartre wrestled for some years with the attempt to provide an ethical answer to it, believing that it must be possible to steal from the envelope of absolute freedom, the core of moral order that it hides. In his posthumously published *Cahiers pour une morale*, composed in 1947–8, Sartre explored the idea that by justifying my own freedom as the absolute foundation of personal life I justify your freedom too.[12] But in his published work he rejected all such compromises, in favour of the absolute demand of authenticity.

A sceptic might respond by arguing that this authenticity that Sartre so greatly values, like the freedom that creates the need for it, is an illusion. Maybe there is no such thing as an absolute freedom, no unconditioned starting point for each individual journey towards commitment. Or if there is such a thing, maybe we should see it as Kant saw it: as the transcendental foundation of an objective morality, which binds us to others in a relation of universal respect and bows us in submission before the moral law. But Sartre, while sympathizing with Kant's position, saw only inauthenticity in that last step of submission to the law that governs others. That is just another way in which the world poisons our endeavours, by compelling us to identify with what is not ourselves.

What, it might be asked, is the true source of Sartre's revulsion towards his own incarnate existence – a revulsion exhibited now in a sense of obscenity, now in the *post coitum triste* of a desire that is nauseated by its own consummation? What is this feeling that focuses so specifically, and yet which also erupts in Roquentin's dismissal of the 'bourgeois' normality, and in a metaphysical nausea that embraces the whole of creation?

It seems to me that St Augustine presented a better answer to that question than the one suggested by Sartre. For Augustine it is the

[12] Paris, Gallimard, 1983, tr. David Pellauer as *Notebooks for an Ethics*, Chicago, Chicago University Press, 1992.

sentiment of original sin that is the cause of our disgust at the world. We are ashamed at our incarnation whenever brought directly face to face with it, and we feel our inner freedom as 'defiled' by its fleshly prison. We see ourselves as exiles in the world, constantly overcome by the stench of mortality. Moreover, St Augustine added, it is in the sexual act that the sense of original sin most completely invades us. For in sexual arousal I am aware that my body is opaque to my will and in rebellion against it. In sex the body dominates and controls me, overwhelming me with shame at my obscene subservience.[13] It is in the act that engenders us that our mortality is most sharply felt, and in which the rotting, slimy character of the flesh is most shamefully presented to consciousness.

If we put together the more powerful of Sartre's observations – and those that play the most important role in his metaphysic of freedom – we are clearly not far from the Augustinian spirit: the spirit of the Christian anchorite raging against the pleasures of this world, and yet uncertain that he has really renounced them. And the chilling awareness of defilement that turns the anchorite to God turns Sartre, who sees no God, to his lonely inner sanctum, where the self is enshrined amid the cluttered icons of its own futile make-believe.

In short, Sartre requires his 'commitment' to fulfil a religious need. The observation has many times been made – not least by the great friend of Sartre's youth, Raymond Aron – that Marxism fills the gap left vacant by religion.[14] But it is in the later work of Sartre that the meaning of this observation is most apparent. According to the metaphysic expounded in *Being and Nothingness*, the correct answer to the question 'To what should I commit myself?' ought to be: 'Anything, so long as you can will it as a law for yourself alone.' But that is not the answer given by Sartre, whose commitment is to an ideal that is in tension with his own philosophy – to revolution in the cause of 'social justice'.

He is taken in this direction, not by the route of affirmation but by the dark path of denial. Having released the genie of authenticity he must do its secret bidding, and its bidding is destruction. Nothing actual can be 'authentic'. The authentic defines itself in opposition to the Other – which means in opposition to the world that others have created and in which they are at home. Everything belonging to others is partial, patched up and compromised. The authentic self seeks the

---

[13] *The City of God*, Book XIV, chs 16–26.
[14] Raymond Aron, *L'Opium des intellectuels*, Paris, 1955.

total solution to the riddle of existence, and one that is his own creation, acknowledging no authority, no legitimacy that is tainted by the unacceptable world of 'them'.

It is this very posture of denial that leads the authentic self to embrace the revolutionary philosophy of Marx. For even if this move is supremely unjustified it nevertheless provides the easiest release from a situation of intolerable pain: the situation of being wholly alone in a godless universe. There are three features of Marxism that endeared it to Sartre. First, it is a philosophy of opposition, through and through saturated by a quasi-religious contempt for the 'bourgeois' order. Second, it is total in its solution and promises a new reality, obedient to a perfect conception of itself. In other words, Marxism abolishes reality in favour of an idea. And this idea is modelled on the transcendental freedom of the 'for-itself'. The promise of full communism is a *noumenal* promise, a ghostly beckoning from the Kingdom of Ends. We know nothing of that Kingdom, except that all its citizens are free and equal, and all its laws authentically chosen.

Finally – and for Sartre this is the most heartening of Marx's promises – the community of the future will be precisely that which the 'for-itself' demands. It will provide the permitted relationship from which the authentic soul is severed by its authenticity, and at the same time it will leave that authenticity intact. The Kingdom of Ends will combine, in a bond that is as incomprehensible as it is necessary, the earthly relation to a labouring proletariat and the transcendental freedom of the existentialist anti-hero. This permitted relationship will be untainted by conventions, roles, rituals – by any form of 'otherness'. And yet it will also be a relationship with the class made sacred by history, whose warm human purpose will compensate for all the disgust that the grim task of authenticity engenders. The noumenal promise that haunts the Marxist philosophy is therefore a promise of redemption.

It is no accident that the emotional force of Marxism is so naturally expressed in the idiom of Kant. As I shall later show in more detail, when considering writers of the Frankfurt School and their contemporary György Lukács, Marxist morality relies heavily on the second version of Kant's Categorical Imperative, the version that enjoins us to treat humanity, never as a means only, but always as an end. In like manner Sartre, whose philosophy begins from a version of Kant's transcendental freedom, seems inexorably drawn towards the philosophy according to which noumenal imperatives will one day govern the world. 'Full communism' is nothing less than the Kantian Kingdom of Ends, and

Marx's promise is of a transcendental freedom made empirically real. This promise offers faith to the existentialist anti-hero; it is the first and only answer to the anguish of Roquentin, for whom, as Iris Murdoch has argued:

> All *value* lies in the unattainable world of intelligible completeness which he represents to himself in simple intellectual terms; he is not (until the end) duped into imagining that *any* form of human endeavour is adequate to his yearning to rejoin the totality... [15]

The existentialist anti-hero who gives himself, with whatever flourish of 'commitment', to a political project in which others too may join is at first sight in bad faith. He sins against the holy of holies, which is the self, the *néant* coiled in the heart of being. But the expiation of this sin is after all not so difficult. The anti-hero need only ensure that his commitment is not to the fragmented imperfection of the actual, but to the purified 'totality' of an abstract idea. It suffices to commit yourself to what Kant called an 'Idea of Reason', but which we might equally describe as Utopia: by doing this you gain a world without losing your freedom. By refusing the fragmented quality of the actual the existentialist earns the salvation that he needs – that of the 'total' viewpoint obtaining in the Kingdom of Ends.

Lest this authenticity be questioned, however, the anti-hero must pay great attention to form. He must ensure that his slavish submission to another's ideology has the appearance of a thorough rejection. Sartre's submission to Marx – his personal *islām* – is therefore presented as a defiant critique of the prophet's doctrine. The pretentiously entitled *Critique de la raison dialectique*, the first volume of which appeared in 1959 and which was never completed, reads like an exercise in intellectual sadism, in which the beloved philosophy is excruciatingly tortured, so that its subjective essence should be offered and abjured.

Marx, it seems, gives us a 'totality', but in forms that have yet to be appropriated for authentic use. Sartre's ambition is to possess this 'totality', to subdue it and control it, and to emboss it with his own authenticity. But it is an ambition that must not appear as though easily achievable; after all 'others' are watching, and those others *must not approve*. Sartre therefore prepares himself for worship at the Marxist altar by a skilful

---

[15] Iris Murdoch, *Sartre, Romantic Rationalist*, London, 1953, p. 22.

litany of meaningless invocations, cursing all the while the God whom he conjures, as do certain tribesmen who have waited too long for the rains. The following is by no means untypical:

> But, through the very reciprocity of coercions and autonomies, the law ends up by escaping everyone, and in the revolving moments of totalisation it appears as dialectical Reason, that is to say, external to all because internal to each, and a developing totalisation, though without a totaliser, of all the totalised totalisations and of all the detotalised totalities.[16]

One word stands out, in that utterance, as particularly burdened by a weight of unconfessed emotion – the word 'totalization', which we will encounter again in the writings of Lukács, and which features throughout the *Critique de la raison dialectique* as the crucial incantation. Like many words with a liturgical use it is not defined but merely repeated – and applied with such mesmerizing meaninglessness as to attract a phalanx of admirers prepared to serve as a priesthood of the faith. Repeatedly in the *New Left Review* during the 1960s and 70s Western culture was criticized for being impermeable to the 'totalizing' worldview.[17] And if the word, clothed as it is in the ardent sentiments of the ideologue, seems threatening, do not be deceived: it is. 'Totalization' is the name of a challenge, which, by its very comprehensiveness, justifies every effort to impose it. Opposition, which signifies only the 'partial', 'serialized' perspective of the ruling class and its lackeys is, when faced with the passionate totalization of the radical leftist, *without right*. It is a mere power, forlorn, friendless and ready for the guillotine. Thus it is that Utopia, endowed with 'totalizing' power, triumphs in advance over every reality.

Martin Jay has argued on behalf of the New Left that the category of totality is *distinctive* of Marxism.[18] Taken literarily such a claim is surely false. One should rather follow Weber, who identifies the significance of 'prophetic revelation' as lying in its ability to represent the world

---

[16] *Critique of Dialectical Reason: Theory of Practical Ensembles*, tr. Alan Sheridan-Smith, ed. Jonathan Rée, London, 1976, p. 39.
[17] Especially by Terry Eagleton and Perry Anderson. See Eagleton's *Exiles and Émigrés* of 1970.
[18] Martin Jay, *Marxism and Totality: The Adventures of a Concept from Lukács to Habermas*, Berkeley, 1984.

as an ordered totality, and who sees the function of the priesthood as one of mediating between this total conception and the disordered fragmentariness of the natural world.[19] Marxism shares the category of totality not only with traditional religion but also with its own arch-enemy and blood-brother, fascism, the political stance that was advocated by Gentile as a 'total conception of life'.[20]

In another sense, however, Martin Jay has touched on an important truth. Neo-Marxism is distinguished not by the category of totality but by the ritual nonsense with which that category is surrounded and by which its liturgical defences are concealed. The rhetoric of totality conceals the empty place at the heart of the system, where God should be. For Sartre totality is neither a state nor a concept but an *action*. It does not reside in the nature of things but is brought to them by the 'totalizing' fury of the intellectual. Totalization is conceived in existentialist terms, as the transcendental action of the self. But it is also a miraculous moment, in which the fissure in reality closes over and the world is healed. This mystic union, like the union of lance and grail, brings together the yearning halves of a sundered universe. When the intellectual reaches down to touch the upward-stretching hands of the proletariat, then is the evil magic of the 'bourgeois' order undone, and the world made whole.

Sartre claims to reject Marxism for its partial and mechanistic account of man's condition. Nevertheless he expresses his 'total' commitment in terms of Marxist categories. The social world is still divided, for him, into bourgeois and proletarian; it is still dependent on 'relations of production'; and this still means that – under capitalism – the extraction of 'surplus value' from the 'alienated' proletariat proceeds by bourgeois 'exploitation', leading to an ever-intensifying 'struggle' between the classes. And Sartre repeatedly and uncritically attaches these Marxist categories to the theories of Marx. His rejection of 'dialectical reason' (a category imported into Marxism by Plekhanov and Engels) is entirely without intellectual substance. Whenever Sartre's prose shifts from slavish submission to would-be criticism it lapses at the same time into mumbo-jumbo. 'The totalizer' then perfects his own 'totalization', by totalizing again de-totalized totalities, emerging at last exactly where we might

---

[19] Max Weber, *Economy and Society*, ed. G. Roth and C. Wittich, tr. Ephraim Fischoff, et al., New York, 1968, vol. 2, p. 451.

[20] G. Gentile, *Che cosa e il fascismo? Discorse e polemichi*, Florence, 1925, p. 39.

have known he would emerge, an unrepentant advocate of 'totalitarian *praxis*'.[21]

Reading the *Critique of Dialectical Reason* is a grim experience. Almost nowhere is this totalitarian dungeon relieved by a shaft of sunlight, and the few pockets of air are those where the spirit of the early Sartre breathes, freely giving itself in lyrical but unsubstantial exhalations. The force of the jargon is to turn the reader's attention away from everything that is truly questionable in the Marxist vision and to create a false conflict in a world of dreams. Nowhere are the real claims of Marxism confronted. Nowhere is the division of society into 'proletarian' and 'bourgeois' questioned, the myth of the 'class struggle' examined, or the theory of 'exploitation' called to account. Even the dead language of Marxian economics performs its mystifying duties unhindered by a critical observation. Nor is this concealed acceptance of Marxist dogma redeemed by the phenomenological imagery:

> The swindle of capitalist exploitation is based on a contract. And though this contract necessarily transforms labour, or *praxis*, into an inert commodity, it is, formally, a reciprocal relation: it is a free exchange between two men who *recognise each other in their freedom*; it is just that one of them pretends not to notice that the Other is forced by the constraint of needs to sell himself as a material object.[22]

Of course, it is always *as* material objects that we relate to one another, and if *Being and Nothingness* is a guide to the human condition then no transition to 'socialist relations of production' could overcome this disability that our very bodies impose. In any case, are we not tired, by now, of this tautologous condemnation of the free economy, which defines that which can be purchased as a *thing* and then says that the man who sells his labour, in becoming a thing, ceases to be a person? At any rate, we should recognize that, of all the mendacious defences offered for slavery, this is by far the most pernicious. For what is unpurchased labour, if not the labour of a slave? We should recognize the enormous onus of proof that lies with the person who condemns the market in labour, in favour of some intellectual alternative. Just who controls in this new situation, and how? Just what elicits labour from the person who would

---

[21] *Critique of Dialectical Reason*, op. cit., p. 317.
[22] Ibid., p. 110.

otherwise withhold it, and how is he reconciled to the absence of a private reward? Such questions are precisely what cannot be answered from the standpoint of a Kingdom of Ends. For they arise from the 'empirical conditions' of human nature, and can be given no 'transcendental' reply.

The argument with Marx is in fact of little genuine concern to Sartre. In countless ways – through vocabulary, through example, through structure, and most of all through style – the *Critique of Dialectical Reason* shows a total rejection of the rules of intellectual enquiry, and a determined flight from the truth. To suppose that the book might fulfil the promise offered by its title is a gross impertinence. The reader is to accept *unquestioningly* all that belongs to Sartre's commitment: henceforth only *unreal* questions may be asked:

> How can *praxis* in itself be an experience both of necessity and of freedom, since neither of these, according to classical logic, can be grasped in an empirical process?
>
> If dialectical rationality really is a logic of totalisation how can History – the swarm of individual destinies – appear as a totalising movement, and how can one avoid the paradox that in order to totalise there must already be a unified principle, that is, that only actual totalities can totalise themselves?[23]

A writer who imagines that *those* are the challenging questions that Marxism has to answer is clearly up to something. He is trying to turn our attention away, not only from the real theoretical critiques of Marxism – which have left the theory of history, the theory of value and the theory of social class more or less in ruins – but also from the terrible practical consequences to which Marxism has led, with its vain millenarian prophecies and its 'totalizing' vision of a 'post-political' Utopia.

The commitment on which Sartre settles is in fact Marxism of a wholly unreconstructed kind. We find emerging from his pages the same destructive fantasies, the same false hopes, the same pathological hatred of the imperfect and the normal, that have characterized all the followers of Marx from Engels to Mao. We are once again to suppose that our world is one of 'bourgeois' control, unified in its opposition to the 'common *praxis* of the workers,'[24] and to imagine that these workers

---

[23] Ibid., p. 79.
[24] Ibid., pp. 213–14.

('the class without property') seek to 'socialise' the means of production.[25] Market relations are not the expression of economic freedom, but the concrete enslavement of man to the diabolical reign of the Other.[26] Otherness poisons all the benefits that 'capitalism' offers us: our democracy is not true democracy but merely 'bourgeois democracy' and when a man votes under our system of government he votes always as the Other and not as himself.[27] Against the background of those worn-out lies, dressed up in the language of Kojève, Sartre tries to induce a knee-jerk acceptance of the Marxist view of modern history.

The erosion of truth by communist Utopianism is seen at its most effective not in the *Critique of Dialectical Reason* but in the subsequent essays, collected in *Situations* VIII and IX, and published in English as *Between Existentialism and Marxism*.[28] In this astonishing work Sartre repeats the standard excuse for the cruelties of the Bolsheviks (made necessary by 'anti-communist encirclement'). He blames the persistence of communist cruelty on Stalin, and subsequently on the fact that the Communist Party became an *institution* – in other words, one of those focal points of 'otherness' (or 'seriality', as the work of the Devil is now called), which resist the 'totalizing' project of the enlightened intellect. Such a criticism is extremely useful in saving what it purports to condemn. The Communist Party is bad, but only in the way that the Boy Scouts, the Sorbonne or the fire brigade are bad – by requiring collective and inauthentic action according to institutional norms. The Party's real work of murder and destruction is unimportant in comparison with this feature, which it shares with every lasting social endeavour.

Thus we should not be surprised by Sartre's commentary on the Soviet invasion of Czechoslovakia. The root cause of the 'Czech problem,' he argues, was not socialism but the imposition of a socialism that was not 'home grown'. 'The reasons why a people choose socialism matter comparatively little; what is essential is that they build it with their own hands.'[29] The fault of the Soviet Union was to prevent this natural process from occurring. It is inevitable that a modern Jacobin should use the word 'people' as Sartre uses it – as a word of Newspeak, to denote an abstract unity that can 'choose socialism' and build it with its own collective, or

---

[25] Ibid., pp. 215–16.
[26] Ibid., p. 291.
[27] Ibid., p. 351.
[28] *Between Existentialism and Marxism*, tr. J. Matthews, London, 1974, reissued 1983.
[29] Ibid., p. 86.

at least collectivized, hands. And it is inevitable that this 'people' should be seen as a form of unanimity. The alternative – collective action in the absence of total agreement – looks too much like an 'institution' for Sartre to recognize it for what it is, namely, the best that mere humans can do.

Nevertheless, it is a little surprising, in the light of the Czech experience, that a humanist intellectual should still close his mind to the all-important fact: that the majority of a 'people' may actually *reject* socialism, for its promises as much as for its real achievements. A 'people' may realize that it does not want 'socialisation of the means of production', and may be suspicious of an 'equality' that deprives them of opportunities and freedoms that they have hitherto taken for granted. For Sartre, as for Hobsbawm, the cruelties of revolutionary socialism stem from 'the necessities of the time' (but who created those necessities?). The error of the Soviet Union was simply to compel the Czechs to adopt a system that was appropriate only for 'Russian peasants of 1920' and not for 'Czech Workers of 1950'[30] – a theory that shows more contempt for the Russian peasants than respect for the Czechs.

The Czech reform movement figures interestingly in Sartre's perception. This movement achieved, he argues, the longed-for 'unity of intellectuals and the working class'.[31] Its mystical goal was the creation of 'a concrete totalisation continually de-totalised, contradictory and problematic, never closed back on itself, never completed, yet nevertheless one single experience'.[32] The Czech workers were 'not calling for a return to bourgeois liberalism, but, since truth is revolutionary, were claiming the revolutionary right to tell the truth'.[33] Casting spells in this way Sartre fortifies his faith. All truth becomes the property of the revolution, and no worker in his hour of truth can do anything but join the revolution. The possibility of being a 'bourgeois liberal' or an anti-socialist has been finally stolen from him. The old Leninist war-cry is now shouted in reverse: he whom we are with is not against us, even when he fights to the death against what we do.

The worker is supposed to gain from his relation with the intellectual. But it is primarily the intellectual who benefits from a relationship in which he alone dictates the terms. The intellectual's compassionating zeal (as Rousseau described it) is based on an emotional need too vast and

---

[30] Ibid., p. 100.
[31] Ibid., p. 111.
[32] Ibid., p. 109.
[33] Ibid., p. 111.

too urgent not to be tyrannical. If intellectuals prove ruthless towards the workers on whom they conduct their experiments it is partly because, seeing the world from the 'totalizing' perspective of the Kingdom of Ends, they cannot perceive the real, but empirical, existence of their victims. The worker is reduced to a mere abstraction, not by the drudgery of capitalist production, but by the fiery rhetoric of the intellectual left. The worker is the means to the intellectual's exultation, and can be abolished without scruple should he fail to perform his task. It is this wholly *intellectual* annihilation of the merely empirical worker that made possible his mass extermination in the merely empirical world.

What is remarkable in Sartre's later writing – at least in that part that is taken up in the *jihād* of 'commitment' – is the copious flow of 'totalizing' Newspeak. Only one subject seems seriously to engage his emotions – sufficiently seriously, at any rate, to lead him to write as though meaning something – and that is his inner identity with the proletariat. This identity is the final outcome of the total war against the bourgeoisie that he had launched in the person of Roquentin. In his satanic commentary on the writer Jean Genet Sartre had described good as 'a mere illusion', adding that 'evil is a nothing (*néant*) that produces itself on the ruins of the good'.[34] And in that book he outlines his deep attachment to *la morale du Mal*. By the mystical device of equivalences Sartre implies that nothing can be said of the good that might not also be said of evil and that the 'authentic' choice between these two must hold them in an equal balance. By the logic of defiance, it must then cast in its lot with the evil that shatters the bourgeois reality.

Sartre follows in the path of Baudelaire (another of his obsessions, and the one to whom he is most spiritually akin). His path is that of a soul longing for the good, but whose pride (which will accept as good only what is his own creation) forces him always to destroy the good. The good comes to him defiled by the taint of 'otherness', and so threatens the authenticity of the self. Hence he must use evil to annihilate the good. The distant identity with the proletariat is a kind of paradisal promise, the vision of an innocence too sacred to be described, lying beyond good and evil, and glimpsed only in rare, holy moments, as at the barricades of 1968.

However, the longed-for identity cannot really be attained. To enter the Kingdom of Ends the proletarian must first be shorn of his empirical

---

[34] *Saint Genet, comédien et martyr*, Paris, 1952, p. 690.

conditions – which are the accoutrements of slavery. In doing so, however, he ceases to be a proletarian. The meeting of the intellectual with his god is therefore a purely inner episode, a private devotion from which the actual proletarian, with his desire for comfort, property and the things of this world, must be permanently shut out.

It is natural therefore that Sartre's discussions of modern politics should centre on the position of the intellectual, and the question of how he should prepare himself for the rite of passage to the promised kingdom. The intellectual, he argues, must reject all 'class sensibility' – and in particular the sensibility of his own class, which is that of the *petite bourgeoisie* – in favour of 'human relations of reciprocity', in which he and the proletariat will be united in a holy tie.[35] The intellectual's enemy in this process of lustration is not the actual, empirical proletarian – who has no say in the matter – but the 'false intellectual', a 'type created by the dominant class to defend its particularist ideology by arguments which claim to be rigorous products of exact reasoning'.[36] With those words Sartre dismisses unnamed such writers as Raymond Aron, Alain Besançon and Jean-François Revel who have tried to puncture the leftist illusions and who have met always with anger, contempt or blank disregard.

Sartre's venture towards 'commitment' therefore comes full circle. He longs for an authenticity in which the self is both *causa sui* and *primum mobile*. But he comes, by persuasive steps, to believe in 'system', in the world created according to an abstract idea. This 'totalized' world is the paradisal arbour of his transcendental marriage. Here he joins at last with the proletarian of his dreams. But this paradise is abstract, insubstantial, and fraught with contradiction, and the intellectual is locked at once in combat with the person who tells him so. Reaching out towards the proletariat, therefore, Sartre encounters in the end only his old intellectual rival, with whom he joins, as ever, in a deadly yet inconclusive affray:

> The true intellectual, as a *radical* thinker, is neither a moralist nor an idealist: he knows that the only peace worth having in Vietnam will cost blood and tears: he knows that peace will only come ... *after* the American defeat. In other words, the nature of his contradiction obliges him to *commit himself* in every one of the conflicts of our time,

---

[35] *Between Existentialism and Marxism*, op. cit., p. 251.
[36] Ibid., p. 252.

because all of them – class, national and racial conflicts – are particular effects of the oppression of the under-privileged and because, in each of these conflicts, he finds himself, as a man conscious of his own oppression, on the side of the oppressed.[37]

Revel remarks on the regularity with which leftist intellectuals have, in their fight against oppression, placed themselves on the side of it.[38] And we see this process at work in Sartre's prose. By reducing his 'commitment' to a purely intellectual matter, a combat with the false prophets who rebut his arguments, he reduces the victim of oppression to a purely abstract idea – an *excuse* for his own heroic posturing. The lot of no one actual could ever be improved by Sartre's noumenal exertions.

The case of Vietnam is but one example of this. When the 11 members of the Israeli team sent to the Munich Olympics were murdered in 1972 Sartre was loud in justification of the crime, a fact that caused a certain hesitation among those who normally rushed to endorse his judgements. In 1984, four years after Sartre's death, Marc-Antoine Burnier gathered together the many instances of Sartre's revolutionary folly.[39] It is with a sombre incredulity that one reads of his support for exterminating regimes that unite the intellectuals and the proletariat only in the places of 're-education' where they gasp out their last miserable hours. 'By means of irrefutable documents we learned of the existence of actual concentration camps in the Soviet Union' – so Sartre wrote, 20 years after the truth was common knowledge among those who did not wilfully shield themselves from it. And yet still he could urge his countrymen to 'judge communism by its intentions and not by its actions'.

In all the campaigns that the Soviet Union waged against the West, at whatever cost in human life and happiness, Sartre took the Soviet side, or else criticized the Soviet Union only in language that reiterated its own favoured mendacities. Following the World Peace Congress in Vienna in 1954 he travelled at Soviet instigation to Moscow, returning to relate that 'there is total freedom to criticize in the USSR' – a remark that is perhaps easier to understand when we remember the significance that Sartre attached to the word 'total'. He was subsequently stunned by the Soviet intervention in Hungary, so stunned that he turned his attention to praising the work of communism elsewhere – first in Cuba and then

[37] Ibid., p. 254.
[38] Jean-François Revel, *Comment les démocraties finissent*, Paris, 1983, Ch. 1.
[39] Marc-Antoine Burnier, *Le Testament de Sartre*, Paris, 1984.

(when his eyes were opened) in China, whose sole distinguishing virtue was that it was as yet unknown. Only at the end of his life, when he came out in support of the refugees from communist Vietnam – publicly shaking hands over the matter with Raymond Aron after a breach of many years – did he seem to have given up the struggle. But by then his work was done.

Sartre's anti-bourgeois rhetoric changed the language and the agenda of post-war French philosophy, and fired the revolutionary ambitions of students who had come to Paris from the former colonies. One of those students was later to return to his native Cambodia and put into practice the 'totalizing' doctrine that has as its targets the 'seriality' and 'otherness' of the bourgeois class. And in the purifying rage of Pol Pot it is not unreasonable to see the contempt for the ordinary and the actual that is expressed in almost every line of Sartre's demonic prose. '*Ich bin der Geist, der stets verneint*', says Mephistopheles. The same can be said on behalf of Sartre, for whom *l'enfer, c'est les autres* – hell is other people, meaning that other people are hell (*Huis clos*, 1947). Like Milton's Satan, Sartre saw the world transfigured by his own pride – and it is this pride that caused him to scorn the Nobel Prize, since tributes originate in the Other and are therefore beneath the notice of the authentic Self.

For all his moral defects, however, there is no denying Sartre's stature as a thinker and a writer. If any work shows this it is *Les mots*, published in 1963, a book written in reaction to the cult of Proust, and designed to rectify the growing misconception, as Sartre saw it, of the place of words in the life and growth of a child. Childhood for Sartre is not the lifelong refuge evoked by Proust, but the first of many mistakes, in which all subsequent mistakes have their premonition. He writes with a sardonic succinctness that is in itself a rebuke to Proust, and the result – strongly influenced by the surrealist Michel Leiris – is a masterpiece of autobiography, to be compared with De Quincey's *Confessions of an English Opium Eater* and Sir Edmund Gosse's *Father and Son*. *Les mots* showed Sartre's true powers as a writer, and in it he temporarily emancipated himself from the grim, jargon-ridden prose of the *Critique de la raison dialectique*. It is written by a man who was capable of laughter – and who might have permitted himself to laugh, were laughter not a weapon in the hands of the Other. However, life, for Sartre, was no laughing matter. Wanting only what was abstract and 'totalized', he condemned what is actual to misery and servitude. The totalized totality is, in the end, what it seemed to be in the beginning: the total commitment to 'totalitarian *praxis*'.

Looking back over twentieth-century France from the vantage point offered by Sartre one is immediately struck by two distinctive features of the French left: enmity and revolutionary fervour. A deep disappointment with reality and a desire to tear it down in the name of Utopia has been the default position of left-wing thinking in France from the Jacobins to the present day. But the twentieth century added a new dimension of disillusionment – a belief that all ideals and loyalties are merely invitations to betrayal, and that redemption lies within the individual, to be bestowed on himself by himself alone.

In the ensuing quest for authenticity there is a permanent need for an enemy. The *gauchiste* knows the illusoriness of values, and finds his identity in a life lived without the easy deceptions that rule the lives of others. Since he has no values, his thought and action can be given only a negative guarantee. He must fortify his position by unmasking the deceptions of others. Moreover this unmasking cannot be done once and for all. It must be perpetually renewed, so as to fill the moral vacuum that lies at the centre of existence. Only if there is some readily identifiable and, so to speak, renewable opponent can this struggle for authenticity – which is in fact the most acute struggle for existence – be sustained. The enemy must be a fount of humbug and deception; he must also possess elaborate and secret power, power sustained through the very system of lies that underscores his values. Such an enemy deserves unmasking, and there is a kind of heroic virtue in his assailant, who frees the world from the stranglehold of secret influence.

We have met this enemy already in the writings of Sartre; but it is to the aristocratic France of Louis XIV that we owe the contemptuous label by which he is known. The renewable opponent is the 'bourgeois': the pillar of the community, whose hypocritical respectability and social incompetence have inspired every variety of renewable contempt. Of course, this creature has undergone considerable transformation since Molière first ridiculed his social pretensions. During the nineteenth century he acquired a complex dual character. Marx represented him as the principal agent and beneficiary of the French Revolution – and also the new enslaver, whose tentacles reach into every pocket of influence and power – while the café intellectuals continued, in more bitter accents, the scathing mockery of the aristocracy. *Épater le bourgeois* became the signature of the disaffected artist, the guarantee of his social credentials whereby he demonstrated his aristocratic entitlement, and his contempt for the usurpatory dominion of the rising middle class.

In German the term 'Bürger' has no comparable significance, and the Enlightenment idea of 'civil society', as the realm of free citizenship under a legitimate rule of law, reappears in Hegel as *bürgerliche Gesellschaft*. For this reason the French term, with its tainted history of disdain, has always been preferred on the European left. Under the dual influence of Marx and Flaubert the bourgeois emerged from the nineteenth century as a monster transformed out of all recognition from his humble origins. He was the 'class enemy' of Leninist dogma, the creature whose dominion we are commanded by history to destroy. He was also the repository of all morality, all convention, all codes of conduct that might hamper the freedom and ebullience of *la vie bohème*.

The Marxist theory of ideology tried to knit the two halves of the portrait together, describing the 'comfortable' values as the social disguise of real economic power. But the theory was vague and schematic, lacking the concrete quality that is required by a rewarding and renewable contempt. Much of the effort of the French left in the twentieth century has therefore been devoted to completing the portrait. The aim has been to create the perfect enemy: the object against which to define and sharpen one's authenticity, by transforming it into wit.

The work of defining the ideal bourgeois, which Sartre began in *La nausée*, was completed in 1952 with the publication of *Saint Genet*, a masterpiece of modern Satanism, in which the bourgeois is characterized by an extraordinary complexity of emotions, ranging from rooted heterosexuality to a hostility to crime. The bourgeois finally emerges as the champion of an illusory 'normality', concerned to forbid and to oppress all those who, in challenging this normality, challenge also the social and political dominion that it conceals.

The anti-bourgeois sentiment that lies at the root of French left-wing thinking partly explains its rejection of all roles and functions that are not creations of its own. Its main power base has not been the university but the café: for to occupy positions of influence within the 'structures' of the bourgeois state was for a long time incompatible with the demands of revolutionary rectitude. Whatever influence the *gauchiste* enjoys must be acquired through his own intellectual labour, producing words and images that challenge the status quo. The café becomes the symbol of his social position. He observes the passing show, but does not join it. Instead he waits for those who, attracted by his gaze, separate themselves from the crowd and 'come over' to his position.

By the same token we must recognize the emerging dependency that began to exist between the *gauchiste* and the true middle class. The *gauchiste*, in the wake of Sartre's scandalous narrative, began to be seen as the confessor of the middle class. He presents an ideal image of that class's sinful condition. The 'bourgeois' of Sartre's iconography is a myth; but he bears a resemblance to the ordinary city-dweller who, seeing himself distorted in this portrait, is troubled by the thought of moral possibilities. He admits to owning property, to being married, to striving to be a semi-faithful husband and conscientious father. He enthusiastically confesses to purely hypothetical crimes. And he begins to extol the *gauchiste* as the absolver of his corrupted conscience. The *gauchiste* therefore becomes the redeemer of the class whose illusions he has been appointed to unmask.

Hence, at a certain point, and despite his rudeness – which is, in truth, no more than the necessary virtue of his profession – the *gauchiste* began to enjoy abundant social privileges. He began to be born aloft on the shoulders of the bourgeoisie whose habits he tramples, and to enjoy again the aristocrat's place in the sun. At the best Parisian parties he would appear in person: but even the meanest reception would take place against bookshelves loaded with his writings. So close, indeed, is this symbiotic relation between the *gauchiste* and his victim as to resemble that previous, seemingly indissoluble, bond between aristocrat and peasant. The major difference is this: the aristocrat both exalted the peasants in his words (creating the idealized 'shepherd', whose virtues were incessantly paraded on the theatrical stage at court), and at the same time oppressed them in his actions. The *gauchiste* judiciously reverses the priorities: he does no more than bark at the hand that feeds him. In this he shows a greater wisdom, and a healthy instinct for survival.

Such indeed were the *gauchistes* whose writings prepared the way for the student protests of May 1968. Julia Kristeva, Phillipe Sollers, Roland Barthes, Marguerite Duras, Alain Robbe-Grillet and the proponents of the *nouveau roman* – all were smooth representatives of an establishment, whose Marxism was veneered with structuralist linguistics and given a decidedly literary appeal. Some were attached to institutions of learning. But none made a boast of academic titles, and all maintained the aloof and bohemian manner bequeathed to them by Flaubert and Baudelaire. Among this generation of fashionable intellectuals by far the most influential has been Michel Foucault, the social philosopher and historian of ideas, who carried forward the anti-bourgeois rhetoric of Sartre and made it into a foundational component of the curriculum, at first in France and then subsequently all around the world, not least in America.

I identify Foucault as a leading thinker of the New Left, but it should be pointed out that his political position was constantly shifting, and that he was always glad to reject any convenient label. Unlike Sartre he was a critic (although, until his later years, a fairly muted critic) of communism. Nevertheless he was the most powerful and ambitious of those who took up Sartre's agenda. He devoted his work to unmasking the bourgeoisie, and showing that all the given ways of shaping civil society are reducible in the last analysis to forms of domination.

It is as difficult to do justice to the achievements of Foucault as it is to those of Sartre. His imagination and intellectual fluency have generated theories, concepts and insights by the score, and the synthesizing poetry of his style rises above the murky sludge of left-wing writing like an eagle over mud-flats. Moreover, this flamboyant adoption of the higher vision is a large part of Foucault's appeal. He is unable to encounter opposition without at once rising, under the impulse of his intellectual energy, to the superior 'theoretical' perspective, from which opposition is seen in terms of the interests that are advanced by it. Opposition relativized is also opposition discounted. It is not what you say, but that you say it, that awakens Foucault's interest. '*D'où parles-tu?*' is his question, and his stance remains beyond the reach of every answer.

The unifying thread in Foucault's earlier and most influential work is the search for the secret structures of power. Behind every practice, every institution and behind language itself lies power, and Foucault's goal is to unmask that power and thereby to liberate its victims. He originally described his method as 'an archaeology of knowledge', and his subject-matter as truth – truth considered as the product (rather than the producer) of 'discourse', taking both form and content from the language in which it is conveyed. A problem at once arises, and proves to be something more than a problem of terminology. What is meant by a 'knowledge' that can be overthrown by new experience, or by a 'truth' that exists only within the discourse that frames it? Foucault's 'truth' does not exist in the world independently of our awareness of it but is created and re-created by the 'discourse' through which it is 'known'.

Thus in *Les mots et les choses* (1966)[40] we are told that man is a recent invention: truly an original and troubling idea! On inspection it turns

---

[40] *The Order of Things: An Archeology of Human Sciences*, tr. Anon, London, 1970.

out that Foucault means no more than this: that it is only since the Renaissance that the fact of being a man (rather than, say, a farmer, a soldier or a nobleman) has acquired the special significance that we now attribute to it. By such arguments we could show that the dinosaur too is a recent invention.

Of course, there is a point to Foucault's remark. He means to emphasize the extent to which the sciences that have taken human beings as their object are recent inventions, and already giving way to other forms of 'knowledge' (*savoir*).[41] The idea of man is as fragile and transitory as any other idea in the history of human understanding, and must give way under the impulse of a new *episteme* (a new structure of knowledge) to something that we cannot yet name. Each *episteme*, for Foucault, is the servant of some rising power, and has had, as its principal function, the creation of a 'truth' that serves the interest of power. Hence there are no received truths that are not also convenient truths.

The theory of the *episteme* is a rerun of the Marxist theory of ideology. It offers to characterize each form of thought, each system of concepts, images and narratives, in terms of its function of embedding and maintaining the power structure on which the social order depends. The power in question is not necessarily that of a ruling class, although those on top are its inevitable beneficiaries. The power is what holds things together, defining dominant and subordinate positions, and in general maintaining the hierarchies that distribute privileges unequally across the social spectrum.

Marx contrasted ideology with science, arguing that ideology is to be understood through its function, and science through its truth. Hence science belongs to the material infrastructure on which all institutions depend, while ideology is a mere by-product of the system. Foucault, however, makes no clear contrast between *episteme* and some other, objective or explanatory form of 'knowledge'. There seems to be no privileged position from which the *episteme* of an era is discernible that

---

[41] While '*savoir*' admits of a plural, 'knowledge' does not, a clear sign that the two words do not mean the same. There can be rival *savoirs* but not rival 'knowledges'. Nevertheless the translators often write as though we humans have competing 'knowledges', an idiom that already relativizes a concept that emerged precisely to anchor our thought in a reality independent of itself. The question of what is meant by *savoir* therefore becomes an issue, not only in the work of Foucault, but also in that of other French thinkers who play fast and loose with this term. See also Badiou, discussed in Chapter 8 below. I will continue to translate '*savoir*' as 'knowledge', using inverted commas when required.

is not imbued by an *episteme* of its own. This raises the question – not, I think ever answered by Foucault – as to the method that would justify his observations, and whether or not he has obtained the impartial standpoint that would really entitle him to make them.

There are certainly many insights in Foucault's early writings. But the relativist method – which identifies reality with a way of apprehending it – must lead us to doubt that they are hard-won. For this method allows him to jump across to the finishing line of historical enquiry, without running the hard track of empirical enquiry. Consider what would *really* have to be proved by someone who believed man to be an artefact, and a recent one at that – more recent even than the medieval and renaissance humanists who extolled man's virtues. A proper assessment of Foucault's thought must therefore try to separate its two components: the relativist sleight of hand (which would lead us too simply to dismiss him), and the 'diagnostic' analysis of the secret ways of power. It is the second that is interesting, and which is expressed in Foucault's claim that each successive form of 'knowledge' is devoted to the creation of a discourse favourable to, and symbolic of, the prevailing forms of domination.

In *Histoire de la folie à l'âge classique* (1961) Foucault gave the first glimpse of this thesis.[42] In that book Foucault traced the confinement of madmen to its origins in the seventeenth century, associating this confinement with the ethic of work and the rise of the bourgeoisie. Foucault is impatient with ordinary causal explanations, and replaces them with a kind of idealist metaphysics, implying that it is our way of thinking things that brings them about, since things are not really distinct from our conceptions. Thus he does not say that the economic reorganization of society brought about the confinement of the insane. Rather, he writes that 'it was in a certain experience of labour that the indissolubly economic and moral demand for confinement was formulated'.

More important is the new slant given not only to the ideas of Marx but to those of Kojève's Hegel. In the period that Foucault describes, in this book and henceforth, as the 'classical age', the madman is 'other'. He is other because he points to the limits of the prevailing ethic, and alienates himself from its demands. There is, in his refusal to be 'normal', a kind of virtuous disdain. He must therefore be brought to order. Through

---

[42] Translated as *Madness and Civilisation: A History of Insanity in the Age of Reason*, tr. R. Howard, New York, 1965.

confinement madness is subject to the rule of reason, which is another name for the preferred form of domination. The madman now lives under the jurisdiction of those who are sane, confined by their laws, and instructed by their morality. The recourse of reason in this close encounter is to reveal to madness its own 'truth' – the truth through which reason 'knows' it. To lack reason is, for 'classical' thought, to be an animal. The madman must therefore be made to act the part of an animal. He is confined in a cage and used as a beast of burden. By this confrontation with his 'truth' he is made whole.

Each successive age finds a similar 'truth' with which to confront those who defy its conventions. And each age defines sanity in the way required by the prevailing system of power: sanity is the form of behaviour that respects the established structures of domination. But, Foucault suggests, the stock of the 'truths' with which madness can be confined is now exhausted. Madness is out of the cage, and confronting us with *our* 'truth'. At the end of Foucault's drama the gods of the French post-war Olympus enter stage left, to stick out their tongues at the bourgeoisie in the stalls. Goya, de Sade, Hölderlin, Nerval, Van Gogh, Artaud, Nietzsche, all are proof, for Foucault, that the voice of unreason (*déraison*) can no longer be silenced, and that the reign of bourgeois normality is over.

What should we make of this encomium of unreason? It was clear to the eighteenth century, according to Foucault, that, while madness was seeking to express itself, it had no language with which to do so besides that provided by reason. The only phenomenology of madness lies in the consciousness of those who are sane. Surely then, the eighteenth century had one sound intuition about the nature of madness. The province of language and the province of reason are coextensive, and if madness contains its own 'truths', as Foucault claims, these are essentially inexpressible. Foucault claims that there is a 'language' of unreason and that we must attune our ears to it. Yet such a language would be one in which self-reference is impossible. It would be a delirious monologue, delivered by a voice that *belongs to no one*. It would be nothing like the voice of Nietzsche in *Twilight of the Idols* or that of Nerval in *Les chimères*, which speak to us directly of the world that we share.

During the nineteenth century, according to Foucault, the experience of 'unreason' characteristic of the 'classical' period becomes dissociated: madness is confined within a moral intuition, and the fantasy of an unceasing monologue of madness, in a language inaccessible to reason, is forgotten, to be resuscitated, however, at the beginning of the twentieth century in the Freudian theory of the unconscious. In the nineteenth century, on Foucault's view, madness became a threat to the whole structure of bourgeois life, and the madman, in his failure to submit to the prevailing norms, was marked out as guilty. The greatest offence of madness is against the 'bourgeois family', and it is the experience of this family that dictates the paternalistic structure of the asylum. The ethos of judgement and reprobation in the asylum is part of a new attitude to madness – madness is at last *observed*. It is no longer thought that the madman has anything to say or symbolize; he is an anomaly in the world of action, responsible only for his visible behaviour.

In the asylum the man of reason is presented as an adult, the madman as a child, so that madness may be construed as an incessant attack against the Father. The madman must be brought to recognize his error, and to reveal to the Father a consciousness of his guilt. Thus there is a natural transition from the 'confession in crisis' characteristic of the asylum, to the Freudian dialogue, in which the analyst listens to and translates the language of unreason which sounds from the unconscious, but in which madness is still forced to see itself as a disobedience and a transgression. Finally, Foucault intimates, it is because psychoanalysis has refused to suppress the family structure as the only one through which madness can be seen or known, that its introduction of a dialogue with madness leads to no understanding of what the madman is trying to say.

Beneath all this fascinating analysis – part insight, part exuberant fiction – it is possible to discern a persistent and simplifying historical perspective. Despite his apparent scholarship Foucault remains wedded to the mythopoeic guide to modern history presented in *The Communist Manifesto*. The world divides conveniently into the 'classical' and the 'bourgeois' eras, the first beginning at the late Renaissance and ending with the 'bourgeois revolution' of 1789. It is only thereafter that we witness the characteristic features of modern life: the nuclear family, transferable property, the legally constituted state, and the modern structures of influence and power. Engels made a heroic attempt to give credence to the idea of the 'bourgeois family', and this has proved useful to left-wing demonology ever since.[43] But Engels's icon is now threadbare and faded, and only marginally more persuasive than the idea that the French Revolution involved a transition from 'feudal' to 'capitalist' modes

---

[43] See Engels's contributions to *The Holy Family*, a collection of polemics published by Marx and Engels in 1845.

of production, from an 'aristocratic' to a 'bourgeois' social structure, and from entailed to transferable property.

Less persuasive still is the idea that the 'classical' outlook of Racine and La Fontaine is the principal index of post-Renaissance, pre-Revolutionary culture in France. All this is based on an elaborate and (for a historian) culpable simplification of the historical data. Foucault's rhetoric is calculated to mesmerize us into a sense that there is some intrinsic connection between 'bourgeois', 'family', 'paternalistic' and 'authoritarian'. Historical facts – such as that the peasant family is more authoritarian and the aristocratic family more paternalistic than the family called 'bourgeois', or that the middle class shows an ability to relax the temper of domestic life that has seldom been matched at the upper and lower ends of the social scale – such facts are kept out of mind.

The reader finds no argument about evidence, no search for instances or counter-instances that might sow the seeds of doubt. For they blur the figures and erase the outline of the necessary icon. When the image fades, so too does the idea: we can then no longer believe that the secret power that created the categories of mental illness, which confined the innocent sufferer and moralized him into 'abnormality', also generated the family, the home and the norms of modern life. Far less can we believe that the nature of this power is summarized in the single word 'bourgeois', which is introduced as part of a liturgy of denunciation.

This schematic historiography nevertheless survives through all Foucault's earlier works. In particular he makes abundant use of the concept of a 'classical' époque. But in subsequent works the enemy who stalks through his pages seems somehow to lose his respectable clothing. He appears as naked power, without style, dignity or status. If the term 'bourgeois' is sometimes applied to him it is a flourish, like an insult thrown by a wrestler to his opponent. There is no longer the same liberating confidence in the enemy's identity. Nevertheless, the method and the results remain, and each of Foucault's subsequent books during the 1960s repeats the hidden agenda of his *Histoire de la folie*.

In *Naissance de la clinique: une archéologie du regard médical* (1963),[44] Foucault extends the ideas of 'observation' and 'normality', so as to explain, not only the confinement of madmen, but also the confinement of the sick. (He will shortly extend the analysis further, to prisons and

---

[44] *The Birth of the Clinic: An Archeology of Medical Perception*, tr. A. M. Sheridan, London, 1973.

punishment. If he stopped short of schools and universities it was not for want of conviction.) That patients should be gathered together for observation shows a need to divide the world into the normal and the abnormal, and to confront the abnormal with its 'truth'. The need is also for a classification of illness, a 'measured language' with which to distinguish each disease and make it visible.

Now there is truth in those ideas: who would deny that the growing understanding of disease arose from isolation, observation and selective treatment? But what a simple truth, and what an innocent fact! Clearly it needs unmasking, as one aspect of the all-pervasive bourgeois conspiracy. So here, in characteristic language, is what the hospital – surely one of the more benign of human accomplishments – becomes:

> Over all these endeavours on the part of clinical thought to define its methods and scientific norms hovers the great myth of a pure Gaze that would be pure Language: a speaking eye. It would scan the entire hospital field, taking in and gathering together each of the singular events that occurred within it; and as it saw, as it saw ever more clearly, it would turn into speech that states and teaches; the truth, which events, in their repetitions and convergences, would outline under its gaze, would, by this same gaze and in the same order, be reserved, in the form of teaching, to those who do not know and have not yet seen. This speaking eye would be the servant of things and the master of truth.[45]

There is an accomplished rhetoric here, a rhythmic movement, which, feeding on the simple fact of scientific observation, becomes a haunting and persecuted awareness of the hidden source of power.

Behind this concept of the Gaze – *le regard*, the term introduced by Sartre and Merleau-Ponty to signify the most potent revelation of the Other's otherness – lurks a great suspicion, the same suspicion of human decencies that inhabits the pages of *Being and Nothingness*. It tells us not to be deceived, not to believe that anything is undertaken or anything achieved except in the interests of power. Yet when Foucault, dying of AIDS, was in June 1984 taken to La Salpêtrière – the hospital whose former use as an asylum for the insane he had so maliciously characterized in *Histoire de la folie* – it was in order to escape the public Gaze, and to

---

[45] Ibid., pp. 114–15.

receive in his last days the compassion that he needed, and which he had dismissed twenty years earlier as one of the masks of bourgeois power.

The same urge to hunt for the power behind the mask takes a further step in Foucault's most brilliant book, *Surveiller et punir*, subtitled 'The birth of the prison'.[46] (The '*surveiller*' of the title is hard to translate, but refers again to the Gaze of the guardians.) It is natural that the near-simultaneous rise of the prison system, the hospital and the lunatic asylum will not go unnoticed by the suspicious iconographer of the bourgeoisie. And there is something persuasive in Foucault's initial analysis of the transition from the exemplary punishments of Renaissance Europe to the system of physical confinement. To call the first 'classical', the second 'bourgeois' is of little interest. But it is surely illuminating to see the earlier system as embodying a kind of corporeal language of crime. The aim of torture was to imprint the crime on the culprit's body, in the living language of pain, so as to make the evil visible. Foucault contrasts the prison system, which, he argues, is founded on a juridical conception of individual rights, and under which punishment has the character of a forfeit. The contracting individualist can be legitimately made to suffer in no other way. And even capital punishment under the new regime of prison has an abstract juridical character:

> The guillotine takes life almost without touching the body, just as prison deprives of liberty or a fine reduces wealth. It is intended to apply the law not so much to a real body capable of feeling pain as to a juridical subject, the possessor, among other rights, of the right to exist. It had to have the abstraction of the law itself.[47]

Foucault proceeds to draw the usual surprising and not so surprising conclusions. It is surprising to be told that punishment is an element in the genealogy of the human soul, so that the Cartesian ego is precisely what is conjured on the rack: the gazing subject who exists as the observer of this pain. It is surprising to learn that the modern soul is a product, if not of the prison system, at least of the juridical idea of the subject, as a complex of legal rights.

It is somewhat less surprising to be told that criminal justice operates in the 'production of truth', and that it is one of those systems

---

[46] *Discipline and Punish, Birth of the Prison*, tr. A. M. Sheridan, London, 1977.
[47] Ibid., p. 13.

of 'knowledge' which, for Foucault, exist because they express and legitimize power. Nor is it surprising to find that punishment undergoes the same transition as medicine, from a system of symbolism to a system of surveillance. In an impressive description of Bentham's 'panopticon' (a *machine à corriger*, in which all prisoners could be observed from a single post), Foucault relates the discipline of the prison to the newly emerging power of the invisible over the visible, which is, if I understand him, the power expressed in law. The law is the invisible possessor of that 'normalizing gaze' which both singles out the criminal as an abnormal specimen, and also deprives him of his rights until such a time as he should once again be able to take up the burden of normality.

There then occurs one of those forced, *marxisant* explanations that mar the poetry of Foucault's far from prosaic writing. We are told that the prison disciplines exhibit a 'tactics of power', with three fundamental purposes: to exert power at the lowest cost, to extend power as far and as deeply as possible, and 'to link this "economic" growth of power with the output of the apparatuses (educational, military, industrial or medical) within which it is exercised'.[48] All that is meant to suggest a connection between prison and the 'economic take-off of the West', which 'began with the techniques that made possible the accumulation of capital'.[49]

Such impulsive observations are produced not by scholarship or empirical evidence but by the association of ideas, the principal idea being the historical morphology of the *Communist Manifesto*. And if we ask why that discredited morphology is still accepted by so sophisticated a modern thinker, the answer is to be found, I believe, in the fact that it provides the preliminary sketches for the portrait of the enemy. It inspires such passages as the following:

Is it surprising that the cellular prison, with its regular chronologies, forced labour, its authorities of surveillance and registration, its experts in normality, who continue to multiply the functions of the judge, should have become the modern instrument of penalty? Is it surprising that prisons resemble factories, schools, barracks, hospitals, which all resemble prisons?[50]

---

[48] Ibid., p. 218.
[49] Ibid., p. 220.
[50] Ibid., pp. 227–8.

No, it is not surprising. For if we unmask human institutions far enough, we will always find that hidden core of power by which Foucault is outraged and fascinated. The only question is whether this unmasking reveals the truth about its subject, or whether it is not, on the contrary, a new and sophisticated form of lying. We must ask ourselves whether the one who observes 'at the very centre of the carceral city, the formation of the insidious leniencies, unavowable petty cruelties, small acts of cunning, calculated methods, techniques, "sciences" that permit the fabrication of the disciplinary individual'[51] – whether such an observer is not in fact the inventor of what he claims to observe.

But it is not easy to unmask this observer. That his writings exhibit mythomania and even paranoia is, I believe, patent. But that they systematically falsify and propagandize what they describe is more difficult to establish. A writer who can glibly declare that 'the bourgeoisie could not care less about delinquents, about their punishment and rehabilitation, which economically have little importance';[52] that 'the bourgeoisie is perfectly well aware that a new constitution or legislature will not suffice to establish its hegemony';[53] that '"dangerous" people had to be isolated (in prison, in the Hôpital Général, in the galleys, in the colonies) so that they could not act as a spearhead for popular resistance'[54] – such a writer is clearly more concerned with rhetorical impact than with historical accuracy.

However, I believe that it would be a mistake to dismiss Foucault on the evidence of such pronouncements. As I have argued, we must separate Foucault's analysis of the workings of power from the facile relativism that opens such easy paths to theory. And paranoia is no more than localized relativism – a specific and focused manifestation of the desire that reality be subservient to thought, that the other have an identity entirely determined by one's own response to him. What is important is not the disposition to find, in human thought and action, the smiling masks of persecution, but rather the idea that, by unmasking them as forms of power, we come closer to an understanding of their nature. It is precisely this that I doubt.

---

[51] Ibid., p. 308.
[52] *Power/Knowledge: Selected Interviews and Other Writings, 1972–77*, ed. Colin Gordon, Brighton, 1980, p. 102.
[53] Ibid., p. 156.
[54] Ibid., p. 15.

In a pair of lectures delivered in 1976,[55] Foucault deliberates over what he means by 'power', and distinguishes two approaches: the Reichian (which argues that 'the mechanisms of power are those of repression'), and the Nietzschean, which holds that the 'basis of the relationship of power lies in the hostile engagement of forces'.[56] In an obscure account of this distinction Foucault aligns himself with the second approach, and he tries to show (in the first volume of *L'Histoire de la sexualité*, 1976)[57] how this conception of power enables us to see even sexual relations as instances of the 'hostile engagement of forces'. But Foucault offers no real explanation of what he means by 'power'. The 'Reichian' and the 'Nietzschean' approaches are entirely compatible, and both are explained in terms – 'repression', 'force' – which are at least as obscure as the 'power' that they are supposed to illuminate.

At that period in his life Foucault repeatedly emphasized that he was concerned with power in its 'capillary' form, the form that 'reaches into the very grain of individuals'.[58] But he did not reveal who, or what, is active in this 'power'; or rather, he revealed it, but in terms that carried no conviction. In an interview Foucault admitted that, for him, 'power is coextensive with the social body'.[59] And it is of course indisputable that social order, like every order, embodies power. A society, like an organism, can sustain itself only by constant interaction among its parts. And all interaction is an exercise of power: the power of a cause to produce its effect. But that is merely trivial.

What is not trivial is the entirely unwarranted and ideologically inspired idea of dominance with which Foucault glosses his conclusions. He at once assumes that if there is power then it is exercised in the interests of some dominant agent. Hence by sleight of hand, he is able to present any feature of social order – even the disposition to heal the sick – as a covert exercise of dominion, which furthers the interests of 'those in power'. He writes: 'I believe that anything can be deduced from the general phenomenon of the domination of the bourgeois class'.[60] It would be truer to say that he believed that the general thesis of the domination of the bourgeois class can be deduced from anything. For

[55] Ibid., pp. 78–108.
[56] Ibid., p. 91.
[57] *The History of Sexuality, vol. 1: An Introduction*, tr. R. Hurley, New York, 1978.
[58] Power/Knowledge, op. cit., p. 39.
[59] Ibid., p. 142.
[60] Ibid., p. 100.

having decided, along with the *Communist Manifesto*, that the bourgeois class has been dominant since the summer of 1789, Foucault deduces that all power subsequently embodied in the social order has been exercised by that class, and in its interests. Any fact of social order will therefore necessarily bear the fingerprints of bourgeois domination. The triviality of the argument needs no comment; what is astounding is the philosophical naivety that underlies it.

In a remarkable discussion with a group of 1968 Maoists Foucault draws some of the political consequences of his analysis of law, as yet another 'capillary' mode of power, yet another way of 'introducing contradictions among the masses'.[61] The revolution, he assures them, 'can only take place via the radical elimination of the judicial apparatus, and anything which could reintroduce the penal apparatus, anything which could reintroduce its ideology and enable this ideology surreptitiously to creep back into popular practices, must be banished'.[62] He recommends the banishment of adjudication, and every form of court, and gestures towards a new form of 'proletarian' justice, which will not require the services of a judge. The French Revolution, he tells us, was a 'rebellion against the judiciary'; and such, he implies, is the nature of every honest revolution. Had he proceeded to mention the historical facts – the Revolutionary Tribunals in which judge, prosecutor and witness were one and the same and the accused had no right of reply, the thousands of executions, the genocide in La Vendée, and all the other calamities that flowed from the 'rebellion against the judiciary' – then his remarks might have been taken as a warning and not, as he intended them, as an endorsement.

But it is not only the French Revolution that illustrates what follows, when the judiciary are removed from office. When there is no third party present at the trial of those accused, no one with the duty to sift the evidence, no one to mediate between the parties or to look impartially on the facts, then 'justice' becomes a 'life and death' struggle, in which one side has all the weapons. Such was observed at the Moscow Show Trials, as well as at the Revolutionary Tribunals of the French Revolution. As a historian Foucault must have known this. Yet he willingly subscribed to a form of 'proletarian justice' that removes all defence from the accused. To think, as he seemed to think, that such a form of justice

---

[61] Ibid., p. 14.
[62] Ibid., p. 16.

will free society from the blight of domination is to overlook all that he had reason to know. If social order is composed of the substance that Foucault called 'power', then the rule of law is the best and most mitigated form of it.

Reading Foucault the *soixante-huitard* one inevitably asks, could he have been serious in saying those things? And the answer, I think, is – yes, he was serious. But things rapidly changed for him. Through his studies of the asylum and the clinic, and through his comprehensive 'archaeology of knowledge', he had tried to show the ways in which normality is manufactured in the interest of the ruling structures of power, and how normality shifts as power is transferred from the aristocratic to the bourgeois class. But there was one area that he had yet to explore, and which had been made central to the study of bourgeois normality by Sartre in *Saint Genet* – the area of sexuality. It was an area of particular personal concern to Foucault, whose active homosexuality led him into well-known excesses, including visits to the sado-masochistic bathhouses of San Francisco, a practice that he exuberantly justified in terms that recalled the spooky encomium to sado-masochism in *Being and Nothingness*.[63]

In 1976 he published the first, introductory, volume to a *History of Sexuality*, in which he sketches the view that his readers would naturally expect from him, namely, that the distinction between normal and abnormal sexual conduct, and the view of sexual activity as intrinsically 'problematized', are to be explained in terms of the prevailing structures of domination.[64] Intellectually the book was not much of an advance on *Saint Genet*, but it promised a three-volume sequel, addressed to the following question: 'Why does sexual behaviour, and why do the activities and pleasures which pertain to it, form the object of a moral preoccupation? Why this ethical concern?'[65]

By the time those subsequent volumes began to appear Foucault was suffering from AIDS, and had begun to shake off his former persona as an *enfant terrible*. The Solidarity movement in Poland made a deep impression on him: not only as the first genuine working-class revolution in history, but as one directed *against* communism and in favour of a

---

[63] See Didier Eribon, *Insult and the Making of the Gay Self*, Duke University Press, 2004, pp. 314–16.
[64] *Histoire de la sexualité, vol. 1: La volonté de savoir*, Paris, Gallimard, 1976, tr. Robert Hurley, *History of Sexuality*, vol. 1: *The Will to Knowledge*, London, Allen Lane, 1978.
[65] *L'Usage des plaisirs*, Paris, 1984, p. 16.

national identity. Foucault spoke out in favour of Solidarity, and tried, in vain, to influence the government of François Mitterrand to take punitive measures against the communist authorities in Poland. And in volumes 2 and 3 of the *History of Sexuality* he began to write in a new way, giving careful accounts of the ancient texts that interested him, and referring at every point to the work of other scholars. In volume 2, entitled *L'Usage des plaisirs*, he studies a variety of ancient texts dealing with sexual attraction, attempting at first – as the title of the book indicates – to identify the primary sexual phenomenon as *pleasure*. But the texts that he studied are not about sexual *pleasure* at all. In the sexual act, as in the relations that made it possible, the human being was seen by the Greeks and Romans as shaping and symbolizing his or her social position. Sex was therefore *intrinsically* 'problematized'. Concepts of honour and virtue creep in behind the first impulse of desire, and even relations between men and boys raised, for those who practised them, the question of how to distinguish the honourable from the dishonourable way of enjoying them, Plato famously arguing that the element of sensual pleasure must be transcended and replaced by the desire to educate.[66]

In volume 3, *Le souci de soi*, Foucault argues that, in the ancient world, sexual activity, at first conceived as a symbol of the social status of the participants, is gradually 'privatized', so as to be governed by the 'care for the self'. This, he suggests, is the source of the growing emphasis on purity, virginity, and fidelity in marriage. But, as he recognizes, 'the intensification of the care for the self goes hand in hand with the valorization of the other'.[67] And by the end of the book the reader is made aware that sex, in the world of Pliny and Plutarch, was not about pleasure, still less about power and domination, but about mutual dependence and the care of children. Of course Foucault does not draw any moral from this, and adopts a position of detachment, as though pleasure remained the primary *subject-matter* of sexual conduct, and social structures the peculiar avenues through which people passed in order to reach it. But the style is hesitant, circumspect and without the former belligerence. And by taking the position of women and children seriously, he comes close to recognizing the truth, which is that it is not power but love that makes the world go round.

---

[66] *L'Usage des plaisirs*, op. cit., pp. 235–6.
[67] *Le souci de soi*, Paris, 1984, p. 175.

The impression created by these later works is of a Foucault who has been 'normalized'. His command of the French language, his fascination with ancient texts and the by-ways of history, his flamboyant imagination and beautiful style – all have been put, at last, to a proper use, in order to describe the human condition respectfully, and to cease to look for the secret 'structures' beneath its smile. It helps that his subject-matter is the ancient world, and the works of authors who cannot be dismissed or debunked as merely 'bourgeois'. But it helps too that Foucault had, by this time, been 'mugged by reality', and was being cared for in the institution which he had once scoffed at for its habit of confronting its inmates with the 'truth' of their condition.

It was when confronted with the truth of *his* condition that Foucault at last grew up. He had gone down with Sartre into the hell where the Other resides. But he had recognized his own otherness too, and returned to the real world in a posture of acceptance. And, reading these later works, I was constantly drawn to the thought that Foucault's belligerent leftism was not a criticism of reality, but a defence against it, a refusal to recognize that, for all its defects, normality is all that we have.

5 TEDIUM IN GERMANY: DOWNHILL TO HABERMAS

After the war, in what was then West Germany, the universities were in crisis, and the question what to teach, and how, was the urgent preoccupation of all serious academics. It was partly through the universities that Nazism had instilled its poison into the minds of the young, and it was understandable that all those who had gained or retained their academic positions during the Hitler years should be regarded with suspicion. In some cases the suspicion was justified, and the notorious case of Martin Heidegger reminds us that even a great philosopher can throw in his lot, when the moment comes, with the forces of destruction.

Had Heidegger attached his great ego to the cause of international socialism, he would have enjoyed the whitewash granted to Sartre, Merleau-Ponty, Hobsbawm and the other apologists for the Gulag.[1] But the cause of *national* socialism could enjoy no such convenient excuse, and the sin was compounded, in Heidegger's case, by the fact that it was precisely the *national*, rather than the *socialist* aspect of the creed that had attracted him. In his own way, however, Heidegger represented a real and indigenous contribution to the intellectual tradition channelled by the German universities, and it was imperative to find some rival source of ideas and arguments with which to justify his exile.

Curriculum, syllabus, literature – all were fumigated, and the tawdry idols of national socialism cast down from their pedestals into the gutter from whence they came. In their place came a new idol – the Marxist humanism of the pre-war Frankfurt School. The idol was crudely wrought at first, from materials that had been hastily shipped to America during the pre-war turmoil. But gradually the process of

---

[1] Maurice Merleau-Ponty's justification of the Soviet show-trials and prison camps was published as *Humanism and Terror* in 1946.

manufacture was refined, and along with the post-war boom in German industry came the new Frankfurt intellectual, smooth, polished and produced like the BMW in many complementary varieties, each technically perfect and each with a performance chart that outstripped those of the French and British rivals. Typical of these functionally perfect bureaucrats of the German Left has been Jürgen Habermas. Born in 1929 into a National Socialist Family, Habermas studied in Göttingen and Bonn, before gravitating to the Institute for Social Research in Frankfurt, and spending time in the late 1950s as assistant to its most important surviving guru, Theodor Adorno. Appointed Professor in Frankfurt in 1964, he has since enjoyed prestigious positions in universities around the world. He is known and read in departments of sociology, philosophy, literature and political science, on account of his endless and soporific attempt to synthesize the contributions of modern philosophers and sociologists to the consensual politics of the post-totalitarian left. Awarded the Hegel Prize in Stuttgart in 1976, he has continued to receive accolades for books that have achieved a rare prestige in Germany, and which are printed in luxury editions for the better class of living room. Few people have read these books from cover to cover; few of those who have read them remember what they say. Nevertheless, with somewhat greater frequency than the lines of Shakespeare that fall from the monkey's typewriter, interesting ideas surface in the great waste-paper basket of Habermas's prose, and any account of the German left establishment must take his writings seriously.

The left in the German-speaking lands grew, like the French left between the wars, from the context of defeat – the catastrophic defeat of the First World War, which destroyed both the German and the Austro-Hungarian Empires and imposed a humiliating peace treaty together with a grid of invented boundaries across the east of our continent, so ensuring that central Europe would remain unstable for the foreseeable future. The two most influential leftists writing in German during the first half of the twentieth century were both highly cultivated products of the upper class. Theodor Adorno (1903–69) began life as a musical prodigy, studied composition in Frankfurt and later under Berg in Vienna. He wrote a doctoral thesis on the philosophy of Edmund Husserl and made an early reputation as an eager defender of radical modernism in music. György Lukács (1885–1971) was a writer and philosopher who, by the time of his death, had become accepted as the major literary critic of the international left, and a leading exponent of the neo-Marxist theory of society. He was also the prime mover of the 'Marxist humanism' that was later to crystallize in the Frankfurt School. No account of German leftism can ignore these two seminal figures, and it is therefore from them that I begin.

A friend of writers, musicians, painters and philosophers, Lukács belonged securely in the world that was soon to go under. He esteemed little or nothing in the Austrian inheritance: the saccharine nobility of Strauss and Hofmannsthal, the nostalgia of Josef Roth, the 'spontaneous order' of Hayek and Wittgenstein, the visionary perspectives on sexual chaos in the writings of Musil and the paintings of Klimt and Schiele – all left him cold. He experienced only a fanatical urge to be rid of such relics, along with all the laws and customs that had nurtured them.

This contempt for existing social realities was by no means peculiar to Lukács; similar sentiments can be found in the works of many of his Austro-Hungarian contemporaries – in the nihilistic satire of Karl Kraus, in the expressionistic atonality of Schoenberg's *Erwartung*, in the cold architecture of Loos and the meaningless laws and offices imagined by Kafka. However, Lukács gave to these sentiments an original and dangerous turn, lifting them out of the realm of speculation and attaching them to the deed of Sarajevo. Hence, although the self-destruction of the Habsburg Empire finds its psychical expression in many of his contemporaries, Lukács adds a vindictiveness of his own. Nothing actual had sense for him: only the future was worth fighting for, and the future belonged with the proletariat. The task of the critic was to invent the proletariat, and to set it up as the true inquisitor of culture.

Lukács was not the creator of the socialist critique of culture. As he repeatedly acknowledges, the idea was a favourite of Lenin's. Nevertheless, he was the first exponent of the idea who was sufficiently well educated to carry it to fruition, and to deliver results that would appear credible to those for whom culture remained a source of secular validity. When the radical academics of the 1960s began to look for the authorities that would justify their censoriousness, it was to Lukács that they turned. Not only had he compiled the first credible Marxist index of modern literature; he had also devised a critical invective that situated culture at the centre of the 'world struggle' between revolution and reaction. He showed his literary followers that their intellectual concern was identical with the universal aim of the proletariat: the liquidation of reactionary elements. In short, he justified culture to the Marxists by showing how to condemn it in Marxist terms. And in doing so he provided crucial concepts to Adorno and the thinkers of the Frankfurt School – concepts that were later to emerge as the basic repertoire of 'Marxist humanism'.

Lukács's father was a wealthy Jewish banker, who had been ennobled by the Emperor and who used his influence to obtain privileges for his son – including exemption from military service during the First World War. Lukács devoted his protracted youth to reading widely in philosophy and literature. Along with the Marxist classics he immersed himself in the writings of the anarcho-syndicalist Georges Sorel, whose apology for violence made a deep impression, and was often used in later years in defence of revolutionary terror. He joined the Hungarian Communist Party shortly after its foundation in 1918, and served as deputy Commissar for Education in the short-lived Hungarian 'Soviet'. He was later to look back with satisfaction at the heroic deeds of that time, when he began the work of dismissing all non-communist professors from the Hungarian universities. He was to return to this work on his return from Moscow after the Second World War, becoming part of the new communist administrative machine, with a responsibility for denouncing non-communist writers and intellectuals and banning their publications. It is thanks in part to Lukács that the most important Hungarian philosopher of the twentieth century – Béla Hamvas – was expelled from his position as a librarian and forced to work as an unskilled labourer in a power plant.

Meanwhile, fleeing Hungary for Vienna in 1919, Lukács had begun his literary career in earnest, publishing his seminal collection of essays – *History and Class Consciousness* – in 1923, and actively cooperating with other members of the Communist Movement then resident in the Austrian capital, including Viktor Serge and Antonio Gramsci (see Chapter 7 below). Summoned to Moscow in 1930, he spent the war years confined to the Marx-Engels Institute, being one of the small number of Hungarian communists in the Soviet Union who survived Stalin's purges, a feat that he achieved partly by denouncing everyone who had been placed on the index, himself included.

Not surprisingly, Lukács's reputation in Hungary today is not as high as it was in Paris in 1968. But his school – Agnes Heller, Ferenc Féher, György Márkus, János Kis and many more – continued to relay the message of 'Marxist humanism', either from their comfortable positions in leftist university departments abroad, or, after 1989, in Hungary itself. It is partly thanks to Lukács's enduring influence that Hungary has, at the present time, a right-wing government, elected twice in succession with a two-thirds majority. The cause of this is not the special virtue of Viktor Orbán and his Fidesz Party, but the awfulness of the alternative, in which the seething resentment of Lukács lives on.

In an autobiographical interview, Lukács makes two remarks that epitomize the outlook of his early years:

> At the time we all felt a bitter hatred for capitalism and all its forms. We wanted to destroy it at all costs and as quickly as possible.[2]

> You cannot just sample Marxism... you must be converted to it.[3]

The two remarks should be taken together. After his 'conversion' to Marxism – when he had become, as he put it, a 'messianic sectarian'[4] – Lukács could see only the hateful presence of 'capitalism', and nothing in his surrounding world had any independent validity. The Dual Monarchy was no longer, in his eyes, a system of laws and institutions; stripped of its true identity, as a carefully negotiated solution to a recurrent problem of multi-national government, it had no aspect besides that of the economic 'system' that supposedly maintained it in being. The root fallacy of Marxism, the belief in a real 'essence' of which our social life is only an 'appearance', had colonized Lukács's brain, and taken the form of an immovable religion. From this moment the surrounding world lost all claim over Lukács's conscience. All was to be swept away in the refining fire of revolution. The law had no greater validity than any other aspect of the political process: 'the question of legality or illegality reduces itself... for the Communist Party to a *mere question of tactics*,' he wrote, adding that 'in this wholly unprincipled solution lies the only possible practical and principled rejection of the bourgeois legal system.'[5]

What was true of the legal system was true too of every other feature of the 'bourgeois' world: economic practices, social relations, emotions, ambitions, even morality itself. In reply to a contemporary enquiry Lukács asserted that 'Communist ethics makes it the highest duty to accept the necessity to act wickedly', adding that 'this is the greatest sacrifice the revolution asks from us.'[6]

---

[2] György Lukács, *Record of a Life*, ed. Istvan Eörsi, tr. R. Livingstone, London, 1983, p. 60.
[3] Ibid., p. 63.
[4] Ibid., p. 76.
[5] *History and Class Consciousness*, tr. R. Livingstone, London, 1971, p. 264.
[6] See Frank Borkenau, *World Communism*, New York, 1962, pp. 172–3.

'Wickedness', after all, is a bourgeois conception, and everything bourgeois must be overthrown. Indeed the entire human psyche is so deformed by capitalism that 'it is not possible to be human in bourgeois society',[7] so that 'the bourgeoisie possesses only the semblance of a human existence'.[8] At the time Lukács penned that last remark Hitler was speaking in similar terms of the Jews; but Lukács chose his language deliberately.

With Lukács we have to do not with the anti-bourgeois snobbery of a Foucault, nor with the disdain for ordinary customs of a Dworkin or a Galbraith. We have to do with hatred. And while this hatred embraces all the 'appearances' of the 'bourgeois' world, it is directed beyond and behind them, to the hidden devil that they conceal. The devil is 'capitalism', and hatred of capitalism is total and unconditional, justifying every moral breach.

But why? What is so bad in 'capitalism'? It is Lukács's major achievement to have found what was to become – first for the Frankfurt School and subsequently for the post-war New Left – the canonical answer to that question. Lukács discovered the language in which capitalism could be represented as the greatest of social evils, to a generation that had experienced the abundance, the freedom, the social provisions and opportunities of a 'mixed capitalist economy'. And he was able to present his critique as the true 'hidden agenda' of *Das Kapital*. For he had discovered the survival, in the guise of economic theory, of the 'Young Hegelian' criticism of Marx's youth.

Marxian economics is a muddled but fascinating concoction, taken partly from Ricardian political economy and partly from what Lukács called 'classical German philosophy' – i.e. from Kant, Schiller, Fichte, Hegel and Schelling. *Das Kapital* opens with a disastrous argument, to the effect that if two commodities exchange against each other their 'exchange-value' must be 'the mode of expression, the phenomenal form, of something contained in [them], yet distinguishable from them'.[9] The remark, phrased already in the tendentious idiom of 'classical German philosophy', is justified by an important fallacy:

Let us take two commodities, e.g. corn and iron. The proportions in which they are exchangeable, whatever these proportions may be, can

[7] *History and Class Consciousness*, op. cit., p. 190.
[8] György Lukács, *Essays on Realism*, ed. R. Livingstone, tr. D. Fernbach, London, 1980, p. 133.
[9] Karl Marx, *Capital*, Standard edition, Moscow, 1962–6, vol. 1, p. 45.

always be represented by an equation, in which a given quantity of corn is equated to some quantity of iron, e.g. 1 quarter corn = x cwt of iron. What does this equation tell us? It tells us that in two different things – in one quarter of corn and x cwt of iron – there exists in equal quantities something common to both. The two things must therefore be equal to a third, which in itself is neither the one nor the other. Each of them, so far as it is exchange-value, must therefore be reducible to this third.[10]

Thus Marx launches himself on the path that leads to 'socially necessary labour' as the 'hidden' value within every equation of exchange.

Now the only *logical* conclusion to be drawn from the fact that two commodities exchange at a given rate is that they exchange at that rate. If a money value is assigned to the given equation then this is simply another fact of the same kind. The value of any commodity can be seen as an 'equivalence class'. Just as a geometer would define the direction of a line as the set of all lines that are identically directed, and just as Frege and Russell defined the number of a class as the class of all classes that are equinumerous with it, so might the economist define the value of a commodity as the class of all commodities that exchange equally against it. The assumption of a ghostly 'third' item, in terms of which this equivalence is to be defined, is strictly redundant – a purely metaphysical commentary upon facts that provide no independent support for it.

By that fallacious a priori argument Marxian economics takes as its subject-matter, not empirical data, but an occult entity that is in no way implied by them. It then makes of this occult entity ('value') the main object of a new pseudo-science – a 'science' which, in the nature of things, must stand at one remove from the empirical data that could confirm or refute its findings. While modern economists take *price*, empirically defined, as their explanandum, Marx tries to explain another, hidden variable, of which 'price' is the mere 'phenomenal form'. Not surprisingly, such 'phenomenal' entities as supply and demand (which explain price) cannot explain the hidden 'essence' of 'value', nor even provide us with reasonable grounds for its existence.

In view of the success of modern price theory – and in particular of the theory of marginal utility, whose emergence in the later nineteenth

---

[10] Ibid.

century destroyed much of the impact of *Das Kapital* – it might seem surprising that interest in Marx's labour theory of value should have been retained. But Marx's fallacy remains appealing. It opens up that philosophical, critical and political perspective without which the landscape of economic theory seems desolate and meaningless. Marx's promise of a 'political economy' is fulfilled at the very outset of his argument, precisely in his use of the language of 'classical German philosophy'. For this language suggests that the data of economics conceal a hidden 'meaning'. The so-called science of 'bourgeois' economics stands in need of an *interpretation*, if we are to grasp the social reality to which it refers. Marx then makes his decisive intellectual move, arguing that 'bourgeois' economics precisely does not explain economic reality but rather conceals it, by turning attention away from its hidden essence. 'Bourgeois' economics is not science but ideology, and true economics – the political economy of *Das Kapital* – rests its scientific claims precisely in its *philosophical* method, which enables it to penetrate behind appearances to the social essence that they conceal.

If the argument were correct then it could be repeated for every scientific theory known to man. All would be dismissed as ideological devices, precisely through their disposition (implied in the very idea of scientific method) to explain appearances and to pay no attention to the 'metaphysical' core. Set theory, for instance, could be dismissed as the 'ideology' of mathematics since it studies, not numbers (the Platonic essences concealed behind our equations) but the 'equivalence classes' that substitute for them in every meaningful formula. Physics would become the 'ideology' of matter, and biology the 'ideology' of life. It is thus, indeed, that Engels constructs his 'dialectic of nature': a preposterous replacement of the laws of physics with ramshackle metaphysics, by which he claims to 'reveal' what 'bourgeois' physics conceals.[11]

This disreputable reasoning – which justifies ideology as 'science' and condemns true science as mere 'ideology' – had great appeal for Lukács, who made it, in effect, the cornerstone of his philosophy. 'The "marginal utility" theory of the imperialist period', he writes, 'is the

---

[11] F. Engels, *Anti-Dühring* and *Dialectics of Nature*. Alain Besançon has drawn attention to the fun that Flaubert might have had at the expense of Bouvard and Pécuchet, had his characters discovered these works: *The Intellectual Origins of Leninism*, tr. Sarah Matthews, Oxford, 1989, p. 49.

acme of [the] abstracting and formalistic evacuation of the real contents of economics'[12] – and in the word 'imperialist' he tries to summarize and condemn an entire age of intellectual endeavour. He goes on: 'Whereas in the classic period the prevailing effort was directed towards understanding the connection between social and economic problems, the era of decay built up an artificial, pseudo-scientific and pseudo-methodological barrier between the two.'[13] Thus the part of economics that has justified itself as science, through its real predictive power, is condemned as 'pseudo-scientific'. In the same terms, Lukács explains away the 'bourgeois' science of sociology: 'The new science of the era of decay, sociology as a special science, arose because the bourgeois ideologists wanted to view the laws and history of social development separate from the economy.'[14]

The meaning of that (slightly paranoid) utterance should not be taken lightly. Indeed, we see in it one of the reasons for Lukács's appeal: his provision of the inquisitorial instruments whereby non-Marxist thought, called to the bar of critical analysis, can be forced to confess its crimes. It is in vain for the 'bourgeois' scientist to consult the facts: in the absence of the 'total' vision of Marxism he who refers to the facts merely condemns himself as an empiricist, and empiricism is 'an ideology of the bourgeoisie'.[15]

> The fundamental assertion of the dialectical method is the Hegelian theory of the concrete concept. This theory states, in brief, that the whole is prior to its parts: the part must be interpreted in the light of the whole, and not vice versa... [16]

If the facts serve to refute the 'total' theory of Marxism, then 'so much the worse for the facts'.[17]

Philosophers of science are familiar with the thesis of Quine and Duhem, that any theory, suitably revised, can be made consistent with any data, and any data rejected in the interests of theory. But what

---

[12] *Essays on Realism*, op. cit., p. 127.
[13] Ibid.
[14] Ibid.
[15] *New Left Review* (1971), reprinted in *Record of a Life*, op. cit., p. 174.
[16] *Tactics and Ethics: Political Essays, 1919–29*, New York, 1975, p. 25.
[17] Ibid., p. 30.

Lukács proposes is the rejection of data in the interests of a philosophy that disparages empirical observation altogether, as the last refuge of the ideologist. Hence he is able to rescue Marxism from the assaults of reality, and set it above the domain of science, over which it may henceforth rule in empty triumph.

Philosophical readers of modern economics often sympathize with the Marxian enterprise. For the bare facts of 'price', 'profit', 'supply' and 'demand' are also human realities, connected with our profoundest social experiences: labour, exchange, gift, ownership, household, consumption and peace. The philosopher is drawn to conceptions that commemorate those fundamental experiences and which imprint them indelibly upon our economic algebra, like the head of the sovereign impressed upon his coin. Hence a philosopher might be drawn to Lukács's reading of Marx, in which the labour theory of value is represented in its true colours – not as a continuation of empiricist economics but as a reappearance, in 'scientific' clothing, of the major theme of 'classical German philosophy': the theme of subject and object. By restoring this lost significance to the Marxian algebra Lukács moralized it in a way favourable to the revolutionary goal. Behind the mask of economic theory he saw the living drama of the human subject, locked in his 'life and death struggle' with the 'object' that threatens always to overcome and destroy him. In other words, he saw again the outlines of the Hegelian dialectic, in something like the form that Kojève had relayed it to the disenchanted intellectuals of Paris.

Lukács also introduces another idea that we have already encountered in the later writings of Sartre: the idea of totalization. To understand the capitalist system, Lukács argues, we must see it in its 'totality', and one can do that only with the help of a 'total' theory – a theory that sees the whole of things, and sees them whole. This total theory is Marxism, conceived according to the 'dialectical' interpretation. From the standpoint of this 'total' theory we are able to see that the 'production relations' of capitalism are reflected, not only in capitalist laws, institutions and ideology, but in the very structure of capitalist consciousness. Capitalism is not only in our bodies; it is in our minds. In particular, capitalist consciousness is prone to 'fetishistic illusions'. The effect of this is to introduce a condition that Lukács called the 'reification' of consciousness.

The term 'reification' (*Versachlichung* or *Verdinglichung*) is taken from *Das Kapital*, as are the theories of 'commodity' and 'capital fetishism', which it is used to generalize. These intellectual devices were given only a secondary role by Marx; Lukács, however, converts them into the principal tools of his anti-capitalist critique. According to Marx, capital is 'not a thing but a social relation between persons, mediated through things'.[18] However, capital appears as an objective *force*, which acts independently of the 'social relations' from which it grows. To attribute this force to an entity called 'capital' is to be the victim of fetishism: it is to attribute purely human powers to inhuman objects – to promissory notes, machinery and coins.

The most pernicious form of this fetishism, the one that most completely masks the social reality of capitalist production, is that which attaches to interest. Under capitalism, Marx argues, it appears

> as though interest were the typical product of capital, the primary matter, and profit, in the shape of profit of an enterprise, were a mere accessory and by-product of the process of reproduction. Thus we get a fetish form of capital, and the concept of fetish capital. [In the process whereby capital becomes capital-plus-interest] we have the meaningless form of capital, the perversion and objectification of production relations in their highest degree, the interest-bearing form, the simple form of capital in which it antecedes its own process of reproduction. It is the capacity of money, or a commodity, to expand its own value independently of reproduction – which is a mystification of capital in its most flagrant form…a form in which the source of profit [viz. the exploitation of the labourer] is no longer discernible, and in which the result of the capitalist process of production – divorced from the process – acquires an independent existence.[19]

The emotional force behind Marx's prose is more evident than the argument, and it is this same force that animates Lukács, in his borrowing of Marx's terminology. 'Reification', 'alienation' and 'fetishism' become the besetting sins of the capitalist system.

Just as there is 'capital fetishism' so too is there 'commodity fetishism', which mystifies the human relations of the marketplace and conceals the exploitation upon which commodities feed. The victim of commodity fetishism sees commodities as endowed with a peculiar power, exchanging

---

[18] *Capital*, op. cit., vol. 1, p. 766.
[19] Ibid., vol. III, pp. 384–5.

as though under the influence of autonomous and objective laws. Viewed in that way commodities do indeed have power – power over the person who fetishizes them and who comes to see himself as governed by their inherent magic. Under capitalism man too is a commodity, exchangeable in accordance with the 'objective' laws of the system. Hence, Lukács argues, the 'objective' world is fetishized, while the subjective world is 'reified'. Objects parade before us as though endowed with a dominating will-power, while the human subject is degraded to the status of a thing, swept along by the 'objective' laws of the market:

> *Objectively* a world of objects and relations between things springs into being (the world of commodities and their movements on the market). The laws governing these objects and their movements are indeed gradually discovered by man, but even so they confront him as invisible forces that generate their own power. The individual can use his knowledge of these laws to his own advantage, but he is not able to modify the process of his own activity. *Subjectively* – where the market economy has been fully developed – a man's activity becomes estranged from himself, it turns into a commodity which, subject to the non-human objectivity of the natural laws of society, must go its own way independently of man, just like any consumer article.[20]

The same inexorable process of capitalist production compels the development of detail labour and hence the fragmentation of the subject – his division into separate skills and functions and the absorption of his life into some particular skill that determines his value as a commodity. According to Lukács, this fragmentation of labour changes production into a species of contemplation. As a mere cog in the machine that dominates and controls him, the labourer loses his status as a human agent and adopts towards his own behaviour the purely contemplative stance of the anatomist, who studies the workings of a body.[21]

Through constant repetition of such arguments, Lukács is able to persuade himself that fetishism, alienation and reification define the prevailing spiritual condition of capitalist society. They are manifest in the enslavement of the workforce, in the debasement of art and language,

---

[20] *History and Class Consciousness*, op. cit., p. 87.
[21] Ibid., p. 89.

in the perversion of sexual relations – in short, in the universal separation of man from his essence. Such 'insights' suggest that the suffering and sinfulness of humankind need no other explanation than the persistence of the capitalist system. But they are far from hard-won, being more or less mechanical applications of 'classical German philosophy' and in particular of the drama of 'subject and object' that was later to have such a profound impact in Paris. To understand what Lukács is getting at we should therefore return to the root of 'classical German philosophy'.

As subjects, Kant argued, we are essentially free, and exercise our freedom in practical reason, which is the source of the categorical imperative that motivates and justifies our conduct. Hegel agreed, but followed Fichte in arguing that the subject is not given absolutely but is rather self-generated, through a process of negation and 'determination' (*Bestimmung*). The subject realizes himself, and so earns his freedom, only through the successive positing of objects that are other than himself, and which provide his field of action. This process of *Selbstbestimmung* is social: I realize myself through my relations with others, from whom my freedom is won. From the 'life and death struggle' with the other either of us might emerge as master or as slave. The slave is a mere object for the master; but, argues Hegel, the master also becomes a mere object for himself, being severed from the world of action by the constant mediation of his slave, and forced to take a purely contemplative stance towards his own existence. True freedom comes only by restoring the unity between contemplation and action, and by overcoming the antagonistic relation that deprives both master and slave of the recognition that they crave.

The process of self-realization exemplifies the structure of the dialectic. The 'immediate', 'indeterminate' subject – the empty 'I' – passes out of itself, is 'objectified' and estranged. In all self-knowledge there is this first moment of negation – the conversion of the subject into an 'object' of its own contemplative awareness. (This is the moment of *Entäusserung*, or becoming 'other'.) Only in the completion of the dialectic is the self restored to itself, so as to become consciously and determinately what it was before only abstractly and potentially.

Thus I gain my moral awareness and my freedom in two stages. First I pass from the immediate 'I want' of childhood to the alienating perception of myself as an object enslaved by desire; then I incorporate this self-awareness into my own subjective nature. I will myself to be a fully self-determining subject, able to overcome desire and to act from a conception of the good. I thereby achieve a unity of contemplation and action: I become a true agent, motivated by a conception of myself, entitled to my own and others' respect.

The rich philosophical implications of that argument cannot detain us. What is of immediate importance is its subsequent history, and in particular its travesty by Ludwig Feuerbach. In his exploration of the 'unhappy consciousness' – 'spirit in self-estrangement' – Hegel had many interesting things to say about religion. He argued that a particular kind of religion – that which regards God as irremediably transcendent, the locus of all virtue and holiness, and the world as eternally separated from God with man himself as 'fallen' – is the reflection of a 'self-alienated spirit'.

Feuerbach applied that observation to all religion, and to Christianity in particular.[22] In Christianity human beings locate all virtue in a heavenly sphere and therefore find no virtue in themselves. Feuerbach here borrows from Kant's philosophy of religion the crucial concept of the 'fetish'. In fetishism, Kant argued, man attributes his own powers to objects that are outside him and is therefore set at one remove from his own will. Christianity too is fetishism, argued Feuerbach, in which man attributes his virtue, freedom and happiness to an unreal 'spiritual' realm, and so lives out his material existence in a state of hopeless separation from his true nature and powers. Virtue could be regained, were we to recognize that its reality lies here, in our material, social existence – in our 'species being' (*Gattungswesen*) as Feuerbach tendentiously called it. In religion we make our virtue into an object, and then worship it as our master. Hence we are 'alienated' from ourselves and separated from our fulfilment. In this way our fetishistic consciousness deprives us of our powers, by investing them in unreal objects.

In the 1844 manuscripts Marx adds a further twist to the story, using the same intoxicating rhetoric to mount a critique of private property. In property, Marx argues, man objectifies his will, endowing a mere object with his own subjectivity and thereby losing it. Property holds sway over him, by virtue of the power that it has appropriated from his own activity and will. In property, therefore, man endows objects with a human soul and becomes a mere object to himself. He is 'restored to himself' only by overcoming the institution of property, so that his relations with others are no longer mediated by the alienating world of things. Man returns from 'object' to 'subject' by rejoining at a higher, more self-conscious level, the 'species being' from which property had sundered him.

---

[22] Ludwig Feuerbach, *The Essence of Christianity*, 1841, tr. Marian Evans, London, 1854.

The 1844 manuscripts were discovered only after Lukács had published *History and Class Consciousness*: he himself helped to prepare the first edition of them during his period of exile in the Soviet Union. However, the Hegelian parable of man's spiritual journey – from innocent self-immersion, through alienation to self-fulfilment in true social life – remained the driving force behind all of Marx's speculations. Lukács had the imagination and the insight to perceive this, and to bring Marx's deeper meaning to the light of day. And he too was spell-bound by the force of the Hegelian parable.

As science the theory of commodity and capital fetishism is hollow: it adds nothing substantial to the explanation of capital accumulation or commodity exchange. Even as social criticism it is more sensational than sensible. For who in fact is really deceived by the illusion that commodities and capital have autonomous powers, the first to exchange, the second to grow? The 'bourgeois' economist explains these phenomena in terms of aggregate supply and demand: in other words, in terms of the social actions of human beings. So what force is there in the claim that the 'laws' of 'vulgar political economy' represent capital as 'an independent source of value'?

Nevertheless, the concept of 'fetishized consciousness' continues to inspire revolutionary thoughts. The Hegelian theory of alienation is not merely an account of man's path to self-awareness. It is a substitute for theology. In the hands of Hegel and Feuerbach it offers a secular theory of original sin. The evil that is 'abroad' in the world, which haunts us and vitiates our actions, is a sign and product of man's self-estrangement. Man is an object, who should be a subject, and his consciousness is through and through permeated by the 'triumph of things'. All power seems to him to reside outside himself, and nowhere does he encounter the spontaneity, the inner validity, of a free human will. To show that capitalism is the necessary and sufficient condition for this state of self-alienation is to justify the holy work of revolution, even (and indeed especially) in an age that has seen the material comforts that the market economy can bring.

This, then, is Lukács's main achievement: to have revealed and endorsed the theological significance of Marxian economics, and to have thereby adapted Marx's theories to the post-war world – both the world after the First World War, in which Central Europeans were looking for a new identity and hoped to find it in the promise of socialism, and the world after the Second World War, when the new styles of consumption spread from America across the globe. His ideas inspired the writers of the Frankfurt School – and Adorno especially – to see through the specious abundance of the American dream, to the 'inner' and 'subjective' alienation that was concealed by it. And he inspired the radicals of the 1960s to look for an 'inner' liberation from the norms of bourgeois order.

Of course, rationally speaking, the theory of 'reification' is no more capable of generating a political programme than any other of the romantic critiques of private property. For what is the alternative? Under what conditions will man escape the prison of a 'reified' consciousness, and how are those conditions to be secured? Why, in particular, should public ownership – or 'social ownership' – be the decisive change? In what way has the socialist critique of capitalism really advanced beyond the Kantian formulation of the sin of worldliness?

Consider Kant's words: 'In the Kingdom of Ends everything has either a *price* or a *dignity*. If it has a price, something else can be put in its place as an *equivalent*; if it is exalted above all price and so admits of no equivalent, then it has a dignity.'[23] In what way has the Marxian critique of capitalist exchange translated that moral maxim into real politics? It is true that the metaphysical idiom of 'subject' and 'object' revitalized the *rhetoric* of socialism – to such an extent that 'reification' became an important cult word during May 1968 in Paris. But the subsequent discussions of the term in the *New Left Review* added nothing to the rhetoric except pseudo-theory: a morose prowling of the intellect around an inexplicable shrine.[24] The lamest observation, expressed in the language of subject and object, could excite the most solemn respect. Marx's declaration that 'the bureaucrat relates himself to the world as a *mere object* of his activity' is typical: trite, snobbish and slightly precious in suggesting that one is less an object the more time one spends in the British Museum Reading Room. But the remark is greeted by Erich Fromm – a product of the Frankfurt school and the great vulgarizer of Marxist humanism – as a 'profound definition', from which a whole morality is seen to flow.[25]

---

[23] *Groundwork of the Metaphysics of Morals*, ed. and tr. Mary Gregor, Cambridge, CUP, 1998, pp. 42–3.

[24] The discussion was effectively begun by Peter L. Berger, Stanley Pullberg and Ben Brewster in *New Left Review* 35 (January–February 1966).

[25] Erich Fromm, *The Sane Society*, London, 1956, p. 127. For a critique of the rhetoric of 'objectification' and 'alienation', and a useful reminder of the Hegelian thesis that man can exist and be happy only if he does release himself *into* the world and become an object of his own perception and striving, see Helmut Plessner, 'De Homine Abscondito', in *Social Research* 36 (4) (1969).

Lukács is no better than his successors: he too believes that the theory of reification *says it all*, so that it ceases to be necessary to delve into the workings of capitalism. The beast has been thoroughly anathematized, and must henceforth be put out of its misery, and out of our misery too. But where are we to turn for the alternative? Lukács rests his communism in a curious addition to the theory, which is held, if not to justify the leap of faith, at least to illuminate the chasm that yawns beneath it. According to Lukács the reified consciousness of the bourgeoisie neutralizes human action and forestalls genuine change, by representing the social world as bound by inexorable and 'objective' laws. So long as we remain within the confines of bourgeois thinking, therefore, we shall be wedded to the status quo of capitalism, unable either to aim for, or even to perceive, the social condition that will dispel the cloud of unknowing.

In the capitalist dark, however, a rival consciousness is growing, the consciousness of the proletariat, which possesses a unique epistemological privilege. By virtue of their proximity to the process of production, the workers 'can become conscious of the social character of labour' so that, to their consciousness, 'the abstract, universal form of the societal principle as it is manifested can be increasingly concretised and overcome'.[26] Hence:

> The knowledge yielded by the standpoint of the proletariat stands on a higher scientific plane objectively: it does after all apply a method that makes possible the solution of problems which the greatest thinkers of the bourgeois era have vainly struggled to find and, in its substance, it provides the adequate historical analysis of capitalism, which must remain beyond the grasp of bourgeois thinkers.[27]

Lukács expands on this idea at considerable length, in prose of supererogatory greyness. But what is he asking us to believe? Apparently the working class, unlike the bourgeoisie, '*always aspires towards the truth*, even in its "false" consciousness, and in its substantive errors'.[28] To understand our situation, therefore, we must see it through proletarian eyes.

Who then should be our authorities – the articulate offspring of the true working class? D. H. Lawrence, Conrad, Céline? Don't be ridiculous!

---

[26] *History and Class Consciousness*, op. cit., p. 171.
[27] Ibid., p. 164.
[28] Ibid., p. 72.

says Lukács, who devotes many pages to anathematizing such counter-revolutionary lackeys of the bourgeoisie. It seems that proletarian thinking is not to be found in the works of proletarian writers, but only in the Marxist classics. The promised 'method' is the dialectic, bequeathed from Fichte to Hegel to Feuerbach to Marx and Engels to Lenin and Lukács. But when did Marx dirty his hands with manual labour? Or Engels, the factory owner, or Lenin, the gentleman in exile? Or Lukács himself – hereditary baron of the Austro-Hungarian Empire, heir to a banker's fortune, scholar, aesthete and relentless conspirator among ruling elites? A *proletarian* thinker? Consider his remedy for reification:

> It can be overcome only by *constant and constantly renewed efforts to disrupt the reified structure of existence by concretely relating to the concretely manifested contradictions of the total development, by becoming conscious of the immanent meanings of these contradictions for the total development.*[29]

Is that an authentic proletarian utterance? Come off it, mate!

Things are actually worse than that implies. Not only is the proletariat identified with Marxism. Every modern thinker who disagrees with some critical tenet of Marxism is denounced as 'bourgeois', while every true Marxist writer is praised as 'proletarian'. These labels are in fact not the names of social classes at all, but expletives. Because the label 'bourgeois' concentrates into itself every human evil, and the label 'proletarian' all human good, Lukács imagines that he has provided himself with the perfect instrument of censorship. Furthermore, he makes it clear that the proletariat, which speaks historically through the mouths of bourgeois intellectuals like Marx and Engels, speaks in the present only through the Communist Party, which is its established church. Only in the Party, with its essentially *organized* structure, is the unity between theory and practice accomplished. Hence: 'it is the great accomplishment of Russian Bolshevism to incorporate, for the first time since the Paris Commune, the consciousness of the proletariat and its self-knowledge in terms of world history'.[30]

To cap it all, anyone who actually consults the ideas of ordinary working-class people commits a heinous communist error, the error

---

[29] Ibid., p. 197, (Lukács's italics).
[30] *Tactics and Ethics*, op. cit., p. 36.

of 'opportunism'. This consists in *'mistaking the actual, psychological state of consciousness of proletarians for the class consciousness of the proletariat'.*[31] In other words, the Party is the sole spokesman for the proletariat, and the Party is infallible. Praxis – the new form of knowledge that shows itself simultaneously in the dissolution of reified consciousness and the engagement in revolution – is the pure equivalent of faith, and obedience to the Party the outcome of a Pascalian wager. Just so long as you do not commit the supreme 'opportunist' error, of consulting actual members of the proletariat, you can persuade yourself that, in performing these mental acrobatics, you disown the polluted consciousness of the bourgeoisie and join the revolutionary struggle of the true working class.

Summoned to Moscow in 1930 Lukács found himself living under the eyes of the Party whose infallible consciousness he had previously defended. He prepared himself with a grovelling act of self-castigation. *History and Class Consciousness* had been vehemently condemned by Bukharin and Zinoviev at the Fifth Congress of the Communist International in 1924. The usual charges – 'revisionist', 'reformist', 'idealist' – had been levelled. And Lukács himself repeated them in Moscow. *History and Class Consciousness*, he said, is an 'idealist' work, adding that idealism is the ally of fascism and its social-democratic 'bedfellows', and thence the true enemy of the proletariat.[32] Earlier 'opportunism' had been the principal enemy. Later it was 'nihilism',[33] while during the high summer of Stalin's paranoia it was 'Trotskyism' that identified the forces of reaction.[34] In *The Meaning of Contemporary Realism* (1957) Lukács gives an instructive history of the enemy's disguises:

The enemy, in Heine's time, was German Chauvinism. Later, it was aggressive Imperialism; still later, Fascism. Today it is the ideology of the Cold War and the preparation for nuclear war. The fight against the common enemy, which has led to close political alliances in our age, enables the critical realist to allow for the socialist perspective of history without relinquishing his own ideological position.[35]

---

[31] *History and Class Consciousness*, p. 74 (Lukács's italics).
[32] See Leszek Kołakowski, *Main Currents of Marxism*, Oxford, 1978, vol. 3, p. 279.
[33] György Lukács, *The Meaning of Contemporary Realism*, tr. J. and N. Mander, London, 1963, p. 63.
[34] *Essays on Realism*, op. cit., p. 34.
[35] *The Meaning of Contemporary Realism*, op. cit., p. 109.

None of those changes in the description of the enemy shows a real change of mind. For although the enemy may change his name, he does not change his nature. He remains the bourgeois, master of the actual world, locked in a life and death struggle with the proletarian, who is guardian of the future. Even after the death of Stalin, and after the ensuing invasion of Hungary in 1956 (when Lukács, despite being a member of Nagy's government, characteristically escaped with his life), he continued to divide the world between the 'bourgeois' and 'proletarian' antagonists,[36] and to apply his energies to denunciations of actually existing literature, and of 'modernism' in particular, in favour of the undisclosed ideal of socialist realism.

It is true that Lukács did not, in his later years, sink quite to the depths of *The Destruction of Reason* – the major document of his 'Stalinist' period – in which virtually all of German post-romantic philosophy was dismissed as proto-Nazi. Indeed, he produced criticism that is not without merit, recognizing, for example, the historical significance and psychological penetration of Balzac and Scott. However, his leniency towards such 'reactionary' observers was made possible by the historical circumstance that they lived before Marxism. Their 'reactionary' critique of the values of the French Revolution could therefore be appropriated by the new revolutionary, who was able to wash away the stain of false consciousness.

The same leniency could not be extended to any modern writer – and hence the lifelong torment caused by Thomas Mann, the former friend who had portrayed Lukács (in a manner distinctly flattering to his intellect) as Naphta in *The Magic Mountain*, and whose novels must surely be counted as among the great artistic achievements of the twentieth century. Mann was a lasting problem, corresponding to the problem that Eliot posed for Leavis. But he was a problem that Lukács contrived to put out of mind, in the interests of the necessary belief that, since Marx, literature is either revolutionary or reactionary, either proletarian or bourgeois, either socialist or fit for the flames. The censorious fervour with which his views were expounded, and the extraordinary propensity to condemn by labels, justify Kołakowski's accusation (in *Main Currents of Marxism*, vol. III) that Lukács was an intellectual Stalinist, one for whom an opponent sacrifices, by his very opposition, the right to exist.

---

[36] Ibid., p. 14.

Consider the following passages of supposed literary criticism:

We have seen how the anti-violence ideology stretches from the sham-revolutionary phase [of expressionism] through to open counter-revolutionary capitulation before the bourgeoisie's white terror.[37]

With Malthus... [the] decay of the romantic critique of capitalism appears very early on in its most repulsive and meanest forms, as an expression of the ideology of the most reactionary section of the English bourgeoisie. [The ensuing] crisis reduced one of the most talented and shining representatives of anti-capitalism, Thomas Carlyle, to a decadent cripple, a mendacious apologist for capitalism...[38]

Whole passages of Lukács's critical writings show this one-dimensional vision, dominated by dichotomizing invective and written in the style of the Albanian *au pair* girl imagined by Peter Simple.[39] Literary criticism is nothing if not the active engagement with an intellect and a sensibility other than one's own. For Lukács, as for all truly orthodox communists, such engagement was impossible and his criticism therefore null, thoughtless and ultimately repulsive in its inquisitorial zeal. At every point where argument is necessary a smothering cloud of labels is blasted in the face of the enemy, and the familiar communist slogan – who is not with us is against us – is shouted from the page.

In an interview given to the *New Left Review* in 1969, but not published until after his death, Lukács dismisses 'bourgeois democracy' in the following words: 'Its defining principle is the division of man into the *citoyen* of public life and the *bourgeois* of private life... its philosophical reflection is to be found in de Sade.' He then opposes 'bourgeois democracy' to 'socialist democracy':

Because the socialist economy does not spontaneously produce and reproduce the man appropriate to it, as classical capitalist society naturally generated its *homo economicus*, the divided *citoyen/bourgeois* of 1793 and de Sade, the function of socialist democracy is precisely the *education* of its members towards socialism.[40]

---

[37] *Essays on Realism*, op. cit., p. 101.

[38] Ibid., p. 121.

[39] 'Peter Simple's diary', written by the late Michael Wharton, appeared pseudonymously in the *Daily Telegraph* and *Sunday Telegraph* during the 1980s and 1990s and was devoted to satirizing the intellectual and political fashions of the day.

[40] *Record of a Life*, op. cit., p. 172.

Lukács here displays the Stalinist method in its essential vacuity. With the stupid allusion to de Sade he is able to dismiss all Western political institutions in a single gesture, and to return to his favoured terrain of brutalizing dichotomies: capitalism versus socialism, reaction versus revolution, reproduction versus education, bourgeois versus proletarian, Lukács versus the enemy.

Safe behind such tangled barbed wire, Lukács continued to ruminate on the true significance of 'classical German philosophy'. In his last work – *The Ontology of Social Being*, a strange lugubrious dance of shadows in the graveyard of German metaphysics – he takes note of real religion, and attributes the discovery of this phenomenon to Hegel. In a sentence that is no less meaningful than any other in this curiously written work, he writes that 'Hegel's historical recognition of religion as an effective mental reality constantly increases, but even so, this never results in a more profound internal relation to its contents.'[41]

Had Lukács been interested in the proletariat, not as the imaginary vehicle of his own glorious hatred, but as a real class of actual human beings, he might have encountered religion not only in the pages of Hegel but also in reality. And confronting the honest source of proletarian morality he might have recognized in himself an inverted and destructive form of the same emotion. He might have noticed his own hatred of God, his refusal of trust, humility and atonement, and his overweening violence towards the created world. But he would have noticed, too, how much his 'messianic sectarianism' remained wedded to the deed of Sarajevo, how much the annihilating labels – 'ideologist', 'nihilist', 'reactionary', 'nostalgist' – which he threw so indiscriminately at the imaginary enemy might have been rightly attached to himself, and how much he remained to the last what he was in the beginning, a privileged remnant of a vanished ruling class.

That description might be equally applied to Adorno, who took over Lukács's analysis of capitalism, and applied it in the wholly new context of the critique of popular culture. Born in 1903, the son of a wealthy wine-merchant, Adorno's first love was music, which he studied in Frankfurt (home of his parents) and then, after 1925, with Berg in Vienna, where he met Lukács. He had been radicalized by the First World War and the support offered to German aggression by the established intellectuals

---

[41] György Lukács, *Hegel's False and His Genuine Ontology*, tr. D. Fernbach, London, 1978, p. 59.

such as Max Weber, Max Scheler and Georg Simmel. In Vienna he moved in revolutionary and Marxist circles, gradually turning his attention to philosophy, while writing in defence of atonality and the musical avant-garde.

He returned to Frankfurt in 1931, to take up a position as lecturer in the University, delivering an inaugural lecture at the independent Institute for Social Research. This Institute, the home of the Frankfurt School, had been founded in 1923, and published an influential journal, the *Zeitschrift für Sozialforschung*, in which Adorno's writings now began to appear. It was home to leading intellectuals, including Max Horkheimer (the Institute's director from 1930), Herbert Marcuse and Erich Fromm. In 1933, following closure by the Nazis, the Institute went into exile, first in Geneva and then, in 1934, in New York, where it became affiliated to Columbia University. After Hitler's rise to power Adorno fled first to London and Oxford and then to New York, where he settled for a while before following Horkheimer, Fromm and Marcuse to California, there to live, when war broke out, under partial curfew as an enemy national. The Institute for Social Research returned to Frankfurt in 1951, and Adorno soon followed, becoming Director on Horkheimer's retirement in 1953.

Horkheimer introduced into the Frankfurt School agenda some of the conservative and pessimistic currents of thought which had found a home in the writings of Simmel and Scheler. But the fundamental posture of the school was again defined by 'classical German philosophy', applied in its Marxist interpretation. The recurrent idea is contained in the title of a book written by Horkheimer during the years of exile in Columbia: *Zur Kritik der instrumentellen Vernunft*, 'Towards the Critique of Instrumental Reason'.[42] According to Horkheimer the capitalist world exhibits the triumph of reason, or rather, of the specifically 'bourgeois' kind of reason, by which all things are remade in the image of the rising middle class.

'Instrumental reason' reduces every problem to one of means, and its world is a world without end. In this world the worker is alienated, fragmented, torn loose from true human nature, by a social order that condemns him to the drudgery of production for exchange. In the bourgeois order the product of labour is a means to that for which it is exchanged, and the commodity itself has no meaning beyond its value in

---

[42] Max Horkheimer, *Zur Kritik der instrumentellen Vernunft*, Frankfurt, 1967, originally published in English translation as *Eclipse of Reason*, New York, 1947, p. 20.

exchange. Money, which is in Marx's words, 'crystallized exchange-value', is the symbol of instrumental reason, and in a world structured by money human life is tyrannized by the rule of things. In this way Horkheimer is able to recycle Lukács's main ideas, describing the reified consciousness and fetishism of commodities in the bourgeois order as resulting from the triumph of instrumental reasoning. Under capitalism the means abolishes the meaning, and the human will, detached from the ends of existence, wanders free and purposeless from thing to thing.

On this basis Horkheimer founded what he called 'critical theory', which was to be the systematic critique of capitalist culture, by relating it to the 'bourgeois relations of production' on which it depends. Reason, he argues, is corrupted by the capitalist order and loses its natural focus in human life. Humanity can never be a means only, but must always be understood as an end in itself. For bourgeois reason, therefore, humanity is strictly *imperceptible*. The true critical philosophy is the one that, by turning the gaze of philosophy on philosophy itself, sees the poisoned sources of its own polluted reasoning.

The true critical philosophy, in other words, is that of Marx – not the later Marx of *Das Kapital* but the earlier Marx, and his Hegelian account of the Fall. By returning philosophy to its 'material' base, by exposing the secrets of its own production, we see that a mode of reasoning may merely tacitly confirm the corrupt social order that produces it. We then pass beyond philosophy into 'critical theory' and discover the true possibility of emancipation, which begins with the emancipation of thought itself. Thought must be freed from the dominion of instrumental reasoning, and hence from the hidden tyranny of things.

The intellectual ancestry of that view is impeccably German, and impeccably bourgeois too. The critical theory of Horkheimer is really the critical philosophy of Kant, recast as an instrument of social criticism, and shaped by the hammer blows of Marx. To the categorical imperative, which enjoins us to treat humanity as an end and never as a means only, is added the Marxian theory of intellectual production. The synthesis had been effected before – notably by Georg Simmel in his great treatise on *The Philosophy of Money*, 1908. But it acquires, in Horkheimer, a distinctively modern melancholy, as well as a new erudition, incorporating in its statement not only the Marxist humanism of Lukács but many of the conceptions of Weberian sociology, along with references to the great culture of Germany that preceded the Nazi eclipse. Horkheimer shows the way back to an authentic German criticism, which might revitalize and render fit for modern consumption the romantic vision of Hegel and the early Marx.

Style is parochial, but truth the property of Everyman. The 'critique of instrumental reason' contains insights; but they are for the most part detachable from the language used to express them. For English readers these insights come clothed in the idiom of Arnold and Ruskin. They have been associated, in our time, not with a Marxian theory of bourgeois rationality but with the conservative defence of the Great Tradition by F. R. Leavis, whose critique of 'Benthamite' civilization expresses in a more concrete, more historically pregnant language, the same abiding sense of the uprootedness of *homo technologicus*. This critique, being common to radicals and conservatives, attaches Horkheimer to neither camp. Without his Marxizing he says nothing unacceptable to an Ernst Junger or a Heidegger. Indeed, Heidegger's discussion of 'technē' delivers, from the point of view of that philosopher's dark phenomenology, just the same vision of modernity as does the 'critique of instrumental reason'.

The Frankfurt vision of instrumental reason has something in common not only with the social criticism of Ruskin and Leavis, but also with Weber's theory of bureaucracy, and has a similar appeal for those oppressed by the vastness of the modern world, whose laws of motion seem so carelessly to disregard us. Introduced into the receptive environment of the American campus, the new critique had an immediate success. In the run-up to the liberation movement of the 1960s Marcuse captured the Frankfurter market with catchy slogans, such as 'repressive tolerance' (his name for the system that paid him a large professorial salary for denouncing it) and 'the totalitarian universe of technological rationality'.[43]

But when the novelty of those jingles – worthy of Orwell's Ministry of Truth – had worn off, Marcuse's disciples found themselves face to face with unanswered and unanswerable questions. The same questions confront the reader of Horkheimer and Adorno, whose more old-fashioned salesmanship fails to conceal the equal shoddiness of their product. Just how is thought to reform itself, merely by reflecting on its social origins? If the false consciousness of the bourgeoisie has poisoned its philosophy, what of the philosophy that says so? Is that not also a bourgeois product? (Compare Lukács, and the attempt to find

---

[43] Herbert Marcuse, 'Repressive Tolerance', in Robert Paul Wolff, Barrington Moore Jr and Herbert Marcuse, *A Critique of Pure Tolerance*, London, 1969, pp. 93–137.

the authentic 'proletarian' voice in philosophy, which should never be confused with the actual voice of the proletariat!)

At this point a certain liturgical quality enters the writings of the Frankfurters. Incantations are uttered against the 'bourgeois' order and the thinking that stems from it, but in a changed tone of voice, indicating the proximity of mystery. Language changes character from the voice of critical theory to the exorcist's spell.

Thus, in a remarkable treatise, Horkheimer and Adorno extend their critique of bourgeois reasoning to the Enlightenment itself: for enlightenment belongs to a world dominated by 'bourgeois justice and commodity exchange'.[44] The assault on bourgeois rationality has now taken on a distinctly hysterical tone. Enlightenment is the real producer (did not Hegel say it?) of 'the herd'; 'enlightenment is totalitarian'; 'abstraction, the tool of enlightenment, treats its objects as did fate, the notion which it rejects: it liquidates them'.[45] The spells are cast one after another, but still the ghost will not vanish. For not only is the Enlightenment here to stay (a fact for which, when you think about it, we should all be grateful); but the Frankfurters' belief in the redemptive role of critical reflection is one form of it.

Enlightenment was anathema to Horkheimer and Adorno in part because it was synonymous with technology and mass production. In place of the humility of the awe-struck man who bowed down to nature's eternal order, the Enlightenment presented the strutting arrogance of the entrepreneur, the person typified by the fathers of Adorno and Horkheimer, who had the solution to hand for every problem, and recognized no problem that was not a matter of technique. The Enlightenment had replaced mystery with mastery. And in doing so it had cut mankind off from the true meaning of culture, which is the self-knowledge and inner truth which only the arduous path of high art can disclose to us.

Culture, according to the later Marx, belongs to the institutional and ideological superstructure of society. It is the by-product of economic processes that it does not seriously influence. The ideological battles are so many 'storm clouds in the political sky': history is unaffected by them, since it is driven by economic forces and the inexorable laws of

---

44 Theodor Adorno and Max Horkheimer, *Dialectic of Enlightenment*, New York, 1944, German edition, Frankfurt, 1969, p. 7.
45 Ibid., p. 16.

their development. Against that vision, which seems to relegate culture and the arts to the historical side-lines, Horkheimer and Adorno argued that a properly theoretical approach to criticism would undermine the false consciousness of 'bourgeois relations of production', and replace the false enlightenment with the true one. The enslavement exerted by capitalism is exerted at every level – the mental, institutional and cultural as much as the economic – and by adopting a critical stance at each of these levels we open the way to a true and liberating understanding of our condition.

Adorno took his cue from Lukács, using the concept of 'commodity fetishism' as part of a comprehensive cultural critique. In a capitalist economy, he suggested, people are enslaved not by others but by themselves, falling victim to the charm with which they invest the commodities that glitter all around them. Their 'false consciousness' exposes them at every turn to the same enchantment, and their real freedom is confiscated by the illusory freedoms of the consumer culture. Adorno had witnessed the result in Hollywood and had been appalled not only by its vulgarity, but by the easy-going way in which Americans seemed to enjoy the rubbish that enslaved them.

Mass culture is a commodity whose function is to neutralize the critical spirit and induce an illusory acceptance of an illusory world. It is an 'ideological' product in Marx's sense – a veil drawn across the social realities, so as to present a comforting illusion in their stead. In other words, mass culture is part of the false consciousness of capitalist society, and Adorno set out to show how its devices short-circuit the path to emotional truth, leading always to clichés and a kind of routine sentimentality.

Adorno's hope, as a composer and a musicologist, was to contrast the creative logic of the masters, who wrestled with realities, who had found the style that comprehended them, and who had never shirked the pain of a real musical argument, with the kitsch that looks for the short cut to comfort, as a popular song slops home to the tonic chord. The cultural fetish is marked by its 'standardized' nature, its routine presentation of pre-digested material, and its refusal to question its own status as a commodity.[46]

---

[46] 'On the Fetish-Character in Music and the Regression of Listening', 1938, reprinted in Andrew Arato and Eike Gebhardt, *The Essential Frankfurt School Reader*, New York, Continuum, 1985.

Adorno followed Lukács in connecting the theory of commodity fetishism with that of reification, meaning the way in which people lose their subjective freedom by investing it in objects outside themselves. As their freedom is spilled out and ossified in objects, Lukács had argued, people are reified: their freedom is transferred to, and captured by, the objects that represent them. Institutions, laws, relationships – all are prone to reification, which voids the world of human meaning, by putting mechanical relations between things in place of free relations between people. Art too is reified, becoming an ornamental addition to the bourgeois inventory, and so losing its authentic nature as a critical instrument.

Bringing together the two ideas of commodity fetishism and reification we conclude that, in a capitalist culture, free relations between subjects, on which our human fulfilment depends, are overlaid and replaced by routine relations between objects. Such was the grand way of putting the point – the way of classical German philosophy: in the mass culture of capitalism subjects become objects and objects become subjects! No wonder Adorno believed that he had seen through the veil of mass culture to the underlying reality.[47] And he extended the jargon of subject and object into the study of the classical tradition in music. Here is how he applied it to Bach, for example:

Bach…renounced his obedience, as antiquated polyphonist, to the trend of the times, a trend he himself had shaped, in order to help it reach its innermost truth, the emancipation of the subject to objectivity in a coherent whole of which subjectivity was the origin. Down to the subtlest structural details it is always a question of the undiminished coincidence of the harmonic-functional and of the contrapuntal dimension. The distant past is entrusted with the utopia of the musical subject-object: anachronism becomes a harbinger of things to come.[48]

That passage makes a perfectly standard observation – namely, that in Bach the logic of counterpoint and that of functional harmony coincide,

---

[47] The idea is spelled out at length, in the context of Hegel's original argument, by another member of the Frankfurt School, Ernst Bloch, in *Subjekt-Objekt: Erläuterung zur Hegel*, Berlin, Suhrkamp Verlag, 1977.
[48] 'Bach Defended against his Devotees', in *Prisms*, tr. Samuel and Shierry Weber, Cambridge, MA, MIT Press, 1983, p. 142.

so that neither seems to be imposed upon the other. But this observation is reworked to imply that Bach was somehow announcing the 'utopia of the musical subject-object'. Such a reworking is typical of Adorno's sleights of hand. The jargon merely *evokes* a conclusion that Adorno fails to prove, namely that Bach is great because his music, contrary to its antique style, is on the right side of history – the side that seeks Utopia, and which preserves, in objective form, the real freedom of the subject.

Why was writing of the kind that I have just quoted so influential? This question returns us to the revolutionary spirit of the 1960s and 70s. The advocates of 'liberation' were aware in their hearts of the benefits that they had received from the market economy. They belonged to a generation that enjoyed freedom and prosperity on a scale that young people had never previously known. To dissent from the 'capitalist' order in the name of freedom seemed faintly ridiculous, when the contrast with the Soviet alternative was so vividly apparent.

What was needed, in order to vindicate the new spirit of revolution, was a doctrine that would show capitalist freedom to be an illusion, and which would identify the *true* freedom that the consumer society denied. That is what Adorno, Horkheimer and Marcuse provided. Adorno's attack on mass culture belonged to the same movement of ideas as Marcuse's denunciation of 'repressive tolerance'. It was an attempt to *see through the lies*. The theories of fetishism, reification, alienation and repression that circulated in the wake of 1968 all had one overriding aim, which was to show the illusory nature of capitalist freedom, and to perpetuate the thought of a critical alternative, of a liberation that would not lead merely to another and darker form of the 'state capitalism' which supposedly ruled over East and West.

By constantly notching up the critique of American capitalism and its culture, and making only muted or dismissive references to the real nightmare of communism, those thinkers showed their profound indifference to human suffering and the unserious nature of their prescriptions. Adorno does not explicitly say that the 'alternative' to the capitalist system and the commodity culture is Utopia. But that is what he implies. And Utopia is not a real alternative. Hence his alternative to the unreal freedom of the consumer society is itself unreal – a mere noumenon whose only function is to provide a measure of our defects. And yet he was aware that there was an *actual* alternative on offer and that it involved mass murder and cultural annihilation. For Adorno to dismiss this alternative merely as the 'totalitarian' version of the same 'state capitalism' that he had witnessed in America was profoundly dishonest.

Having said that, it is only fair to add that the Frankfurt critique of the consumer society contains an element of truth. It is a truth far older than the Marxist theories with which Adorno and Horkheimer embellished it. Indeed it is the truth enshrined in the Hebrew Bible, reformulated time and again down the centuries: the truth that, in bowing down to idols, we betray our better nature. The Torah sets before us a vision of human fulfilment. It tells us that we are bound by the law of God, who tolerates no idolatry, and wishes for our absolute devotion. By turning to God we become what we truly are, creatures of a higher world, whose fulfilment is something more than the satisfaction of our wishes. Through idolatry, by contrast, we fall into a lower way of being – the way of self-enslavement, in which our appetites shape themselves as gods and take command of us.

Of course, Adorno did not believe in God and had little time for the teachings of the Torah – less time than his hero Arnold Schoenberg who, in his unfinished and unfinishable masterpiece, *Moses und Aron*, attempted to dramatize the thoughts that I have just expressed. But his attack on mass culture should be seen in the Old Testament spirit, as a repudiation of idolatry, a reaffirmation of the age-old distinction between true and false gods – between the worship that ennobles and redeems us, and the superstition that drops us in the ditch. For Adorno the true god is Utopia: the vision of subjects in their freedom, conscious of the world as it is, and claiming that world as their own. The false god is the fetish of consumerism – the god of appetite, who clouds our vision and confiscates our choice.

And here is where Adorno profoundly differed from the revolutionaries of the 1960s, even while speaking a language that they thought they could use. The advocates of 'liberation' were seeking another form of society, in which people would be truly free – free precisely because they had torn away the veil of illusion to begin the construction of a less oppressive world. But the redemption that Adorno promised was not to be achieved by social reform: it was a personal salvation, a turning away from fantasies, on a voyage of self-discovery.

Through fixing his mind on utopia, a person is put in touch with his subjectivity, and acquires true discipline of spirit. Such a person has no motive to avoid hardship and suffering: for he knows that these are the proof of human freedom. Nothing is more repugnant to him than the fetish, which beckons from the land of illusions, and which, by denying tragedy and suffering, denies and destroys the higher life. But the consolations of Cythera stand condemned by the same moral decree, and a 'liberation' that adds sex, sin and idleness to the list of consumer products is merely another name for the old enslavement.

To put the point more exactly, Adorno's outlook is not that of the revolutionary seeking the overthrow of capitalism, but that of Hegel's 'beautiful soul', condemned to live in an idolatrous world, while working always to retain the spiritual discipline that defines his moral apartness. The Hegelian jargon of subject and object points to the real message of Adorno, which is not about the conflict between capitalist 'relations of production' and some emancipated alternative. It is about art, and the difference between true art and its idolatrous substitutes. True art matters because it puts us in touch with what we really are, and enables us to live on that higher plane where freedom, love and fulfilment are given. But we are surrounded on every side by pseudo-art – by sentimentality, cliché and kitsch. And this pseudo-art ties us to the world of 'reifications', in which things with a value are replaced by things with a price, and in which human life loses its worth, to become a thing of repetitive appetite.

Such, as I understand it, is the burden of Adorno's critique of mass culture. Like other such critiques, from Ruskin and Arnold to Eliot and Leavis, it is downstream from the Old Testament condemnation of idolatry. And like them it contains a core of truth. The problems stem from Adorno's use of the Marxist language, and from the resulting implication that he is shaping a *political* alternative to 'bourgeois' society, identifying defects that could be overcome by a Marxist revolution. The only revolution that Adorno can envisage is one that takes place in the world of culture itself – not a political but an aesthetic revolution, an attempt to understand Utopia through art. Moreover, art that places itself directly in the *service* of revolution, like the propaganda art of Brecht and Eisler, surrenders – according to Adorno – the only kind of truthfulness of which art is capable. The utopian urge must be vindicated within art itself, through an internal revolution in the forms of creativity. 'Direct protest is reactionary.'[49] It is precisely in this way that Adorno was able to belong to the revolution of the 1960s, and also to slip out from under its grip, so as to return to the meditations that really interested him,

---

[49] *Aesthetic Theory*, ed. Gretel Adorno and Rolf Tiedemann, tr. Robert Hullot-Kentor, Minneapolis, University of Minnesota Press, 1997, p. 31. See also 'On the Social Situation of Music', *Telos*, 35, 1978.

concerning the fate of tonality, the nature of mass culture, and the reign of kitsch.

Coming on the scene in the aftermath of 'critical theory', and all the fraught emotions that had been invested in it, Jürgen Habermas was in a difficult position. It was by now obligatory to be 'on the left' but not in the manner of Adorno, whose rudeness about popular culture, mass protests, kitsch, jazz and marijuana did not endear him to Frankfurt University's new mass intake. Habermas turned his back on the Frankfurters (who in any case found fault with the thesis submitted for his *Habilitation*), and decided that they were, after all, out of touch with the postmodern world. Moreover, now that Germany had been reconnected to civilization there was an awful lot of reading to do.

Nevertheless the critique of instrumental reason survives in Habermas, in a fortified and bureaucratized form, to become part of a study of 'purposive-rational action', spread over works that touch on every subject under the sun. The style is vague, irresolute and emotionless, in the manner of a sociology PhD:

> As a result of its reflection on the conditions of its own appearance and application, theory understands itself as a necessary catalytic moment within the very nexus of social life which it is analysing. Indeed, it analyses this as an integral nexus of constraints from the point of view of its eventual *Aufhebung*. The theory thus covers a double relation between theory and praxis: on the one hand, it investigates the historical conditions for the constitution of a constellation of interests to which, as it were, the theory still belongs through its acts of cognition; and, on the other hand, it investigates the historical context of action which the theory can itself influence through the way it orients action. On the one hand, it is concerned with social praxis which, as social synthesis, makes knowledge possible; on the other hand, it is concerned with a political praxis which is consciously directed towards overturning the existing institutional system...[50]

Only in that last phrase, where the hidden agenda is momentarily exposed, does Habermas declare himself. The rest is prodigious waffle, and indeed barely intelligible, part of a seemingly endless stream of 'on the one hand/

---

[50] Jürgen Habermas, *Theory and Practice*, 1963, 1971, tr. John Viertel, London, 1974, introduction to 3rd edn.

on the other hand' ruminations, inspired by whatever book or article has just come to Habermas's attention, and littered with sociological jargon.

A reader coming for the first time to Habermas, and confronted with acres of such writing, may well feel a certain astonishment at the thought that here, before him, lies the intellectual core of the German left establishment. Nevertheless it is so, and it is important to see that the bureaucratic style is by no means dispensable. On the contrary it is an integral component of the message. The style is the agent of legitimation, whereby the Habermasian critique of bourgeois society establishes its academic credentials. Tedium is the vehicle of an abstract authority, and the reader waits in the corridors of Habermas's prose like a petitioner to whom truth has been promised, albeit only abstractly, on a document that is perhaps already out of date.

To extract the meaning from Habermas is additionally difficult on account of the structure of his books, which are composed of loosely connected chapters with no argument sustained for more than a page or two. Each chapter reads like an 'assignment' composed by a committee appointed to consider some matter towards which its members are largely indifferent.

The earlier works continue the '*Problematik*' of the Frankfurt School, studying instrumental reason ('purposive-rational action') in all its modes, and the 'legitimation problem' for modern societies in which production and consumption are the dominant goals. But the long stream of books morphs seamlessly into a new theme, which is the search for a 'communicative rationality' that will be '*herrschaftsfrei*' – free from the taint of domination, equivalent in the realm of conversation to the free and equal utopia that was promised by Marx. It is impossible for me to cover all the by-ways and dead ends into which Habermas rambles along the way. But it is important to see, nevertheless, that, in crucial respects, neither the method nor the agenda has changed since the first stirrings of Marxist humanism in the writings of Lukács.

Three early works – *Theory and Practice*, 1963, *Technology and Science as 'Ideology'*, 1968, and *Knowledge and Interests*, 1968 – announced Habermas's credentials to the world, submitting official reports on Hegel, Marx, Comte, Peirce, Dilthey, Freud, Kant and Fichte, telling us that the authorities are displeased. That which displeases them is the 'instrumental reasoning' that dominates the lives of modern people, and Habermas adds to their ageless lament the confirming rubber-stamp of last year's jargon.

In these works Habermas distinguishes two kinds of social conduct: the 'purposive-rational' and the 'communicative'. The first is the 'instrumental reason' of the man in the street; the second is the 'intellectual production' of the man on the campus. The distinction between knuckling under and shooting your mouth off is dressed up as a profound theoretical insight:

> By 'work' or *purposive-rational action*, I understand either instrumental action or rational choice or their conjunction. Instrumental action is governed by *technical rules*, based on empirical knowledge. In every case they imply empirical prediction about observable events, physical or social. These predictions can prove correct or incorrect. The conduct of rational choice is governed by *strategies* based on analytic knowledge...
>
> By 'interaction', on the other hand, I understand *communicative action*, symbolic interaction. It is governed by binding *consensual norms*, which define reciprocal expectations about behaviour and which must be understood and recognised by at least two acting subjects...[51]

The distinction is immensely laboured, proceeding in that way for several paragraphs. It can be phrased, however, more simply: work is measured by its efficiency, speech by its intelligibility. The rules that guide the first are therefore technical, concerning the choice of means to an end. The rules that guide the second are constitutive, like the rules of a game, and serve to define the meaning of what is done.

Undeniably there are interesting comparisons to be made between the two kinds of action. But we cannot assume that every action is one or the other: to which category should we assign a game of football, for example, a jam session, sexual congress, a church service or a family meal? It is characteristic of Habermas that he does not say whether the distinction is exclusive, exhaustive or absolute. It is equally characteristic that, despite leaving such crucial questions unanswered, he goes on to use the distinction as the principal theoretical instrument of an anti-capitalist critique. Almost everything that is identifiably wrong with bourgeois society can be traced, in the end, to the operation of 'purposive-rational' thought and action, whereas everything that gives us hope for

---

[51] *Technology and Science as 'Ideology'*, 1968, pp. 91–2.

a better world is contained, however secretly, within the paradigm of 'communication'.

Emancipation, Habermas suggests, is first of all emancipation of language – what he later refers to as the 'ideal speech situation'. While the suggestion sounds somewhat paradoxical, coming from a writer whose language is imprisoned by meaningless jargon, it has the distinctive authority of a tradition. It repeats the original aspiration of the Frankfurt School, which is to break the manacles of bourgeois culture through discovering *another form of consciousness*. What is being sought is no longer the authentic voice of the proletariat (not to be confused, remember, with the actual voice of working people) but the ideal voice of the academic, who will, by speaking freely, tell it how it is.

Before examining this revolutionary programme, however, we should observe an important feature of the quoted definition. It is, in fact, a combination of stationary platitudes ('these predictions can prove correct or incorrect'), and radical leaps of unjustified thought. What begins as 'instrumental action' is at once transformed into 'rational choice', which in turn becomes 'technical rules' founded on 'empirical knowledge'. Later the definition is stretched towards 'preference rules' and 'decision procedures', thereby picking up jargon from new books, disciplines, articles and conferences in the academic milieu. Similar associative movements occur in Habermas's other works of this period. For example:

> Empirical analysis discloses reality from the viewpoint of possible technical control over objectified processes of nature, while hermeneutics maintains the intersubjectivity of possible action-orienting mutual understanding…In the behaviour system of instrumental action, reality is constituted as the totality of what can be experienced from the viewpoint of technical control. The reality that is objectified under these transcendental conditions has its counterpart in a specially restricted mode of experience. The language of empirical-analytic statements about reality is formed under the same conditions…[52]

Although it is difficult to understand the precise meaning of such passages (supposing they *have* a precise meaning), it is relatively easy to

---

[52] *Knowledge and Human Interests*, 2nd edn, tr. J. J. Shapiro, London, 1978, p. 191.

divine their purpose. They gather together, within the scope of a single dichotomy, all the subsidiary distinctions that will provide substance to Habermas's critique of contemporary capitalism. Radical thought is dichotomizing thought, and 'advances' in radical theory consist in the amalgamation of oppositions within a single over-arching divide. The divide will be expressed in countless ways: capitalism versus socialism; bourgeois versus 'producer'; technical reason versus critical theory; rational purpose versus communication. But the meaning remains the same: the actual world is a fallen world, a world of means, while the world to which we left intellectuals aspire is a redeemed world, a kingdom of ends.

In Habermas the dichotomy is bureaucratized, and expressed in the official language of German sociology. The instrumental is aligned with the technical, the empirical, the analytic, the behavioural, the 'decisionistic', the 'objective', and pitted against the 'communicative', the 'hermeneutic', the 'intersubjective', the normative. But the purpose remains unchanged. By this alignment, which is no more than a substitute for thought, Habermas builds a kind of judicial machine, which accuses bourgeois society of every dehumanizing failure, and attributes to the undisclosed ideal of communicative action the lost human success.

On the assumption of this easy-won critique of capitalist society Habermas is able to reaffirm, from time to time, the old radical promise, namely:

The 'pursuit of happiness' might one day mean something different – for example, not accumulating material objects of which one disposes privately, but bringing about social relations in which mutuality predominates and satisfaction does not mean triumph of one over the repressed needs of the other...[53]

But such direct expressions of the old agenda are comparatively rare, and increasingly absorbed into Habermas's advocacy of chatter as the true goal of politics. In the later 1970s, Habermas began to develop his account of the 'ideal speech situation', as the remedy to the alienating social structures of the capitalist economy. In three dense and laboured works (*Communication and the Evolution of Society*, 1976, *On the*

---

[53] *Communication and the Evolution of Society*, tr. Thomas McCarthy, London, 1979, pp. 198–9.

Pragmatics of Social Interaction, 1976, and *The Theory of Communicative Action*, 1976) he gives a new account of 'communicative rationality' and the 'argumentation' on which it depends. Having absorbed all of academic sociology he sets out to absorb anthropology, linguistics and analytical philosophy too, phrasing his position as a 'theory of universal pragmatics'.[54] And the socialist utopia must now be glimpsed through the haze of Oxford philosophical jargon: 'The structure of communication itself produces no constraints if and only if, for all possible participants, there is a symmetrical distribution of chances to choose and to apply speech-acts.'[55] If we were to take such pronouncements seriously – and the adoption of a consciously 'scientific' language suggests that we should – we cannot fail to draw some remarkable conclusions. Linguistic emancipation means shooting your mouth off, in a world where everyone has an equal opportunity to do the same.

But freedom, defined as 'symmetrical chances' is also a dubious asset. For you can achieve it merely by making sure that everyone is equally constrained: for instance, by commanding universal silence. The real question of liberty, which is that of human nature and the institutions required for its proper fulfilment, is simply by-passed by Habermas's argument, with its empty technicalities and its strange obsession with 'communication' between beings whose social nature and historical situation is never concretely defined. Here is a fragment of *The Theory of Communicative Action*, which proceeds in this way over 800 pages of relentless abstraction:

> …the rationality proper to the communicative practice of everyday life points to the practice of argumentation as a court of appeal that makes it possible to continue communicative action with other means when disagreements can no longer be repaired with everyday routines and yet are not to be settled by the direct or strategic use of force. For this reason I believe that the concept of communicative rationality, which refers to an unclarified systematic interconnection of universal validity claims, can be adequately explicated only in terms of a theory of argumentation.

---

[54] 'What is Universal Pragmatics?', in ibid.
[55] 'Vorbereitende bemerkungen zu einer Theorie der kommunikativen Kompetenz', in J. Habermas and N. Luhmann, *Theorie der Gesellschaft oder Sozialtechnologie: Was leistet die Systems Forschung?*, Frankfurt, 1971, p. 137.

We use the term *argumentation* for that type of speech in which participants thematize contested validity claims and attempt to vindicate or criticize them through arguments. An *argument* contains reasons or grounds that are connected in a systematic way with the *validity claim* of a problematic expression. The 'strength' of an argument is measured in a given context by the soundness of the reasons... [56]

As is surely apparent from that instance, the scientific idiom is no more than a twitch: a new rubber-stamp which Habermas has not quite got the hang of and which he applies upside down. After a few hundred pages of this writing, in which definitions are swallowed by tautologies swallowed by definitions in seemingly endless sequence, the reader experiences an urgent need to get to the heart of it. What exactly is Habermas saying, and what is he telling us to do? There is no concrete answer. Real human beings fall through the net of his argument, and only speech in the abstract remains. We are to aim for a *herrschaftsfreie Diskurs* – a discourse without domination – but about what, and for what purpose? He tells us elsewhere that we are to be liberated by a 'consensus achieved in unrestrained and universal discourse'.[57] But consensus about what, and in the cause of what?

In the ideal world there will be a kind of universal expressive abandon, in which a symphony may be distantly heard: 'In so far as we master the means of the construction of [this] ideal speech situation, we can conceive the ideas of truth, freedom and justice, which interpenetrate each other – although of course only as ideas.'[58] But what is the value of truth, freedom and justice, if they remain no more than ideas? What exactly does this *herrschaftsfrei* discourse achieve, beyond itself? What does it bring, for example, to my taciturn farmer neighbours, who know how to do things, but waste no time discussing them? Habermas is adamant that our existing speech habits are intolerably constrained, not least because they 'prevent questions that radicalise the value-universalism of bourgeois society from even arising'.[59] But, in so far as the phrase means anything, 'radicalising the value-universalism of bourgeois society' is just about all that goes on in the academic departments with which Habermas is

---

[56] *The Theory of Communicative Action*, p. 45.
[57] 'Towards a Theory of Communicative Competence', *Inquiry* (1970): 370 (adaptation of the chapter referred to in note 55).
[58] Ibid.
[59] *Communication and the Evolution of Society*, op. cit., p. 198.

familiar. Isn't that what the 'critique of instrumental reasoning' and the 'dialectic of Enlightenment' were all about?

Although Habermas purports to be describing an 'ideal speech situation', however, his prose gestures continually towards a new, and in some way liberated, social order, in which the poison of bourgeois consciousness would be washed away. In this new order communication would no longer be distorted by prejudice, by deference to authority, by vanity or self-doubt. A 'communicative ethics' would emerge which would 'guarantee the generality of admissible norms and the autonomy of active subjects'.[60] This new order, which was a preoccupation of Habermas in his earlier work on the idea of legitimation, would be brought about by the adoption of norms 'on which everyone affected agrees (or would agree) without constraint if they enter into (or were to enter into) a process of discursive will-formation'.[61]

Agree, or would agree? Actual contract or merely hypothetical? Habermas claims to be writing about language: in fact he is prowling around the old idea of the social contract, raising, without addressing, the question raised by Kant, whether a hypothetical contract is enough to secure legitimacy, and whether an actual contract is in any case ruled out. But his muddled and bureaucratic language obscures this very pertinent question and also conceals the reef on which his own critical enterprise must founder. Either people are free to contract in their present condition, in which case could we not say that they have implicitly accepted the 'capitalist' order? Or else they are not free, and our criterion of the preferred social order is given only by what people *would* choose, in ideal circumstances. The problem then is, how do we define those circumstances? How do we arrive at the *herrschaftsfrei* social choice?

The only cogent answer that has ever been given to that question is precisely the one from which Habermas flees: namely the truly free and autonomous choice is the one that respects the sovereignty of the individual, by granting him the right to dispose of his will, his labour and his property as his own. It is the answer given by the Enlightenment, enshrined in the American Constitution, and embellished by the Austrian theory of the market, and the tradition of Western democracy. In other words it is the answer that Marxist humanism had dismissed from the outset as 'bourgeois ideology', and which Habermas himself is constantly

---

[60] *Legitimation Crisis*, tr. Thomas McCarthy, London, 1976, p. 89.
[61] Ibid.

and dismissively referring to, in side-swipes that never come clean as to what they are really swiping at.

In his earlier work Habermas was much occupied by the question of legitimacy, drawing his concepts as much from Weberian sociology as from Marxist philosophy and the analysis of language. In *Legitimationsprobleme im Spätkapitalismus* (1973) he argues that our societies are suffering from a 'deficit in legitimacy' and cannot be rendered legitimate by any of the procedures sanctioned by 'late capitalist' thinking – in other words, the Enlightenment procedures to which I just referred. The language of the title is indicative. The ritual deference to Marxism is not a conclusion of the argument, which has no real conclusion, although it wheezes at a certain point to a halt. It is assumed from the start that terms like 'bourgeois' and 'late capitalist' are adequate to the social phenomena as we confront them; it is assumed that a society may be characterized through its 'production relations', its 'level of the development of the productive forces', its 'ruling ideology' and its available procedures of 'legitimation'. Those assumptions are not questioned – or are questioned only in the desultory manner of an official enquiry carried out by people concerned to whitewash their ineradicable habits. Instead of examining his assumptions Habermas diverts attention from them, by posing endless rhetorical questions:

> Can the new potentials for conflict and apathy, characterised by withdrawal of motivation and inclination toward protest, and supported by subcultures, lead to a refusal to perform assigned functions on such a scale as to endanger the system as a whole? Are the groups that place in question, possibly passively, the fulfilment of important system functions identical with the groups capable of conscious political action in a crisis situation? Is the process of erosion that can lead to the crumbling of functionally necessary legitimations of domination and motivations to achieve at the same time a process of politicisation that creates potentials for action? ... We have not yet developed sufficiently precise and testable hypotheses to be able to answer those questions empirically.[62]

The sudden invocation of scientific method should not be taken seriously. To answer such questions empirically is precisely not to answer them as Habermas requires: for it would mean coming down from the

---

[62] *Theory and Practice*, op. cit., pp. 6–7.

level of abstraction, where he can generate his endless definitions and dichotomies, into the real situations of human choice. In Habermas's volumes you will seldom encounter a real dilemma, an actual institution, a record of some felt community of purpose. All is as in the paragraph just quoted: systems, subcultures, motivations, functions, legitimations, ideologies, forces – abstract entities described in a pan-dynamic Newspeak that removes real human beings from the equation.

Looking back over the landscape that we have travelled in this chapter we encounter a remarkable work of *annihilation*. Following the trauma of Napoleon's invasion, the destruction of the many tiny principalities that had been held in precarious but enduring equilibrium by the Holy Roman Empire, and Napoleon's eventual defeat, the German-speaking people strove to build a national self-consciousness that would reconcile their competing interests and secure them against the threat of subjugation. In fiction, poetry, drama and music they celebrated the many ways in which Germans had lived together in mutual affection, building lasting institutions and legal order, and endowing private life with a civic meaning. Hegel's *Philosophy of Right*, with its deep description of marriage, the family, the civil service, the school and the corporations of 'civil society', set a standard in political philosophy that few subsequent writers have lived up to, exploring the many ways in which corporate personality emerges from and organizes the associations of citizenship. German and Austrian literature of the nineteenth century describes a society rich in institutions, corporations and 'little platoons'. Novels like Adalbert Stifter's *Nachsommer* describe in loving detail the immediacy and spiritual depth of the household, of the landscape, of the offices of civil life, even of the *Innigkeit* of bureaucracy. Through the *Bildungsroman*, the lyric song-cycle and the operatic stage Germans and Austrians strove to rescue and to perpetuate the abundance of public spirit by which they were still surrounded, and in one of their greatest artistic achievements – Wagner's *Die Meistersinger von Nürnberg* – we encounter a drama whose central character is not an individual but a corporate person, endowed with all the moral and ceremonial attributes with which our civilization has lifted associations above the life of their members. In *Das deutsche Genossenschaftsrecht*, which appeared in four volumes between 1868 and 1913, the great jurist and social philosopher Otto von Gierke invoked the wealth of civil institutions that had marked the development of the German-speaking countries from medieval times, and showed the ways in which the native common-law tradition had protected and amplified their social power.

All that wealth of social being, which is celebrated still in much of the art and music of the early twentieth century, even at the moment when Loos, Schoenberg, Musil and Kafka were putting it in question, is summarized in the work of Lukács, Adorno, Horkheimer and Habermas in a single, annihilating abstraction: 'bourgeois'. And if you wish to identify the *reality* of which bourgeois life is the *appearance*, then you are given only another abstraction: 'capitalism'. That's it. Nothing of real human life remains. All has been wiped away by Newspeak, to be replaced by the endless bureaucratic mutterings contained in volume after volume of Habermas. Marx's categories have been used to complete the work begun by Napoleon and continued in another and more horrible way by Hitler. They have been used to *remove the German people from history*, and to replace civil society and its meaning with a committee of intellectuals, either speaking like Lukács with the voice of the official 'proletariat', or participating in an 'ideal speech situation' in which only abstractions can be uttered and only leftist bureaucrats take part.

And here it is perhaps worth referring to another curious fact, which is that the 'critique of instrumental reason', which enters a dead end with Habermas's committee-speak, has had a flourishing career, not on the left, but on the right. In their several ways Burke, Hegel and Oakeshott showed the connection between instrumental rationality, the utilitarian mind-set, and the loss of respect towards institutions and cooperative forms of life. Our allegiance to civil society, they argued, is no more provisional than is our allegiance to the family and the legal order, and the state is no more justifiable as a means to an end than is the bond of love in the family. Allegiance to what is established is, therefore, a *given*, from which social criticism departs. It is neither conditional nor purposive, but a form of immersion in the institutions to which one's identity is owed. That is where political thinking starts, in the associations of individuals, as they shape their values and aspirations through the ethos of the little platoon.

Moreover, as Oakeshott has forcefully argued, the model for civil association is not enterprise but conversation, which is not a means to an end but an end in itself, an association that is 'purposeful without purpose', and which confers the attachments without which no society can endure. Conversation shapes us as *joiners*, members of institutions and corporate persons, people immersed in ownership and gift: in short, instances of that despised 'bourgeoisie' which is seen by the Frankfurters merely in abstract and annihilating terms.

It is probably true that Habermas was influenced, in his observation that legitimacy is thrown into crisis by 'purposive-rational' thinking, by a German thinker who dared to draw those conservative conclusions: Arnold Gehlen. In a comparatively lucid essay Habermas pays tribute to Gehlen, while criticizing his addiction to institutions and his 'imitation substantiality'.[63] Gehlen had the courage to utter what, in post-war Germany, had become all but unutterable. His thoughts, absorbed by the machinery of the leftist bureaucrat, are regurgitated in utterable form, severed from their conclusions, and offered as a 'critique' of another 'capitalist crisis'. And yet, in truth, it is only socialists who have wished, in our time, to found the legitimacy of government on its function as a means. It is only socialism that has set up, in the place of the government of men, the faceless 'administration of things' that is to be judged by the 'technical rules' of social engineering. And if there has been, in the contemporary world, a 'deficit of legitimacy' it was greatest where socialism most made its mark, in the former Soviet Empire. Seeing this, we see also that it is not 'late' but 'early capitalism' that Habermas is invoking.

Habermas is no passionate revolutionary. Indeed, he is not a passionate anything. In so far as he has woken to the realities of social conflict it has been to lend tentative support to the 'democratizing' aims of the student protests of the 1960s, and then, in more recent times, to enter into dialogue with the great and the good on behalf of a Euro-centric politics – though one from which conservative and nationalist voices seem always to be excluded. Indeed, in his recent appearances as a public intellectual Habermas has been more concerned to support the project of European integration than any of the old anti-capitalist causes, although always on the understanding that it is not the *free market* that is important in Europe, but rather the workings of the welfare state, the dissolution of national borders and national identities, and the retreat from American imperialism.

And this defence of the emerging soft-left bureaucracy, which is to melt the European people into a homogeneous welfare state striving for an 'ideal speech situation' with its no longer aggressive neighbours, is the natural culmination of the Frankfurt project. The German left establishment is acutely aware of its status as a privileged elite. While it repeats its monotonous condemnation of technocracy, it knows, in its heart, that 'instrumental reason' – described by Habermas in one of

---

[63] 'Arnold Gehlen: Imitation Substantiality', 1970, in *Philosophical Profiles*, tr. Thomas McCarthy, Cambridge, MA, 1983.

his more candid moments as 'work' – is the social condition on which it depends. In the last analysis the criticism of 'purposive-rational' behaviour and the celebration of the 'ideal speech situation' are no more than ideology: the ideology of an elite concerned to turn its back on the real world of modern industry and to uphold the dignity of its own position as a leisure class.

As with every ideology, the principal task is to persuade the lower orders to accept it. And it is a sound instinct to have issued these ideological proclamations in bureaucratic form, while burying within them an obscure promise of emancipation. The worker and the manager are thereby cajoled into thinking of the leftist as a superior civil servant, with an arcane industry of his own. The leftist keeps the cabinet where truth is filed, and must be petitioned for meanings with the same patience as any other civil servant. Indeed it was Hegel, ideologist of 'bourgeois society', who identified the civil servants as its true upper class.

How then should we see Habermas, now that the prizes have been bestowed and his identity as the voice of the new Europe confirmed? As the last living offshoot of the Frankfurt School, Habermas tinkered for many years with Marxist categories and tried to find new ways of shaping the anti-capitalist message. At first he thought that the capitalist 'crisis of legitimacy' could be overcome by the usual alliance of left-wing intellectuals with carefully selected, and duly deferential, members of the working class. To his credit he grew away from that stultifying agenda, advocating dialogue, negotiation and sympathy in the place of the old Marxist 'struggle'. However, the new agenda had the form of a political programme without the content.

Having swept all realities aside in favour of bureaucratic abstractions, he was unable to say what we should communicate about, or how we might give heart to our world. If the *only* message is, let's talk, it is doubtful that we really need volume upon volume of inspissated jargon to convey it. And the dialogues that Habermas now advocates, in the wake of 9/11, are noticeable for the voices that they exclude: no nationalists, no social conservatives, no pre-modernists or fervent free-marketeers will be invited to the table, when the postmodern future of mankind is plotted in the Habermasian bunker. And by excluding so much of ordinary humanity from his chatter-house, Habermas *avoids* the real questions that confront us, recommending that we discuss them only to avoid discussing them. That, I suspect, is what the new Europe is all about.

6 NONSENSE IN PARIS: ALTHUSSER, LACAN AND DELEUZE

The left-wing enthusiasm that swept through institutions of learning in the 1960s was one of the most efficacious intellectual revolutions in recent history, and commanded a support among those affected by it that has seldom been matched by any revolution in the world of politics. This was the age of 'intellectual production', in which the identity of the intellectual as honorary member of the working class was established – precisely when the real working class was disappearing from history and could be guaranteed survival only in this theatrical form.[1]

The revolution of the 1960s was therefore a revolution conducted in laboratory conditions, with hardly a step being taken outside the world of books. For the first time it was possible to observe the 'revolutionary consciousness' from close to, while running no risk of violence other than the violence of words. It was possible, in particular, to observe how quickly and adroitly the left-wing message was encased in dogma, how energetically the new revolutionaries went about the business of inventing spurious questions, barren controversies and arcane pedantries, with which to divert all intellectual enquiry away from the fundamental questions that had – from emotional necessity – been begged in their favour, including the question of revolution itself: what, exactly, *is* a revolution, and what good does it do?

The urgency of the question, and the elaborate ways of begging it, are nowhere more apparent than in the writings of the man who was singled

---

[1] At least one of the revolutionaries of May 1968 – André Gorz – perceived in due course that the working class had effectively disappeared, precisely at the moment when the 'intellectuals' made their most determined effort to unite with it. Compare his *Le Socialisme difficile* (Paris, 1967, tr. as *Revolution and Socialism* by N. Denny, New York, 1973) – a pie-eyed exposition of the *Temps modernes* version of student revolution – with his subsequent *Adieu au prolétariat*, Paris, 1984, a melancholy renunciation of the revolutionary road.

out by the revolutionaries of 1968 as their intellectual leader, Louis Althusser. In Althusser's work there emerged a new species of Marxist dogma: a theory, or rather meta-theory, which iterated in mesmerizing paragraphs the *form* of a dogma, while contriving meticulously to conceal its content. Such meta-dogma, as one might call it, pretends to a methodological sophistication that places it beyond any criticism from standpoints other than its own. And yet it insists that there is only one legitimate goal of all intellectual endeavour, which is the goal of revolution. And throughout all the writings of the *soixante-huitards* and their followers the message is repeated: the goal of intellectual labour is to be *on the side of revolution*, regardless of the consequences.

I begin by considering Althusser at length, since he offers a model of a new and fortified language, in which no question can be posed, and no answer offered, except in terms that are barely intelligible to those who have not renounced their capacity to think outside them. As Orwell perceived, the first target of every revolution is language. The need is to create a Newspeak that puts power in the place previously occupied by truth and, having done this, to describe the result as a 'politics of truth'.

To achieve this new kind of truth it is important to avoid refutation, but not, as science avoids it, by courting and surviving counter-arguments. Refutation must be *evaded*, so that the truth within the dogma can be protected from the malice contained in real things. Hence Althusser's writings – which are exemplary in this respect – engage with nothing written by those outside the Marxist camp, nor do they acknowledge any tradition of social and political thinking that does not bear, from its inception, the stamp of the Marxist dogma towards which it tends. About every serious objection to the theory and practice of Marxism Althusser remains silent.

Thus he praises the labour theory of value and purports to be persuaded by it. What then does he make of the extensive literature critical of that theory?[2] Precisely nothing. Since it begins and ends on

---

[2] Already, in contemporary reviews of Marx's great work, the early marginalists were pointing to its defects. To their criticisms were added those of the Austrian school, notably of Böhm-Bawerk and von Mises. It seems, for example, that the theory cannot account for scarcity rents and that it depends crucially upon a reduction of qualitative differences of labour to quantitative differences – a reduction that could be carried out only by abandoning the terms of the theory. And for the past seventy years it has been widely accepted that it is impossible to construct a theory of price ('exchange-value') which, like the labour theory, makes no reference to demand as an independent variable. There have, of course, been those who have wished to defend the theory. Economists such as Morishima,

a note of refutation he is unable to acknowledge its existence. Instead of addressing it he takes issue, in impenetrable side-swipes, with his fellow dogmatists – Della Volpe and his school, the Soviet theorist Il'enkov, and 'numerous scholars in the socialist countries'.[3] He does not pause to tell us what these writers say, but sets them before us like enigmatic stage props, to be interpreted at will, or in accordance with a drama of which he alone is the central actor. We learn that

> ... it is no slander on Rosenthal's work to reckon it partly beside the point here, since it merely paraphrases the immediate language with which Marx designates his object and his theoretical operations, without supposing that Marx's very language might often be open to this question.[4]

Which question? You will search the text in vain for an answer. The sentence is merely a self-directed gesture, pretending to an authority that it does nothing to establish, and in any case unconcerned by the possibilities of disagreement. For the writer who has chosen to discuss only with his friends, such gestures are more like comradely insults thrown across a meeting-hall, than real signals of opposition.

Disagreement, when it comes, takes the form of total hostility, directed towards an unnamed and caricatured enemy: 'Knowing that *Capital* was under a radical ideological-political edict imposed by bourgeois economists and historians for eighty years, we can imagine the fate reserved for it by academic philosophy!'[5] To which the correct response is: nonsense! The close reading of *Capital* by those 'bourgeois' economists is precisely what has led to the refutation of so many of its major tenets. For Althusser such a truth is unmentionable and must be kept at bay, silenced by ritual cursing. The entire pressure of his style is towards the belief that Marx's texts have a sacred character and can

---

following the lead of Piero Sraffa in *Production of Commodities by Means of Commodities* (1960), have tried to resuscitate some of the central tenets of Marxian political economy. Again, however, it has been powerfully argued (by Ian Steedman, *Marx after Sraffa*, 1977) that the valid points of Marxian economics can be used precisely to *dismiss* the labour theory of value.

[3] L. Althusser, *Reading Capital*, with sequel by E. Balibar, tr. Ben Brewster, London, 1970, p. 77.

[4] Ibid., p. 77.

[5] Ibid., p. 76.

be neither discussed nor understood, except by those who already – by whatever act of faith – accept their main conclusions. How else are we to interpret passages such as the following?

> ...this study [of *Capital*]...is only possible given a constant and double reference: the identification and knowledge of the object of Marxist philosophy at work in *Capital* presupposes the identification and knowledge of the specific difference of the object of *Capital* itself – which in turn presupposes the recourse to Marxist philosophy and demands its development. It is not possible to read *Capital* properly without the help of Marxist philosophy, which must itself be read, and simultaneously, in *Capital* itself.[6]

The first sentence enshrouds the reader in darkness. It seems to accuse him of a lack of penetration; at the same time, with its technicalities and its aura of rational argument, it promises an eventual illumination. The second sentence then provides the 'conclusion' that the reader is supposed to receive as 'justified'.

In plain English, the conclusion is this: you can understand *Capital* only by believing it or, in even plainer Latin, *credo ut intelligam*, as St Anselm put it, when discussing the supreme mystery of God: I believe in order to understand. In other words, we have to deal with religious faith, locked within the thought of its own validity. For the scientific mind belief is the consequence, and not the cause, of understanding. But it is precisely the scientific failure of Marxism that necessitates Althusser's enterprise – that of sacralizing Marx's texts and transforming their content into revealed dogma.

For Althusser, however, dogma is 'revealed' by being concealed. It is the act of concealment, within intellectual structures of impenetrable opacity, which guarantees the truth of every revelation. The axioms of Marxist theory appear in Althusser's prose like blinding flashes of total darkness, within clouds of grey on grey. This 'darkness visible' is like a photographic negative, and Althusser intimates that there is a process that will reverse it, changing dark into light and nonsense into sense. Read *Capital*, he insists, look on this text, look intently at it, hold it upside down, sideways, high in the air, but don't let your eyes stray from it. Then, and only then, will the great reversal occur.

---

[6] Ibid., p. 75.

At the same time, it is not the reversal of dark to light that is required of the believer, but the 'negative revelation' that precedes it. The true revelation consists in the *credo quia absurdum* of the devotee, who sees darkness everywhere and then turns to Marx's text, in order to convert this darkness into light.

Naturally none of this would be capable of attracting a serious following, were it not possible to glimpse the shadowy forms of theories and attitudes in the pervading dark. Althusser supports his meta-dogma, therefore, with what is, in effect, the disembodied form of a Marxist theory. This is presented in *Pour Marx*, 1965,[7] and subsequently 'assumed' – in so far as anything less than everything is assumed – in the work from which I have so far quoted, *Lire le Capital* (*Reading Capital*), 1968.

Like many communist intellectuals, Althusser was dismayed at the turn towards the early Marx on the part of the younger generation. He saw this turn as a threat to orthodoxy – or rather to the meta-orthodoxy that he expresses in his writings. He was particularly opposed to the rewriting of historical materialism and the theory of value in the terms suggested by the 'Marxist humanism' of the 1844 manuscripts and also, in the pre-war years, by Lukács and the Frankfurt school. Since the publication of *Grundrisse* it has become widely accepted that Marx himself would probably have countenanced such a rewriting, and would certainly not have been totally opposed to it.[8] But such a suggestion was intolerable to Althusser, who therefore removed himself from the literature that suggests it.

In answer to the young humanists, Althusser argued for an 'epistemological break' between two distinct phases of Marx's writing, marked by two separate 'problematics'. The early Marx's concerns were 'ideological', the later Marx's were 'scientific'.[9] In order that the reader should greet this interpretation with due solemnity Althusser at once conceals it, burying the technical terms (which he never explains) within paragraphs of Newspeak:

Understanding an ideological argument implies, at the level of ideology itself, simultaneous, conjoint knowledge of the *ideological field* in which a thought emerges and grows; and the exposure of

---

[7] Louis Althusser, *For Marx*, tr. Ben Brewster, London, 1969.
[8] See Karl Marx, *Grundrisse der Kritik der politischen Ökonomie*, 1858, tr. M. Nicolaus, Harmondsworth, Penguin, 1973.
[9] *For Marx*, op. cit., pp. 32–3.

the internal unity of this thought: *its problematic*. Knowledge of the ideological field itself presupposes knowledge of the problematics compounded or opposed to it. The interrelation of the particular problematic of the thought of the individual under consideration with the particular problematics of the thoughts belonging to the ideological field allows of a decision as to its author's specific difference, i.e. *whether a new meaning has emerged.*[10]

The passage illustrates the ponderous, suspicion-laden circularity of Althusser's prose, which goes round and round monotonously on its own heels, like a lunatic trapped in an imaginary cage. The content of the paragraph can be summarized in a few words: to understand an argument is to see its meaning. The endless circle that is built from that tautology has, however, a mesmerizing quality, pointing to another meaning that lies always just out of reach beneath the surface.

From such beginnings Althusser advances towards his interpretation of historical materialism, presented simultaneously as true to Marx's intentions and true to human history. He phrases this interpretation in 'dialectical' terms, believing that this captures the essence of Marx's theory, as an inversion of Hegel. He recognizes that Marx makes no mention of the Hegelian 'dialectics' in his later work, but he makes up for this by a dark reference to Lenin's notebooks, and by copious praise of Mao Zedong's *On Contradiction*. All change, he suggests, is the outcome of 'contradictions', which emerge within the various structures of society. These contradictions may appear as 'class struggles', or as intellectual and ideological confrontations. There is no *one* level at which they emerge and exert their transforming force: contradictions emerge at every level and in every guise. What then remains of Marx's thesis, that base determines superstructure – i.e. that transformations in the economic structure of society determine transformations everywhere?

Two somewhat half-baked emendations to Marx's original hypothesis have proved useful in reconciling it with the recalcitrant facts of human history. The first is the suggestion made by Engels that the economic factor does not determine social development but merely determines it 'in the last instance'; the second is the theory alluded to by Marx and proposed formally by Trotsky as the 'law of uneven development'. The first is tantamount to the admission that history is *not* generated by economic

---

[10] Ibid., p. 90.

change, the phrase 'in the last instance' being no more than an apology for a theory that has never been provided. The second likewise admits the non-conformity of historical processes to the pattern described by Marx, and argues that this is because several transitions in economic structure may take place simultaneously. This invocation of 'economic epicycles' recalls the attempt to save the Ptolemaic astronomy, by protecting the cherished hypothesis from the evidence that seemed to refute it.

Both catch-phrases – 'in the last instance' and 'uneven development' – recur persistently in Althusser's meta-theory. According to Althusser the motor of history is 'structural causation'. The 'principal' or 'general contradiction' (that which is effective 'in the last instance') is the one identified by Marx and exemplified in the conflict between the forces and the relations of production. However, this principal contradiction is inseparable from the total structure of society. The social body contains other contradictions, existing at several distinct levels within the superstructure and interacting systematically, as they strive to align themselves. A vague suggestion is made that contradictions might be 'passed' from one level to another, like geological faults. Because the various contradictions develop unevenly, it is possible that an economically backward country might present the sudden confluence of contradictions necessary for successful revolution (the case of Russia). Althusser described this 'fusion of accumulated contradictions' as 'over-determination', borrowing a term from Freud.

Thus revolution – and indeed any decisive social change – must be seen as the result of many confluent factors, each determining society in the same direction and towards the same total crisis:

> ...the whole Marxist revolutionary experience shows that, if the general contradiction [between productive forces and relations of production] is sufficient to define the situation when revolution is the 'task of the day', it cannot of its own simple, direct power induce a revolutionary situation, nor *a fortiori* a situation of revolutionary rupture and the triumph of revolution...[11]

In such passages of comparative lucidity Althusser reveals that his meta-theory establishes precisely nothing, and is indeed not a theory at all so much as a bundle of incantations. If the 'principal contradiction' fails to

---

[11] Ibid., p. 99.

bring about revolution, but simply makes revolution 'the task of the day', then what *actually* happens is the upshot of human decision. History may take any course, depending on the aims, strengths and methods of the protagonists. The 'principal contradiction' is not really a contradiction at all (otherwise it *would* cause the anticipated collapse): it is merely a problem with which people (rulers and ruled alike) have to deal.

Historical materialism surely requires that the 'principal contradiction' should provide an *explanation* of the contradictions within the superstructure. Otherwise we are not entitled to the distinction between superstructure and base. Althusser's 'theory' is therefore tantamount to a *denial* of historical materialism. (And there are many other examples of so-called amendments to Marx's materialism which, like Gramsci's theory that I discuss in the chapter following, are really ways of rejecting it.)

Elsewhere Althusser argues – on grounds of 'Marxist tradition' – that historical materialism (characterized by the 'famous' phrase 'determination in the last instance') allows us to believe in both the 'relative autonomy' of the superstructure, and in the 'reciprocal action' of the superstructure on the base.[12] But by admitting that political transformations have political causes ('relative autonomy') and that economic structures may be generated by political choice ('reciprocal action'), he allows human thought and intention to be prime causes of historical change. In which case, what remains of historical materialism? Only a strong dose of scientific method could rescue Althusser from this impasse, but nothing in his writings suggests that he has ever seriously considered what scientific method consists in.[13]

Rather than examine just what 'determination in the last instance' might mean Althusser prefers to wrap the phrase in nonsense, thereby shielding it from interrogation. This habit was inherited by his most famous student, Alain Badiou, whose work I discuss in Chapter 8. Here is Badiou's way of contributing to the debate concerning 'determination in the last instance':

If no *instance* can determine the whole, it is by contrast possible that a *practice*, thought in the structure that is proper to it, which

---

[12] L. Althusser, *Lenin and Philosophy and Other Essays*, tr. Ben Brewtser, London, 1971, p. 131.
[13] This is not to say that historical materialism could not be presented as a well-formed scientific hypothesis. But it is no easy matter to develop the necessary concepts, as is shown by G. A. Cohen's impressive attempt, in *Karl Marx's Theory of History: A Defense*, Princeton and Oxford, 1978.

is thus a structure that is so to speak *dislocated* (*décalée*) with regard to the one that articulates this practice as an instance of the whole, plays the determining role with regard to a whole in which it figures in a decentred manner.[14]

I tried to unravel that sentence without success. (The whole what? The structure of what? The determining role in doing, making or effecting what?) I then tried to link it to its neighbours in the text, but was again greeted by failure. Each sentence exhibits the same slightly delirious syntax, embedding a host of unexplained terms in structures that have the shape of thought without the matter. Such, I suspect, was the principal effect of Althusser's teaching.

In fact, Althusser's 'interpretation' makes the theory of history irrefutable. The theory becomes compatible with every course of events, and therefore explanatory of none. It is the mere 'form' of a theory, useful for its incidental terms ('contradiction', 'over-determination', 'revolution') which serve to focus a particular attitude to events, but useless for its predictive power. It simply has no predictive power. But in another sense that is why it is useful. It permits the believer to turn his mind away from the facts of history, save only those that seem to nourish a pre-existing revolutionary fervour. The theory of history becomes a theology of history, a 'hypothesis' which, being compatible with every course of events, is in exactly the same boat as the 'hypothesis' of God's existence, of which Laplace famously said that he had no need.

In order to protect his theory from refutation, Althusser sets out to conceal it instead, adopting the process of 'negative revelation' described above. He takes the key technicalities and transforms them into concentrated nodes of dazzling darkness. The following passage illustrates the process at work:

> Over-determination designates the following essential quality of contradiction: the reflection in contradiction itself of its conditions of existence, that is, of its situation in the structure in dominance of the complex whole. This is not a univocal 'situation'. It is not just its situation 'in principle' (the one it occupies in the hierarchy of instances in relation to the determinant instance: in society, the economy) nor just its situation '*in fact*' (whether, in the phase under consideration,

---

[14] *The Adventure of French Philosophy*, ed. and tr. Bruno Bosteels, London, Verso, 2012, p. 156.

it is dominant or subordinate) but *the relation of this situation in fact to this situation in principle,* that is, the very relation which makes of this situation in fact a *'variation' of the – 'invariant' – structure, in dominance, of the totality.*[15]

Get it? No, you are not really supposed to: what is required is to grasp certain ideas that are singled out for special treatment, by being 'hardened' through immersion in extra-emphatic prose, while crying out 'let *this* not be doubted'. Here is how he hardens 'in the last instance':

> Elsewhere, I have shown that in order to conceive this 'dominance' of a structure over the other structures in the unity of a conjuncture it is necessary to refer to the principle of the determination 'in the last instance' of the non-economic structures by the economic structure; and that this 'determination in the last instance' is an absolute pre-condition for the necessity and intelligibility of the displacements of the structure in the hierarchy of effectivity, or of the displacement of 'dominance' between the structured levels of the whole; that only this 'determination in the last instance' makes it possible to escape the arbitrary relativism of observable displacements by giving these displacements the necessity of a function.[16]

None of which, of course, goes the slightest way towards telling us what 'in the last instance' really means. We can ascribe to Althusser a perverted form of Wittgenstein's imperative: 'Don't look for the meaning, look for the use!' And the use is what I have called 'meta-dogma' – the form of dogma, without specific content.

Below I sketch some other instances of the peculiar convoluted prose with which the *soixante-huitards* kitted out their 'nonsense machine'. However Althusser was not, consciously, producing nonsense; rather he was trying to give voice to a religious sentiment, struggling to find the words that would reach through to others and join them to the faith. Religious belief possesses the structure of Pascal's wager, and this is one way by which we recognize it. It postulates an inestimable benefit to the believer and then, by a piece of deception, persuades him that this benefit is sufficient reason (and not just sufficient motive) to believe. Althusser

---

[15] *For Marx*, p. 200.
[16] *Reading Capital*, p. 99.

follows Gramsci in laying down similar terms for the revolutionary wager. By believing you join the elect: you, the urban intellectual, are united in 'solidarity' with the oppressed workers. Therefore believe.

It is a well-known difficulty for the materialist theory of history that, taken seriously, it seems to deny the efficacy of intellectual labour, to dismiss it as a mere epiphenomenon, a nebulous offshoot of processes over which it asserts no real influence. It is of the first importance, therefore, to give a role to 'intellectual labour' in the 'material conditions' of existence, so making it a genuine 'motive force' in history, unlike the mere 'ideology' of the bourgeois enemy. Hence the distinction between science and ideology: my thought is science, yours is ideology; my thought is Marxist (since only Marxism penetrates the veil of ideology), yours is 'idealist'; my thought is proletarian (Lukács), yours is bourgeois; my thought belongs to the 'material conditions' of production, and can be called 'theoretical praxis', your thought belongs to the false consciousness that arises like a cloud above the place where history is made. My thought is at work in the factory; yours is puffed from the chimney and dissolves into air.

The interest of 'theoretical practice', so described, is twofold. It situates intellectual activity within the economic base (Althusser therefore prefers to speak of 'intellectual production'), so uniting the intellectual with the toiling proletariat. It also provides an exact equivalent of religious faith. As in Pascal's wager, believing becomes a kind of doing, and in this doing lies the moral salvation – the inner identity with the revolution – for which the intellectual craves.

The doctrine of faith begins with deceptive simplicity:

… what do we gain by this 'speculative' investigation that we do not possess already?

One sentence is enough to answer this question: Lenin's 'Without revolutionary theory, no revolutionary practice.' Generalising it: theory is essential to practice, to the forms of practice that it helps to bring to birth or to grow, as well as to the practice it is the theory of. But the transparency of this sentence is not enough; we must also know its *titles to validity*, so we must pose the question: what are we to understand by *theory*, if it is to be essential to *practice*?[17]

---

[17] *For Marx*, p. 166.

That paragraph marks time, awaiting a new consignment of technicalities from the factory of 'intellectual production'. As Althusser recognizes, 'the transparency of this sentence is not enough'. The consignment soon arrives, enabling Althusser to darken his terms:

> I shall call Theory (with a capital T), general theory, that is, the Theory of practice in general, itself elaborated on the basis of the Theory of existing theoretical practices (of the sciences), which transforms into 'knowledges' (scientific truths) the ideological product of existing 'empirical practices' (the concrete activity of men). This Theory is the materialist *dialectic* which is none other than dialectical materialism.[18]

Such passages – received by Althusserians as introducing an important notion of 'theoretical levels' – display the essential vacuity of Althusser's thought. 'This Theory is the materialist *dialectic* which is none other than dialectical materialism.' The neophyte, contemplating such utterances, repeats them to himself in a spirit of awe. They have the same vertiginous quality as Stalin's pleonasm, 'The theories of Marx are true because they are correct', which was once so important an incantation in the dark night of communist doubt.[19] The more tautological the utterance, the more does it seem to conceal, and the more effectively does it induce the state of spiritual readiness that is the prelude to faith.

After a few pages of dense circularities, the reader is finally brought – by an accumulation of non-contradictions – to the crisis of belief:

> The only Theory able to raise, if not to pose, the essential question of the status of these disciplines, to criticise ideology in all its guises, including the disguises of technical practice as sciences, is the Theory of theoretical practice (as distinct from ideological practice): the materialist dialectic or dialectical materialism, the conception of the Marxist dialectic in its *specificity*.[20]

To raise (if not to pose) a better question: what in fact are we being invited to believe? The Althusserian version of dialectical materialism is,

---

[18] Ibid., p. 168.
[19] On the spiritual significance of Stalin's slogan, see Ivan Volgin (pseud.), 'The Magic World of Homo Sovieticus', in *The Salisbury Review* 1 (4) (Summer 1983).
[20] *For Marx*, pp. 171–2.

as we have seen, no more than the form of a theory, and the emphatic conclusions are meta-dogmas, devoid of specific content. In *Reading Capital* we are told that '*theoretical practice* is its own criterion, and contains in itself definite protocols with which to *validate* the quality of its product, i.e. the criteria of the scientificity of the products of scientific practice'.[21] In other words, even the invocation of theoretical practice does not permit Althusser to descend from the 'meta' level, to the level of 'specificity'. It remains impossible to explain theoretical practice, except in terms of itself.

Hence, when Althusser turns to the text of *Capital*, it is partly in order to give vent to religious awe, but also to extract a phrase or a paragraph, which he encases in metaphysical spells, like a drunken mystic commenting on the Gospels. In doing this he claims to be pursuing the 'object' of *Capital* – although it is never certain whether he means this word in the sense of aim, or subject-matter, or content. Once again the major purpose is one of 'negative revelation'; it is a massive attempt to appropriate the meaning of *Capital* by concealing it. The search for the 'object' is an exercise in burial: the object is the sixpence in the Christmas pudding, and Althusser's approach to his reader is to say: eat this pudding, chew this text, and you will bite on its significance.

At the same time, Althusser engages in some fervent expostulations against the enemies of theoretical practice. His totalitarian characterization of these enemies illustrates an interesting feature of Newspeak, noticed also by Petr Fidelius and Françoise Thom: the 'unity of evil' under which all opponents are gathered.[22] For Althusser the enemies of theoretical practice are all 'empiricists', characterized by their belief in 'abstraction'.[23] This accusation is fired at the rationalist Descartes, the absolute idealist Hegel, and Kant, the greatest critic of empiricism. All are gathered in a common grave, representatives of 'empiricism, whether transcendent (as in Descartes), transcendental (Kant and Husserl) or "objective"-idealist (Hegel)'.[24] Someone acquainted with the real history of philosophy might be so astounded by this travesty as to overlook the purpose of Newspeak,

---

[21] *Reading Capital*, p. 59.
[22] Petr Fidelius, 'Totalitarian Language', *The Salisbury Review* 2 (2) (Winter 1984); Françoise Thom, *La langue de bois*, Paris, 1986. Fidelius's brilliant account of communist language, published as *Jazyk a Moc* by an exile press in Germany in 1984, is now available as an e-book, *Řeč komunistické moci*, Prague, Triada, 2010.
[23] *Reading Capital*, p. 35.
[24] Ibid., p. 184.

which is not to describe the world as it is, but to cast spells. Althusser is warning us off from all viewpoints other than 'theoretical practice', whose criterion of validity is itself.

How are we to explain Althusser's influence? It is not enough to dwell on the theological contours that he gives to Marxist materialism, or upon the paradisal reward that he offers to the urban intellectual. It is necessary to recognize the operation of factors that became increasingly important as the revolution of the 1960s and 70s unfolded. First, in the spirit of dialectical materialism, we should examine the material conditions of the disciples of Althusser. For the most part these were young radical lecturers in universities and polytechnics, who had yet to establish their academic credentials, and who were in search of inscrutable pedantries of their own, in which to bury their intellectual faults while revealing their political sympathies. Althusser provided a kind of fortified redoubt of pseudo-scholarship, from which to fire devastating 'proofs' of the futility of traditional learning. He was the first of a whole series of alchemical scholars who helped the new generation of academics in the humanities to put power above truth on their scale of values. By virtue of his and similar writings, political conformity could be disguised as 'ground-breaking research', and so used as the sole test for promotion in the world of scholarship.

Second, and more importantly, we must understand the 'existential posture' implicit in the style. The human world is fundamentally opposed to Althusser. Every institution plays its part in the 'objective' conspiracy that oppresses him. Church, family, school, trade union, culture, press, judiciary – all belong to the 'ideological state apparatus' whose purpose is the 'reproduction' of repressive power.[25] Everywhere about us are the marks of a 'ruling ideology', of 'state violence' and 'class oppression'. Individuals are controlled and subjected, either by the 'direct' method of fascism, or by the 'indirect' method of parliamentary democracy (or rather 'democracy'). Althusser is a lone persecuted voice in a world where 'the communications apparatus crams every "citizen" with daily doses of nationalism, chauvinism, liberalism, moralism, etc....'[26]

It is not the content of those utterances that invites our submission – for they are nothing but slogans – but the tone of voice in which they are uttered, and which is, in truth, the only feature of Althusser's writings

---

[25] *Lenin and Philosophy*, p. 135.
[26] Ibid., p. 145.

that is consistently transparent. His tone is the self-defensive tone of the paranoiac – the tone of someone who has locked himself within his own discourse, and who can communicate with no one who does not accept his dictatorial terms. Within Althusser's linguistic redoubt the opponent does not exist except as the darkly defined enemy, whose identity can be guessed by the boundaries from which Althusser's thought recoils into itself, undefeated, because untried in combat.

Within the inner darkness, however, fierce loyalties impose their law: loyalty to Marx, to Engels, to Lenin, to Mao, to the mythologized 'workers' movement' and above all to the French Communist Party. Those loyalties define the real content of the paranoid vision, whose appeal is not intellectual but emotional. The call to theoretical practice is the call to allegiance, the call to arms, in a self-defensive circle of obscurity that remains closed to those who threaten it. The Althusserian style creates the intellectual equivalent of a totalitarian state, in which all is governed by a single orthodoxy, encased in mesmerizing slogans, with neither opposition nor diversity. All in this state are united around a common loyalty, and 'hostile elements' have been duly liquidated. Althusser expresses, in his meta-dogma, the incipient totalitarianism of the revolutionary consciousness. He therefore shows to the new radicals that they are sufficiently redeemed by their left-wing allegiance to be able to dispense with the need to understand or conciliate their opponents. Their opponents have already been allocated to the 'dust heap of history'; it is only necessary to transport them there.

It is said that Althusser's murder of his wife in 1978 was in response to her 'revisionism'. Whatever the truth in this rumour, it has a certain gruesome logic. The tragic outcome of Althusser's pilgrimage into the heart of darkness seems like the domestic re-creation of the tragedy suffered by the peoples of Russia, China, North Korea, Vietnam, Cambodia and Eastern Europe. It is the tragedy that inevitably follows, when paranoid suspicion displaces the natural law of compromise. The paranoid mentality, seeking to preserve at all costs the illusion of its own absolute correctness, turns itself into a superstition, and persecutes as evildoers all those who will not accept its dominance. It invents a language without meaning, since meaning constitutes a threat, and the syntax of this language is organized by the search for power. It inhabits this language with the absolute vigilance of a tyrant, ceaselessly working to liquidate the poisonous meanings that have seeped into it from the world of 'the Other'.

But here we should acknowledge a third factor in Althusser's appeal to the new generation of radicals. His constant lapse into nonsense is not, in the eyes of his disciples, a fault, but a deep proof of his relevance. He provides a way of writing in which political allegiance is *all that there is*, but which also has the *form* of intellectual enquiry. By writing and thinking like this you put power at the centre of discourse, emancipate yourself from real knowledge, and lose the very possibility of doubt by losing the only language that could be used to express it.

Althusser was therefore enthusiastically endorsed by his Parisian contemporaries, who were, at the time, assembling a nonsense machine that could eliminate the possibility of rational argument, and which could also rephrase every question, however scholarly, as a question of politics. Thanks to the nonsense machine you could plunge into the work of 'intellectual production', and believe that you were already part of the revolution. No need to ask what revolution means or what you might achieve by means of it. Nothing means anything and that *is* the revolution, namely the machine to annihilate meaning. The machine was put together by Jacques Lacan, Gilles Deleuze and a few others, from discarded fragments of Freudian psychology and Saussurian linguistics, and attached to Kojève's Hegelian wind-bag, with which to pump it up with hot air. But it survived its inventors, and a version of it can be found in virtually every humanities department today.

The intellectual history here is complex, and I must content myself with a few brief observations.[27] In his *Cours de linguistique générale* (published posthumously in 1916) the Swiss linguist Ferdinand de Saussure introduced two ideas that were to be used, abused and jargonized throughout the 1960s and 70s: the idea of language as a system of 'differences', and the idea that there is, or could be, a 'general science of signs'. The meaning of a sign, Saussure argued, attaches to it only in the context of the other signs that might replace it in a sentence. The meaning of 'hot' must be understood in terms of the difference between 'hot' and 'cold'. Some went further, arguing that language is *nothing but* a system of differences, each sign owing its meaning to the signs that it excludes. This was taken by Saussure as authority for the view that language has no 'positive terms', but is an endless stream of negations, whose meaning lies

---

[27] For relevant observations, and a powerful response to the whole phenomenon, see Raymond Tallis, *Not Saussure: A Critique of Post-Saussurean Literary Theory*, London, Macmillan, 2nd edn, 1995.

in what is not said, and what cannot be said (for to say it is merely to defer the meaning to another hidden negative).

Jacques Derrida went further still, arguing that therefore no sign means in isolation, and meaning waits upon the 'other' sign, the sign that completes it by opposing it, but which cannot be finally written down. Meaning is never present but always deferred, chased through the text from sign to sign, always vanishing as we seem to reach it; and if we stop at a particular place, saying *now* we have it, *now* the meaning lies before us, then this is our decision, which may have a political justification, but which is in no way dictated by the text. Thus the ambiguous noun *différence* must here be taken in both its senses – as difference and deferral, a fact that Derrida records by misspelling it, as *différance*. That intoxicating (and toxic) piece of nonsense is now as firmly embedded in intellectual history as Newton's mechanics or Kant's Transcendental Deduction.[28]

The idea of a general science of signs – or 'semiology' – was a favourite of Saussure's, and deserves far more treatment than I can give to it here. Briefly, there is a science of fish because fish are similarly constituted, obey similar laws, and have a discoverable nature, over and above the similarities that cause us to classify them together. (Fish constitute a 'natural kind'.) Buttons, by contrast, have no common nature, and are defined not by their constitution but by their function. There can be no general science of buttons, but only a science of their function. Signs are clearly more like buttons than like fish. But can we really identify a *single* function that unites the many things called 'signs' – including words, road signs, gestures, symptoms, costumes, notes in music, the grammar of classical architecture, and signs of the times? I leave the topic there, for what mattered to the builders of the nonsense machine was not the answer but the mystery stirred by the question.

The frame of the nonsense machine was assembled by Jacques Lacan, the cranky psychiatrist whose writings, published in 1966, had an extraordinary impact on the student revolutionaries, with whose cause he publicly aligned himself.[29] Lacan has been described by Raymond Tallis as 'the shrink from Hell', words that aptly characterize the practice of a psychoanalyst who would see ten clients in an hour, sometimes while attended to by his barber, tailor or pedicurist, and whose idea of cure was to teach the patients to speak, think and feel in the same paranoid language

---

[28] For my criticisms, see *Modern Culture*, 3rd edn, London, 2005, Ch. 12.
[29] Jacques Lacan, *Écrits*, Paris, Éditions du Seuil, 1966, enlarged edition 1969.

as their doctor.[30] But maybe we should not be too harsh on Lacan in this respect. People become famed as psychoanalysts not for their therapeutic successes (maybe there are none), but for their ideas. And the fame of an idea arises from its influence, not its truth. So it was with Freud, Jung and Adler; so it has been with Klein, Binswanger, Lacan and many more.

The unconscious, Lacan wrote, is structured like a language. And he set out to interpret this language, borrowing terms from Sausssurian linguistics, together with the idea of the Other, as he had gleaned this from Kojève. He also scattered his writings and his lectures with mathematical jargon, taken from theories that he did not care to understand, but which he referred to casually as 'mathemes', on the analogy with the phonemes and morphemes into which linguists divide the functional parts of language.[31] (In a similar move, Lévi-Strauss at around the same time introduced the 'mytheme' and Derrida the 'philosopheme', a usage that had been anticipated by Schelling.)[32]

There is, Lacan suggested, a big Other (capital A for *Autre*), which is the challenge presented to the self by the not-self. This big Other haunts the perceived world with the thought of a dominating and controlling power – a power that we both seek and flee from. There is also the little other (little a for *autre*) who is not really distinct from the self, but is the thing seen in the mirror during that stage of development that Lacan calls the 'mirror stage', when the infant supposedly catches sight of himself in the glass and says 'ah-ha!' That is the point of recognition, when the infant first encounters the 'object = a', which in some way that I find impossible to decipher indicates both desire and its absence. (Note, however – though Lacan characteristically does not – that blind children become adroit in the practice of distinguishing self and other at the same age as sighted children.)

The mirror stage provides the infant with an illusory (and brief) idea of the Self, as an all-powerful other in the world of others. But this self is soon to be crushed by the big Other, a character based on the good-breast/bad-breast, good-cop/bad-cop scenario invented by Melanie

---

[30] Raymond Tallis, 'The Shrink from Hell', *THES* (3 November 1997).
[31] See the devastating criticism of Lacan's misuse of set theory, topology etc. by Jean Bricmont and Alan Sokal, *Impostures Intellectuelles*, Paris, Odile Jacob, 1997, published in English as *Fashionable Nonsense: Postmodern Intellectuals' Abuse of Science*, London, Profile Books, 1998.
[32] Friedrich Schelling, 'Über Mythen, historische Sagen und Philosopheme der ältesten Welt', *Sämmtliche Werke*, ed. K.F.A. Schelling, Stuttgart, Cotta, 1856–61, 1. 1. 43–83.

Klein. In the course of expounding the tragic aftermath of this encounter Lacan comes up with astounding aperçus, often repeated without explanation by his disciples, as though they have changed the course of intellectual history. One in particular is constantly repeated: 'there is no sexual relation', an interesting observation from a serial seducer from whom no women, not even his own analysands, were safe.[33]

In addition Lacan is credited with the view that the subject does not exist beyond the mirror stage until brought into being by an act of 'subjectivation'. You become a self-conscious subject by taking possession of your world and incorporating its otherness into your self. In this way you begin to 'ex-sist', i.e. to exist outwardly, in a community of others. This is more interesting of course, though why Lacanians give Lacan credit for a thesis expounded far more lucidly and with all due qualifications by Hegel and Kojève is to be explained only by the kind of deification that Lacan not only demanded but also, to the disgrace of human nature, received.

Lacan's ruminations on the Other purport to be part of a 'return to Freud', and a theoretical restatement of the Freudian theory of object-relations, as amplified by Klein and Bion. In fact, as is obvious, the principal influence was Kojève's Hegel. Responding to Kojève's huge success in recruiting the admiration of the Parisian intelligentsia, Lacan established his own seminars in 1953. The influence of these seminars – 34 volumes of which have been transcribed and also translated – is one of the deep mysteries of modern intellectual life. Their garbled regurgitation of theories that Lacan clearly neither explored nor understood, is, for sheer intellectual effrontery, without parallel in recent literature. I give a few examples, because they suggest the true nature of Lacan's achievement. Lacan discovered the infinite power of the meaningless, when the meaningless is used to exert a personal charisma.

In *The Four Fundamental Concepts of Psychoanalysis* (transcribed from lectures and published in 1977) Lacan explains the object = a as follows:

Today then I must keep to the wager to which I committed myself in choosing the terrain in which the *object a* is most evanescent in its function of symbolizing the central lack of desire, which I have always indicated in a univocal way by the algorithm $(-\Phi)$.

---

[33] The study by Elizabeth Roudinesco – *Jacques Lacan*, New York, Columbia University Press, 1999 – contains enough information to damn Lacan as a criminal charlatan; but the judgement is more devastatingly made by Raymond Tallis, in his review of Roudinesco, cited above, note 30.

I don't know whether you can see the blackboard, but as usual I have marked out a few reference points. *The object a in the field of vision is the gaze.* After which, enclosed in a chain bracket, I have written:

$$(in\ nature$$
$$($$
$$(as = (-\Phi)$$

Science promises the truth about reality, and this truth may be useless; but alchemy promises a deeper truth, and one inseparable from power. So it is with the difficult science of linguistics. Here too there is an alchemy, which will decipher mysteries and so give us control over them. In Lacan's seminal text entitled 'The Agency of the Letter in the Unconscious of Reason since Freud', we find something called an 'algorithm' and attributed to Saussure:

To pinpoint the emergence of linguistic science we may say that, as in the case of all sciences in the modern sense, it is contained in the constitutive moment of an algorithm that is its foundation. This algorithm is the following:

$$\frac{S}{s}$$

which is read as: the signifier over the signified, 'over' corresponding to the bar separating the two stages.

He puzzles over Saussure's formula, wondering what it could possibly mean, and concluding that perhaps it means nothing, perhaps indeed that there is nothing in any case to mean:

If the algorithm S/s with its bar is appropriate, access from one to the other cannot in any case have any signification. For in so far as it is in itself only pure function of the signifier, the algorithm can reveal only the structure of a signifier in this transfer.

Lacan gathers confidence on noticing that *barre* is an anagram of *arbre*: 'Let us take our word "tree"...and see how it crosses the bar of the Saussurian algorithm' (*arbre-cadavre*, so to say). He then solves the problem by interpreting the bar as a sign of division, so that the 'S' and the 's' become algebraic symbols:

What we have been able to develop concerning the effects of the signifier on the signified suggests its transformation into:

$$f(S)\frac{t}{s}$$

We have shown the effects not only of the elements of the horizontal signifying chain, but also of its vertical dependencies in the signified, divided into two fundamental structures called metonymy and metaphor. We can symbolize these by, first:

$$f(S\ldots S')S \cong S(-)s$$

that is to say, the metonymic structure, indicating that it is the connection between signifier and signifier that permits the elision in which the signifier installs the lack-of-being in the object relation using the value of 'reference back' possessed by signification in order to invest it with the desire aimed at the very lack it supports…

The reader might well puzzle over such passages: is the 'f' really a function sign? Is the bar really a sign of division, the '$\cong$' of approximate equality, the 'S…S' of a mathematical series? We soon find that the answer is yes. Meaning has indeed been reduced to an equation and in the solution of this equation the signified is found to be identical with the square root of minus one:

$$\frac{S\ (signifier)}{s\ (signified)} = s\ (the\ statement),$$

with S = (−I), produces $s = \sqrt{-I}$

After a few pages of that,[34] convinced that the erectile penis (the primary object of meaning) under bourgeois conditions is no more potent than the square root of minus one (or maybe minus ego, if the ego is less than one, which it probably is), the reader is ready to accept that

---

[34] See p. 317 of *Écrits*.

the distance between the object = a and the ex-sistent = e is no greater than that between Freud and Fraud. Hence 'there is no further need to have recourse to the outworn notion of primordial masochism in order to understand the reason for the repetitive games in which subjectivity brings together mastery of its dereliction and the birth of the symbol'. Exactly.

From Badiou to Žižek the followers of Lacan have rejoiced in the discovery that he bequeathed to us, and it is easy to see why. Derrida had cast doubt, in his theory of deconstruction, on the possibility of meaning anything. Lacan showed that it is not necessary to mean anything anyway. You can go on meaning nothing for page upon page, and as long as a few 'mathemes' are thrown in, and as long as you maintain a posture of inviolable certainty, secure in the revelation of which you are the sole proprietor, you will have done all that is required by way of making a contribution to the emerging 'revolutionary consciousness'.

The frame established by Lacan was, however, somewhat bare in the original version. The big and little others, A and a, were required to do an excessive amount of work, dancing around the bewildered square root of minus one as it strove to catch sight of itself in the glass. It was left to Žižek (whom I discuss in Chapter 8) to systematize the Lacanian aperçus in a comprehensive account of the postmodern condition. Meanwhile, the next generation, including those like Félix Guattari who had sat through Lacan's *séminaires*, and those like Gilles Deleuze who came from a more strictly academic background, began to bolt on to the frame of Lacan's nonsense machine all the accessories that were needed by the new curriculum. The goal of this curriculum is to uphold Lacan's doctrine that the 'subject' does not exist. The 'I' is an absence, striving for 'ex-sistence' in acts of 'subjectivation', but always cancelled by the object = a, and retreating to the condition enjoyed by Lacan, which is not ex-sistence but in-sistence.

Gilles Deleuze (1925–95) has received tributes from many distinguished writers, Foucault going so far as to describe the post-war period as 'le siècle Deleuzien'. Adrian Moore, one of our cleverest and most erudite analytical philosophers, has singled him out as a major metaphysician, seemingly on a par with Frege, Wittgenstein and Quine.[35] I therefore hesitate to say what my conscience nevertheless urges me to

[35] A. W. Moore, *The Evolution of Modern Metaphysics: Making Sense of Things*, Cambridge, 2012.

say, which is that he was just as much a fraud as Lacan. Let the reader judge, however. Deleuze is of interest in the present context primarily for the use that has been made of him, which is to trundle the nonsense machine from subject to subject and topic to topic in the humanities, reducing the entire landscape to the intellectual equivalent of the aftermath of the Somme.[36] And in that aftermath, haunting the scene of devastation, the spirit of revolution rallies the survivors with its call to a new solidarity against the enemy.

Deleuze was not, at first, a political, still less a politicized, thinker, and the nonsense machine that he helped to assemble was put to political use primarily by other and less scrupulous spirits. In a series of books devoted to the classics of Western philosophy Deleuze established his reputation as an academic philosopher, exploring the relevance to our condition of Spinoza, Kant and Nietzsche. But his major treatise, *Difference and Repetition*, published in 1968, shows the true nature of his thinking, presented as a rumination on the words in the title.

This title derives obliquely from Heidegger, whose *Being and Time* was a revelation to philosophers of Sartre's generation, since it seemed to revive the ancient question of being – the question of 'being *qua* being' as Aristotle put it – and to apply it directly to life in the modern world: to the problems of being here and now. Heidegger's work was, in this respect at least, the inspiration for Sartre's great *Being and Nothingness*, and (later) Alain Badiou's *Being and Event*. Deleuze wished to replace the idea of being, and its associated notions of substance and identity, with that of difference. And he took from Nietzsche the view that time is to be in some way transcended through the 'eternal recurrence' of all that happens – in other words through a repetition implanted deep in the order of things. Hence 'Being and Time' becomes 'Difference and Repetition'. That, however, is just about as far as I got.

Deleuze claims that Western thought has hitherto been guided by the concept of identity, and that identity must now give way to difference. What exactly does that mean? Difference and identity (whether numerical or qualitative) are inter-definable, and someone who deploys the one concept necessarily deploys the other. Since Aristotle, however, identity (something's being the thing that it is)

---

[36] See the series published by Bloomsbury, *Deleuze and…* (*Deleuze and Futurism, Deleuze and Art, Deleuze and the Diagram* etc.).

has been treated as logically prior to all predications, including the predication of difference. For identity is presupposed by individuation, the act of singling something out as an object of reference. Reflecting on what that involved led Kant to his view that the fundamental objects of identification are spatio-temporal substances. And Kant's argument has been revived in recent times by Strawson, Quine, Wiggins and Kripke, in works that are clearly and interestingly argued, even if Deleuze (who often hints that he has read everything) does not mention them. In the light of this tradition one may well ask how difference can displace identity from its fundamental position in anchoring the frame of reference. What would it be, to single out difference as more basic than identity, so that 'being different' from other things, rather than identical with a specific thing, is understood as the primary way of being?

Adrian Moore tells us that Deleuze is drawing attention to positive differences, features of the object in which difference cannot be defined qualitatively since it is itself a basic fact. (Thus, in the matter of 'intensive' magnitudes, such as heat and cold, two objects can differ even while having all their qualities in common – they are both hot, for example, even though one is hotter than the other.) However, that does nothing to establish the possibility that 'differences' could provide a new foundation for ontology – a new way of understanding the basic way things are. To attribute these intensive qualities to an object we still need the act of individuation that tells us *which* object we are referring to.

Deleuze's thesis is put forward as deeply subversive: we were imprisoned by sameness and have been released into difference! But does this really subvert the entire previous course of Western metaphysics, and if so, to what effect? Deleuze's language covers the topic in such mystery that it is impossible to say:

> ...rather than the repeated and the repeater, the object and the subject, we must distinguish two forms of repetition. In every case repetition is difference without a concept. But in one case, the difference is taken to be only external to the concept; it is a difference between objects represented by the same concept, falling into the indifference of space and time. In the other case, the difference is internal to the Idea: it unfolds as pure movement, creative of a dynamic space and time which corresponds to the Idea. The first repetition is repetition of the Same, explained by the identity of

the concept or representation: the second includes difference, and includes itself in the alterity of the Idea, in the heterogeneity of an 'a-presentation'...[37]

Deleuze sometimes comes down a notch or two, in order to explain himself to the ordinary reader. But he does so in an endless stream of abstractions, from which all reference to concrete reality and the flow of human life has been excised. He does not argue, but encloses his key words in fortified boxes, which he firmly locks against all questioning before throwing the key away:

> There is a crucial experience of difference and a corresponding experiment: every time we find ourselves confronted or bound by a limitation or an opposition, we should ask what such a situation presupposes. It presupposes a swarm of differences, a pluralism of free, wild or untamed differences; a properly differential and original space and time; all of which persist alongside the simplifications of limitation and opposition. A more profound real element must be defined in order for oppositions of forces or limitations of forms to be drawn, one which is determined as an abstract and potential multiplicity. Oppositions are roughly cut from a delicate milieu of overlapping perspectives, of communicating distances, divergences and disparities, of heterogeneous potentials and intensities. Nor is it primarily a question of dissolving tensions in the identical, but rather...[38]

But rather what? You won't discover from the text, which continues piling abstraction on abstraction with no hint of a real question, still less of an answer. Is the book really about identity and difference? Has it even got as far as Frege's thoughts about identity in 'On Sense and Reference', or taken in the question whether propositions of numerical identity can be contingently true?[39] Who knows? The seamless web of abstractions continues to the very end of the book, at which point Nietzsche, the most concrete and immediate of modern philosophers, is wrapped in more

---

[37] Gilles Deleuze, *Difference and Repetition*, 1968, tr. Paul Patton, London, 1994, Bloomsbury edition, 2004, pp. 26–7.

[38] Ibid., p. 61.

[39] See, for example, the seminal argument in Saul Kripke, *Naming and Necessity*, Oxford, Wiley-Blackwell, 1981.

abstractions and reissued as a philosopher of 'difference', in rebellion against identity:

> Zarathustra is the dark precursor of eternal return. The eternal return eliminates precisely all those instances which strangle difference and prevent its transport by subjecting it to the quadruple yoke of representation. Difference is recovered, liberated, only at the limit of its power – in other words, by repetition in the endless return. The eternal return eliminates that which renders it impossible by rendering impossible the transport of difference.[40]

It is worth repeating that last sentence a few times, and experiencing the strange way in which meaning hovers in it, just out of reach, vanishing with a mysterious gust of cold air as we discover that the eternal return is in fact the rendering impossible of that which renders it impossible.

Incidentally, it would probably not be regarded by Deleuze, and certainly not by all of his followers, as a criticism to describe his works as nonsense. The response will immediately come that, in the *Logic of Sense* and elsewhere, he is explicitly challenging the distinction between sense and nonsense, showing that the true use of language is expressive, not representational, so that nonsense is as much a part of communication as what is normally called sense.[41] He invites us to read *The Logic of Sense* as a psychoanalytical novel, and wraps each sentence in the book so tightly into itself that it is rarely possibly to prise it open with the tools of logic. I doubt that Deleuze would have objected to my description of his style as that of the nonsense machine, and all that I am writing in this chapter might be understood, by a true Deleuzian, as a form of praise.

Still, it is worth reflecting for a little on the last block of prose that I quoted. (Deleuze writes without paragraphs. His pages are like cliff faces from which fragments can be broken away, only to yearn through their jagged edges for the mother stone.) Nietzsche's exuberant invocation of 'eternal recurrence' is not a metaphysical thesis. It is an exhortation to live *as if* everything eternally recurs. Maybe, by living in that way, I 'liberate' difference. But surely, *that* is not why Nietzsche argued as he did. He

---

[40] Ibid., p. 373.
[41] On this point see Helen Palmer, *Deleuze and Futurism: A Manifesto for Nonsense*, London, Bloomsbury, 2014.

exhorted us to live in this other way so as to possess ourselves of our individuality, our identity, our *this*-ness, our knowledge of the deep and irreplaceable sameness of the I. Throughout Nietzsche's life it was identity that obsessed him, and difference only as the most vivid sign of it.

One point, however, is suggested by Deleuze's sentences. In all human societies people have been troubled by time. Things come into being and pass away; but no human community has ever accepted this fact. In all places and times people have believed that there is a way into the eternal, a door out of time into a place where nothing changes and all is at rest within its being. And the key to this door is repetition. That is what sacred rituals, sacred words and sacred places provide: the prayers, chants, costumes, steps and gestures that must be repeated exactly, and for which there is no explanation other than that this is how things are done.

Sometimes, reading Deleuze, I think that he has something like that in mind – the primordial religious experience, which uses repetition as an icon of eternity. However he never *says* as much. The thought is too simple, too near to human realities, too obviously true to merit his attention, and if it is here and there suggested, like a seam of water trapped within the lithological stratum, it is never allowed to flow out into a clear standing pool.

Later, writing with Félix Guattari, Deleuze puts aside the abstractions of metaphysics, and becomes both more psychoanalytical and more political (Guattari was a Lacanian analyst, a Trotskyite and an active participant in all the revolutionary movements of 1968). Their influential book *L'anti-Oedipe* is at one level an attack on the Freudian theory of the Oedipus complex – or rather, an attack on the bourgeois family, the 'daddy, mummy, me' complex, whose inner dynamic and implicit catastrophe Freud had attempted to describe. Psychoanalysis, they suggest, remains fixated on this model, and therefore presents us with a false idea of development, as a return to the bourgeois family, rather than a liberating break with it. They describe the human being as a 'machine désirante' and also as the body voided of its organs, the body awaiting its identity, which it can either forge for itself (or can it?) or assume from the surrounding world of differences (or is it a world of identities? And when is difference an identity and identity a form of difference?).

The point is explained by two practising Deleuzians:

The body without organs is a presupposition of form and meaning, and thus the closest Deleuze ever comes to a figural description of immanence. A smooth space of pure movement and transition, it is impossible to conceive of without the process of organisation that will create shapes from it: the smooth space of the BwO is itself irresistible. What matters then is its relationship to organisation, both of the personal and social bodies, and time is marked out by the machine-like creation of a body or social system...[42]

From which you can understand why Deleuze and Guattari think that they have hit on the true explanation of schizophrenia.

The phrase 'body without organs' (BwO) is taken from the surrealist playwright and director Antonin Artaud, and Deleuze and Guattari use it to denote the body in its virtual state – the body prior to being 'actualized' in relationships. Schizophrenia, they suggest, is exactly what we should expect when the BwO is hit by capitalism: it is how we experience our humanity when the 'oedipianization' imposed by the regime of consumption empties the biological receptacle in which the human being is contained.[43] Of course, some details remain to be cleared up. Referring to Deleuze's *The Logic of Sense*, Slavoj Žižek writes:

> Is, on the one hand, the productive flux of pure Becoming not the BwO, the body not yet structured or determined as functional organs? And, on the other hand, are the OwaB [organs without a body] not the virtuality of the pure affect extracted from its embeddedness in a body...?[44]

Clearly, once this language is adopted a thousand questions can be asked and, even if they have no answers, this only adds to the sense of their relevance and profundity.

The pot is given another stir in *Mille plateaus*, a sequel to *L'Anti-Oedipe*, in which the stench of BwO is overpowering, issuing in rhapsodic belches like this:

> People ask, so what is this BwO? – But you're already on it, scurrying like a vermin, groping like a blind person, or running like a lunatic:

---

[42] Damian Sutton and David Martin-Jones, *Deleuze: A Guide for the Arts Student*, London, 2008, p. 112.

[43] Gilles Deleuze and Félix Guattari, *L'Anti-Oedipe: capitalisme et schizophrénie*, Paris, Éditions de Minuit, 1975, Ch. 2.

[44] Slavoj Žižek, *In Defense of Lost Causes*, London and New York, 2008, p. 368.

desert traveller and nomad of the steppes. On it we sleep, live our waking lives, fight – fight and are fought – seek our place, experience untold happiness and fabulous defeats; on it we penetrate and are penetrated; on it we love. On November 28, 1947, Artaud declares war on the organs: *To be done with the judgement of God*, 'for you can tie me up if you wish, but there is nothing more useless than an organ.' Experimentation: not only radiophonic but also biological and political, incurring censorship and repression. Corpus and Socius, politics and experimentation. They will not let you experiment in peace.[45]

Each particle of that comparatively lucid utterance makes sense. But what is the connection between them? There is no knowing. And that is the point. The reader is being granted brief glimpses of a store of hidden knowledge, to which the authors have the only key. The exultant tone, which one might read as a sign of mental disorder, shows total confidence in the revelation, displayed like a tantalizing ankle beneath a burqa.

There is more to *A Thousand Plateaus* however. As in *Difference and Repetition* Deleuze and Guattari introduce 'key words', two of which have since become every bit as important as the 'difference' of Saussurian linguistics, and the 'Other' of Kojève: 'rhizome' and 'territorialisation'. A rhizome is a plant stem that grows horizontally underground, enabling a plant to spread through its roots, as grass does. In his earlier work Deleuze advanced the view that 'identity' had hitherto characterized Western thinking, and that 'difference' must now replace it. A similar claim is now made for 'rhizomatic' thinking. Instead of the vertical tree – the up/down, cause/effect, root/branch – model of human thinking that has apparently dominated Western civilization hitherto, Deleuze and Guattari propose the rhizomatic model, in which thought spreads sideways, linking, including, growing like a forest, always encountering some other rhizome at its edge.

Western culture, they tell us, has presented a narrative dependent on binary divisions: cause and effect, us and them, one and many, and so on. Its 'assemblages of power' impose 'signifiance and subjectification as their determinate form of expression', and 'there is no signifiance without a despotic assemblage, no subjectification without an authoritarian assemblage'.[46] Worse, 'our semiotic of modern White Men, the semiotic

[45] Deleuze and Guattari, *A Thousand Plateaus*, tr. Brian Massumi, paperback edition, London, 2004, p. 174.
[46] Ibid., p. 211.

of capitalism, has attained this state of mixture in which signifiance and subjectification effectively interpenetrate.'[47] 'Signifiation' does not mean 'signification', but rather the habit of using signs. 'Subjectification' is the 'subjectivation' of Lacan, which we will encounter again in Badiou and Žižek – the process whereby the human being creates himself as a 'for-itself'. Somehow, in the conditions imposed on us by capitalism, our attempts at self-consciousness are fatefully muddled with our use of signs, and therefore with the 'despotic assemblage' and the 'authoritarian assemblage' that the two activities (are they activities, exactly, and are they really two?) in any case involve.

Our situation, in other words, is dire, and we need a remedy. And the remedy is the rhizome, which 'draws a plane that has no more dimensions than that which crosses it; therefore the multiplicity it constitutes is no longer subordinate to the One, but takes on a consistency of its own'.[48] Rhizomatic thinking replaces 'the One and the multiple with a distinction between types of multiplicities', though beware: sometimes the tree strikes back, and produces 'an arborification of multiplicities'.[49] The important point seems to be that rhizomes are connected as planes, strata, and not as trees (hence those who represent language through generative trees, as Chomsky does, have made a fundamental mistake about the available possibilities).

Rhizomatic development establishes a territory. But in doing so it 'deterritorializes' the previous occupants, as when weeds take over a garden, or colonists displace their competitors from the land where they settle. The concept of territorialization is given a vast and flexible extension by Deleuze and Guattari – it is what a flock of birds does as it spreads in flight, what the individual bird does when he marks out his territory with a song, what music does when it establishes a refrain, what people do when they settle down together, what flood water does when it spreads across a field. And in all such cases we witness deterritorialization (as when the flock goes forward on a line before spreading elsewhere, or when the nomads pack their tent and move on, or when you pull the plug from the bath) and a reterritorialization, when things settle into a new formation.

The process of deterritorialization always encounters its opposite, so that deterritorialization and reterritorialization occur together. Deleuze

---

[47] Ibid., p. 213.
[48] Ibid., p. 588.
[49] Ibid.

and Guattari offer a peculiar explanation of this, through the example of a wasp pollinating an orchid:

> How could movements of deterritorialisation and processes of reterritorialisation not be relative, always connected, caught up in one another? The orchid deterritorialises by forming an image, a tracing of a wasp; but the wasp reterritorialises on that image. The wasp is nevertheless deterritorialised, becoming a piece in the orchid's reproductive apparatus. But it reterritorialises the orchid by transporting its pollen. Wasp and orchid, as heterogeneous elements, form a rhizome.[50]

As you can see from that explanation – which is the clearest that is offered in *A Thousand Plateaus* – we are dealing with new words, but not with new concepts. In the place of definitions we are offered associations, and in the place of theories we are given terms that can be stretched from category to category like transparent wrapping, under which everything appears as it was, and yet at the same time strangely transfigured, brought into relation with alien matter like trophies in a shopping spree. Indeed, if you wanted a word to describe the intellectual method of Deleuze and Guattari, there is none more apposite than 'packaging'.

The resulting nonsense, although it cannot easily be deciphered intellectually, can be deciphered politically. It is *directed* nonsense, and it is directed at the enemy. We are to discard the old hierarchies, the binary structures, the 'trees' of the bourgeois family and the capitalist machine, and to reform ourselves as rhizomes, grass-roots communities of underground activists, who will achieve the revolution through the reterritorialization of desire, and the deterritorialization of the existing hierarchies. This revolutionary goal will come about through the new language that Deleuze and Guattari are offering – not the language of psychoanalysis, which merely reconciles the bourgeoisie to their condition, but the language of 'schizanalysis', which is an assault on the existing structures in the name of desire.

It is not just the *existence* of the enemy that is under attack, therefore. The assault is aimed primarily at the language through which the enemy lays claim to the world, the language that we know as rational argument

---

[50] Deleuze and Guattari, *A Thousand Plateaus: Capitalism and Schizophrenia*, tr. Brian Massumi, 3rd edn, London, 1996, p. 10.

and the pursuit of truth, and which is dismissed by Deleuze and Guatarri as mere 'representation', rather than the transformation that their writings herald. 'The love of truth', declared Jacques Lacan, 'is the love of this weakness whose veil we have lifted; it is the love of what truth hides, which is called castration.'[51] The love of truth, therefore, has no independent validity, being merely a disguise worn by the weaker party. There is no real commodity at issue save power. And victory is brought by the magic wand, the square root of minus one which, thrown at the enemy, cuts off his balls. Hence, as Deleuze and Guattari put it, 'the notions of relevance, necessity, the point of something, are a thousand times more significant than the notion of truth, not as substitutes for truth, but as a measure of the truth of what I'm saying.'[52] Truth is subservient to power, and the power is mine, the power of relevance and necessity.

Deleuze and Guattari tell us that 'the BwO is what remains when you take everything away'.[53] And that exactly describes their mode of argument. All normal forms of thought, all empirical observation, all pre-existing knowledge is dissolved in their delirious prose, which ranges over everything and anything, to produce exactly nothing. At the end of every paragraph there is only this mysterious 'body without organs', whose nature is never defined.

The authoritative-sounding language – in which assertoric sentences succeed each other without a break, and with never the slightest nod towards a real or imagined interlocutor – consists of undefined technicalities, imagined 'questions' that cannot be translated into any other idiom, and occasional glimpses of the real world, but so distorted by the language as to be all but unrecognizable. Abundant footnotes, referring to out-of-the-way works in political theory, anthropology, biology, musicology, particle physics, etc., serve further to intimidate the reader, and the undergraduate, faced with the resulting text at the top of his reading list, is given no alternative but to parrot its terms, and to distinguish with a straight face and in a scientific tone of voice:

(1) BwO's, which are different types, genuses, or substantial attributes. For example, the Cold of the drugged BwO, the pain of the masochist

---

[51] Jacques Lacan, *The Seminar of Jacques Lacan*, ed. Jacques-Alain Miller, Book XVII, New York, Norton, 2007, p. 52.
[52] *What is Philosophy*, tr. Hugh Tomlinson and Graham Burchell, New York, Columbia University Press, 1996, p. 130.
[53] *A Thousand Plateaus*, op. cit., p. 176.

BwO. Each has its degree 0 as its principle of production (*remissio*). (2) What happens on each type of BwO, in other words, the modes, the intensities that are produced, the waves that pass (*latitudo*). (3) The potential totality of all BwO's, the plane of consistency (*Omnitudo*, sometimes called the BwO).[54]

If you can reproduce that language – and it is, after all, not so hard, since there are no constraints of logic, truth, observation or sincerity – you will be on the way to the A grade that your tutor will certainly wish to give to an essay that endorses his own claims to be a scholar. The paperback of *A Thousand Plateaus* extends to over seven hundred pages in the English edition, each of which demands hours of attention from the devout. The fact that it has been printed eleven times in the last ten years is a sobering commentary on what higher education in the humanities now amounts to.

Two features of the nonsense machine help to explain its popularity. First is its use in defeating the enemy. This enemy is the bourgeoisie, the class that has (according to the indelible Marxist caricature of history) monopolized the institutions of French society since the Revolution of 1789, and whose 'ideology' has spread through all the channels of communication since then. Behind the patriarchal family excoriated by de Beauvoir, behind the institutions of the prison and the madhouse debunked by Foucault, behind the oedipianized '*machine désirante*' of Deleuze and Guattari and the norms of heterosexual respectability mocked by Sartre in *Saint Genet* has stood the same force, both economic and spiritual and too vast and pervasive to be identical with any merely human group, the force of the bourgeoisie. Even when the dismissal of bourgeois society is tacked on with pins, as in the early works of Deleuze, it is emphatically present, responsible for all that is most lucid in these curious texts. Indeed, it is the only part of the text that addresses the reader rather than communing in a dream syntax with itself.

Second, the nonsense machine has been put together from second-hand parts: ideas that were lying around at the end of the war, when the post-war generation was attempting to shake off the memory of occupation and betrayal. The Saussurian distinctions between 'signified and signifier', between *langue* and *parole*, between phoneme and morpheme, entered the new language, alongside the theories of base and superstructure, use value and exchange value, production and

---

[54] Ibid., p. 183.

exploitation taken from Marx and the theories of repression and the libido borrowed from Freud. The distinctions and theories were welded together by the revolutionary fire, and extraordinary and exciting results often followed, such as Lacan's proof that 'schizophrenia', and I quote from one of his followers, 'designates a purely metonymic form of desire untrammelled by the metaphoric associations of equivalence and meaning imposed on desire by social and/or linguistic codes operating in the name of the father'.[55] Or Guattari's proof that, by getting beyond the signifying semiologies in which we have hitherto been bound to become 'a-signifying semiotic machines' we will 'free desire-production, the singularities of desire, from the signifiers of national, familial, personal, racial, humanist, and transcendent values (including the semiotic myth of a return to nature), to the pre-signifying world of a-semiotic encodings'.[56] The monsters of unmeaning that loom in this prose attract our attention because they are built from forgotten theories, forged together in weird and ghoulish shapes, like gargoyles made from the debris of a battlefield. And always the gargoyles are sticking out their tongues at the bourgeoisie.

Moreover, the machine never casts itself off from that one all-important idea, acquired during the great pre-war self-examination, which has not lost its credibility, an idea that endures because it is not a scientific hypothesis that stands to be refuted, but a philosophical reflection on the nature of consciousness. This is the idea of the Other rescued from 'classical German philosophy' by Kojève. We have seen this idea in Sartre and Foucault. It comes dressed in maternal garb in Lacan, and it reappears in Deleuze and Guattari, who adapt the Other to their own *folie à deux* in prose that it would be hard to caricature:

The Other Person is enough to make any length a possible depth in space, and vice versa, so that if this concept did not function in the perceptual field, transitions and inversions would become incomprehensible, and we would always run up against things, the possible having disappeared...(In) the concept of the other person, the possible world does not exist outside the face that expresses it,

---

[55] Eugene W. Holland, 'From Schizophrenia to Social Control', in Eleanor Kaufman and Kevin Jon Heller, eds, *Deleuze and Guattari: New Mappings in Politics, Philosophy and Culture*, Minneapolis and London, University of Minnesota Press, 1998.
[56] Gary Genosko, 'Guattari's Schizoanalytic Semiotics', in ibid.

although it is distinguished from it as expressed and expression; and the face in turn is the vicinity of the words for which it is already the megaphone...[57]

By the early 1970s, a kind of impenetrable meta-literature, literature about literature about literature, had evolved, incorporating the features I have mentioned, and about which only one thing was clear – namely, what side it was on. If the politics were obvious, then the obscurity of the language was no defect. On the contrary: in these circumstances obscurity could be read as proof of a profundity and originality too great to be encompassed by ordinary words. Hence obscurity served to validate the politics, to show that throwing stones at policemen was the conclusion of a practical syllogism that had the highest intellectual authority for its every step.

In their now famous book *Intellectual Impostures*, Alan Sokal and Jean Bricmont attack the phony expertise of Deleuze, Guattari, Baudrillard, Lacan and many more.[58] You may not be persuaded by their arguments, or by Malcolm Bradbury's *Mensonge*, his brilliant satire of postmodern literary manners.[59] My own criticism of Sokal and Bricmont is not that they are unfair to their targets – in my view they lean over backwards in the effort to find sense in the passages they attack. Nor do I blame them for failing to understand that it is acceptable, in the square mile around the Rue Mouffetard, to treat science as *jouissance*. My real criticism is that they overlook the political significance of the postmodern meta-literature. They identify themselves as men of the left, which is of course necessary if they are to have the remotest chance of influencing those who are tempted to join the stampede towards postmodern meaninglessness. But they fail to point out, and perhaps fail even to see, that being on the left is what it is all about.[60]

The boiling tide of nonsense flows between secure walls on which indelible messages have been chiselled. These tell us that the world is in the hands of the capitalist Other, and is awaiting the great Event of its

---

[57] Gilles Deleuze and Félix Guattari, *What is Philosophy?*, op. cit., pp. 18–19.

[58] Alan Sokal and Jean Bricmont, *Impostures intellectuelles*, op. cit.

[59] *Mensonge: My Strange Quest for Henri Mensonge, Structuralism's Hidden Hero*, London, King Penguin, 1985.

[60] Chomsky, a radical leftist with a genuinely scientific mind, has, it seems, given his own powerful demolition of the nonsense machine. See the conversation circulated in 1995 at http://cscs.umich.edu/~crshalizi/chomsky-on-postmodernism.html.

liberation – the revolution that is to be summoned by the new literature of spells. It does not matter from what source those spells are taken – topology, quantum mechanics, set theory, anything will do so long as it intimidates the enemy. This enemy is the doubter, the one who hesitates before the moment, who does not recognize, as he should, that the call to action is now.

That, in my view, is what is really going on in passages like this:

> …Vice-diction…presides over the distribution of distinctive points within the Idea [and] has two procedures which intervene both in the determination of the conditions of the problem and in the correlative genesis of cases of solution: these are, in the first case, the *specification of adjunct fields* and, in the second, the *condensation of singularities*. On the one hand, in the progressive determination of the conditions, we must in effect discover the adjunctions which complete the initial field of the problem as such – in other words, the varieties of the multiplicity in all its dimensions, the fragments of ideal future or past events which, by the same token, render the problem solvable; and we must establish the modality in which these enclose or are connected with the initial field. On the other hand…[61]

In his role as curious philosopher Adrian Moore puts his ear to the ground beside this rambling and self-vaunting prose, and hears quite another voice inside it – the voice of the metaphysician, wondering whether the world is as it seems and whether our common sense is really a way of 'making sense'. But his is an unusual, not to say eccentric reading. For the mass of commentators (and they do indeed form a mass) Deleuze is to be received as a prophet. His locked-in prose offers, through its very syntactical shackles, the key to liberation. By means of it you can pass beyond the old world of Western thought, into the new world of desire. You become the BwO, the great pseudo-Dionysus, who through endless repetition will triumph in the Now. For such readers it is no surprise that the passage quoted goes on as follows:

> It is as though every Idea has two faces, which are like love and anger: love in the search for fragments, the progressive determination and linking of the ideal adjoint fields; anger in the condensation of

---

[61] *Difference and Repetition*, op. cit., p. 239.

singularities which, by dint of ideal events, defines the concentration of a 'revolutionary situation' and causes the Idea to explode into the actual. It is in this sense that Lenin had Ideas.[62]

Having touched base, so to speak, with the real agenda, the prose then rambles on, by way of the differential calculus, to linguistics, to Saussure's assertion that 'in language there are only differences', to phonology and the work of Gustave Guillaume, and so on and on without pausing to define a question, and picking up terms and technicalities with only the faintest suggestion that their meaning really matters.

Occasionally there is an abrupt and arresting paradox. For example, we are told that 'the Idea knows nothing of negation'; we learn that 'while it is in the nature of consciousness to be false, problems by their nature escape consciousness'.[63] And because these hints are dropped in the course of endorsing (without explaining) the argument of *Das Kapital*, the reader can be assumed to accept them as obvious. Stand back from them, however, and you will surely view them with astonishment. If problems by their nature escape consciousness, how can Deleuze have become conscious of this? No matter, since 'the transcendent object of the faculty of sociability is revolution. In this sense, revolution is the social power of difference...'[64] It is therefore in these moments of abrupt lucidity that the agenda is revealed. It could be that the acute ear of Adrian Moore hears, in the theory of 'difference', an answer to the metaphysics of identity that has taken up such a secure position in analytical philosophy. But Deleuze's followers don't give a toss about that. What excites them is the promise that 'difference' means revolution, and the endless impenetrable technicalities that are adduced in its favour also spell the intellectual defeat of the capitalist enemy.

Emerging from the Deleuzian nonsense machine is a new academic style, which has syntax without semantics. Turns of phrase implying deep concentration and a straining at the limits of abstract and mathematical thought are in constant evidence. When real thought appears, it is out of context, shorn of its foundations, reduced to a scattering of uprooted technicalities.[65] Hence the style enables thought and non-thought to

---

[62] Ibid.
[63] Ibid., pp. 258, 259.
[64] Ibid.
[65] If you need an example, consider the mad meditations on the symbol dx on p. 217 of *Difference and Repetition*.

compete on equal terms, employing the same turns of phrase and the same argumentative structures. The privileges previously enjoyed by truth, validity and rational argument are cancelled at a blow, and the materials now exist with which to build an impressive scholarly career on a foundation of nothing. Moreover, howsoever you build your career, one thing will be certain, you are 'on the left' politically, vindicated by all the righteous causes (whatever they might be) of the day, and therefore immune from serious criticism. Your academic discourse is really play, self-expression, *jouissance*. What matters is where you stand, and in this you are impeccably correct, secure in your academic entitlement, and a worthy recipient of taxes paid by the bourgeoisie.

7 CULTURE WARS WORLDWIDE: THE NEW LEFT FROM GRAMSCI TO SAID

The Parisian nonsense machine was used to mount a ballistic assault on the bourgeois culture, throwing dense blocks of impenetrable Newspeak over the battlements into the public square of the besieged city. The effect was to destroy the conversation on which civil society depends. All delicate ideas concerning law, constitution and the roots of civil order, all the ways in which human beings argue over rights and duties, honour their opponents and seek for compromise, were flattened by mathemes, 'deterritorialized' and buried beneath the debris of the great Event. This was the turning point in a battle that has been raging now for a century – the battle to take possession of the culture, by defining the intellectual life as an exclusively left-wing preserve.

We have already seen how this battle was fought in the German-speaking territories in the wake of the First World War. The 'bourgeois' conception of reality was dismissed as 'false consciousness', 'fetishism' and 'reification', and the revolution was proposed as a kind of intellectual purification, in which the proletarian consciousness would displace the rule of ideology and things would be seen for the first time as they truly are. The battle spread to Italy, where it took shape as a confrontation between communism and fascism, and where the principal weapon was not the impenetrable Newspeak that reached its apogee in Deleuze but the common-sense sociology of Antonio Gramsci. It was from this sociological approach that the cultural ideas of the New Left in Britain and America largely derived, and their influence is probably as great today as it was in Italy before the war.

'Gramsci was an extraordinary philosopher, perhaps a genius, probably the most original communist thinker of the twentieth century in Western Europe' (Eric Hobsbawm). 'If we except the great protagonists of the Soviet revolution, there is no personality in the history of the workers' movement whose person and work have aroused greater interest than Gramsci's' (Norberto Bobbio). 'Who has *really* attempted to follow up the explorations of Marx and Engels? I can think only of Gramsci' (Louis Althusser). Such praise, from eminent members of the intellectual establishment, is but a small part of the tribute that has been offered in recent times to Gramsci. We have seen the founding in Rome of a Gramsci Institute, the publication of virtually all the posthumous works, and the inclusion of Gramsci in a thousand university courses, as a political theorist, a revolutionary, a cultural critic and a philosopher. This is not the result of a few scholarly articles only, but of a vast movement of sympathy, a kind of hunger for moral and intellectual guidance, which singled out Gramsci as its object, which clung to him ardently during the last decades of the twentieth century, and which is only now beginning to wane.

Imprisoned by the fascist government in 1926, Gramsci wrote his most important texts while incarcerated, and died while still confined in 1937, having by then been moved to a public hospital. For the romantic generation of the baby-boomers he was a perfect symbol of their inheritance – the consumptive intellectual, victim of fascism, who had devoted his whole life to composing the case against it. He was the archetypal revolutionary hero, silenced during his lifetime, and surfacing as pure spirit in the words that he left.

The idea of the revolutionary hero is not new. It inspired the Italian Risorgimento and the cult of Garibaldi; it was a recurring theme of literature in nineteenth-century Russia, and the original inspiration for Wagner's *Ring* cycle. But it has always been problematic for the Marxists. Indeed, it is one of the most interesting paradoxes of Marxism that it has combined a theory of history that denies the efficacy of leadership with a revolutionary practice that has depended entirely on leadership for its success, and which has been able to consolidate its hold on power only by establishing habits of reverence towards the revolutionary hero. This paradox – the problem of 'so-called great men', as Engels described it – is one to which Gramsci, in his theoretical writings, directly addressed himself. But he could never have foreseen that a generation of students would one day be taught to see him in the same light and with the same uncritical adulation that they were taught to see Trotsky, Mao, Castro and Che Guevara: as leader, teacher and hero of a worldwide revolutionary movement.

Every critical development on the left requires an atmosphere of 'struggle', such as existed in 1968, which provides the necessary feelings of solidarity. But it also requires a figurehead, who is hero or martyr in the cause of revolution. In order to qualify it is not sufficient to be a resolute leader. It is necessary also to be an intellectual; to claim a theoretical and not just a practical importance. The figureheads of modern left-wing movements have therefore been consistently presented in those terms: the myth concerning the 'brain of Lenin' is but one instance of a permanent hagiographic process, whereby second-rate thinkers (such as Lenin) are presented as paragons of insight and wisdom, whose words are oracles, and whose deeds are inspired by knowledge.

The effect of this process is felt in two spheres. In the sphere of practical politics a left-wing movement is able to present itself as a rescue: it is the way in which real ideas and real knowledge step in to rectify the blunders and corruption of the mere mortals who have hitherto attempted to manage things. The leader personifies truth, in a fight to the death with error. But the process is also felt in the sphere of culture, and felt more profoundly, since culture is a sphere that is largely unguarded against enthusiasm, a massively subsidized theatre whose stage is up for grabs. Hence it was through culture – through universities, art schools, theatres and books – that the New Left had its greatest and most immediate impact during the 1970s.

More impressive, perhaps, than the example of Lenin is that of Mao, whose titanic strength and military genius could never have qualified him for the position of figurehead had it not also been possible to believe in his 'theoretical correctness' and in the intellectual prowess that was displayed by it. Hence a whole generation of students was encouraged to study works of philosophy and political theory which, judged from a point of view outside the hagiographic zeal of Mao's admirers, appear risibly naïve and fraught with the crudest misunderstandings. There are further examples – Ho Chi Minh, Che Guevara and Stalin – but none more vivid to those of us who were students in the 1960s than Gramsci, who did for the sixties what Lenin and Stalin had done for the thirties and forties: he convinced his following that revolutionary practice and theoretical correctness are identical attributes, that learning equals wisdom and that wisdom equals the right to rule.

That idea was identified by Eric Voegelin as the root of Gnosticism,[1] the primal heresy within the Christian worldview, to which all subsequent heresies return. And it partly explains the emotional appeal of Gramsci's

---

[1] Eric Voegelin, *Science, Politics and Gnosticism*, Chicago, 1968.

species of leftism in Catholic countries, in Italy especially. For not only is a 'clerisy' already present in the Italian national culture; there is a widespread belief, fostered by the Church, that leadership is in every sphere the outcome of education. Gramsci took this legacy in a secular direction. With a frankness that would be surprising in a more orthodox Marxist, he devotes a considerable amount of his work to the role of the intellectuals, directly asserting not only that they are the true agents of revolution but also that they owe their legitimacy to the 'correctness' of their views.[2] It follows that I, the critical intellectual, have the right to rule over you, the merely prejudiced person.

The revolutionaries of the 1960s retained their faith in Mao and, by extraordinary contortions, were able to see the Cultural Revolution as something other than a war against the intellect. But they dimly perceived that intellectual leaders are not to be trusted to respect an intellectual following. Stalin had been unmasked, and a certain suspicion was beginning to fall on Lenin. True, there was always Trotsky, but Gramsci possessed an advantage that Trotsky could not claim: he was not only dead, but dead in the struggle against fascism. It is testimony to the success of communist propaganda that it has been able to persuade so many people that fascism and communism are polar opposites and that there is a single scale of political ideology stretching from 'far left' to 'far right'. Thus, while communism is on the far left, it is simply one further stage along a road that all intellectuals must go in order not to be contaminated by the true evil of our times, which is fascism.

It is perhaps easier for an English writer than it is for an Italian to see through that nonsense, and to perceive what it is designed to conceal: the deep structural similarity between communism and fascism, both as theory and as practice, and their common antagonism to parliamentary and constitutional forms of government. Even if we accept the – highly fortuitous – identification of National Socialism and Italian Fascism, to speak of either as the true political opposite of communism is to betray the most superficial understanding of modern history. In truth there is an opposite of all the 'isms', and that is negotiated politics, without an 'ism' and without a goal other than the peaceful coexistence of rivals.

---

[2] *Selections from the Prison Notebooks*, ed. and tr. Q. Hoare and G. Nowell-Smith, London, 1971, pp. 425 ff.

Communism, like fascism, involved the attempt to create a mass popular movement and a state bound together under the rule of a single party, in which there will be total cohesion around a common goal. It involved the elimination of opposition, by whatever means, and the replacement of ordered dispute between parties by clandestine 'discussion' within the single ruling elite. It involved taking control – 'in the name of the people' – of the means of communication and education, and instilling a principle of command throughout the economy.

Both movements regarded law as optional and constitutional constraints as irrelevant – for both were essentially revolutionary, led from above by an 'iron discipline'. Both aimed to achieve a new kind of social order, unmediated by institutions, displaying an immediate and fraternal cohesiveness. And in pursuit of this ideal association – called a *fascio* by nineteenth-century Italian socialists – each movement created a form of military government, involving the total mobilization of the entire populace,[3] which could no longer do even the most peaceful-seeming things except in a spirit of war, and with an officer in charge. This mobilization was put on comic display, in the great parades and festivals that the two ideologies created for their own glorification.

Of course there are differences. Fascist governments have sometimes come to power by democratic election, whereas communist governments have always relied on a *coup d'état*. And the public ideology of communism is one of equality and emancipation, while that of fascism emphasizes distinction and triumph. But the two systems resemble each other in all other aspects, and not least in their public art, which displays the same kind of bombast and kitsch – the same attempt to change reality by shouting at the top of the voice.

It will be said that communism is perhaps like that in practice, but only because the practice has betrayed the theory. Of course, the same could be said of fascism; but it has been an important leftist strategy, and a major component of Soviet post-war propaganda, to contrast a purely theoretical communism with 'actually existing' fascism, in other words to contrast a promised heaven with a real hell. This does not merely help with the recruitment of supporters: it reinforces the habit of thinking in dichotomies, of representing every choice as an either/or, of inducing the thought that the issue is simply one of for or against.

---

[3] On the importance of the element of mobilization, see Leonard Schapiro, *Totalitarianism*, London, 1972, pp. 38–9.

Thus, when Lenin announced that '*the only choice* is: either bourgeois or socialist ideology; there is no middle course',[4] he merely translated into a slogan the Marxist theory of class struggle. He was echoed by the French socialist leader, Jean Jaurès: 'No social force can remain neutral when a great movement is on foot. If they are not with us, they will be against us.'[5] Hence, Jaurès continued, the peasants 'must be willing to sell their produce at the common shop' – i.e. on terms dictated by the socialists. In any other event, they join 'the enemy'.

The same threatening posture ('you *must* be willing') is encountered everywhere in Gramsci's early writings,[6] and is encapsulated in the slogan with which he first led the Italian Communist Party into battle against Mussolini – 'between fascism and communism there is no middle road', with which slogan Mussolini, being an intellectual of similar make-up, was disposed to agree.

There is another reason for Gramsci's canonization, however. He provided the theory that promised both to solve the problem of 'so-called great men', and also to establish the intellectual's right to govern. In *The Modern Prince* and other writings from his prison years[7] he moved on from Leninist sloganizing and devoted himself to the task of reconciling the Marxist theory of history and society with a philosophy of political action.

Gramsci referred to his theory as 'the philosophy of praxis', and developed it in opposition to the 'vulgar materialism' of Bukharin.[8] This vulgar materialism raised the problems that called forth from Althusser the serpentine contortions that I discussed in Chapter 6. If 'base' determines 'superstructure' – if the works of the spirit are by-products of economic processes that they do not control – what place is there for political (and specifically revolutionary) action? And if the base moves ineluctably in response to the growth of productive forces, how can a social system survive the point at which it enters into conflict with economic growth? How can the capitalist order endure, when it begins to 'fetter' the economy?

---

[4] V. I. Lenin, *What is to Be Done?* (1902) in *Selected Works* (Moscow, 1977), vol. 1, pp. 121–2.
[5] Jean Jaurès, *Studies in Socialism*, tr. Mildred Mintum, 2nd edn, London, 1908, p. 124.
[6] See especially the addresses to the Lyons Congress, in *Selections from the Political Writings, 1921–26*, ed. and tr. Q. Hoare, London, 1978, pp. 313–78.
[7] In ibid. and also *The Modern Prince and Other Writings*, tr. L. Marks, The Gramsci Institute in Rome, New York, 1957.
[8] N. I. Bukharin, *Historical Materialism: A System of Sociology*, Moscow, 1921.

Those questions prompted Gramsci's theory of 'hegemony'.[9] A social order can survive through crisis, he argued, because of the complex nature of class domination. Under capitalism the bourgeois class holds power not merely because it controls the means of production but also because it establishes a 'hegemony' throughout civil society and the state, reserving to itself the offices of government and the key positions of influence in all the institutions of civil society. Religion, education, communication, indeed the whole of civil society falls under bourgeois control.

The result of this hegemony is twofold. First, it enables a class to exercise (whether or not consciously) a concerted political will, and thereby to control the effects of an economic crisis, and to ensure the survival of the social order from which it derives its power. Second, it places in the hands of a ruling class the instruments of education and indoctrination, whereby to propagate the belief in its legitimacy. That is how priesthood works: through representing all customs and institutions as ordained of God, and so unalterable. By virtue of this dual influence a ruling class can exert itself to overcome the pressures that rise from the economic base, and the base becomes subject to a reciprocal influence from the institutional and cultural superstructure. To put the point another way: the Marxist theory of history, which explains all historical development as the product of changes in the economic infrastructure, is false. Historical development is as much the outcome of political will (as our 'bourgeois' historians have always insisted) as the outcome of 'material' processes.

Gramsci does not put it in quite that way: he writes of a 'dialectical' relation between superstructure and base,[10] thus using the jargon of Marxism in order to say what its opponents deeply believe, which is that history is on no one's side. Nevertheless, Gramsci's rebuttal of Marxist determinism is fundamental to his own 'philosophy of praxis'. It enables him to do what classical Marxism cannot do, which is to rehabilitate the political sphere. Politics becomes an active principle of change, which can stand against economic pressures and curtail or defeat them.

---

[9] This theory derives from the prison writings and is given in *The Modern Prince* and elsewhere. It is very clear from Gramsci's language that he had always in mind the celebrated preface to *A Critique of Political Economy*, in which Marx delivered in aphoristic form the complete outline of his theory of history.

[10] See also the discussion in Joseph V. Famia, *Gramsci's Political Thought*, Oxford, 1981, Ch. 3.

Communist politics then becomes possible, not as a revolutionary movement from below, but as a steady replacement of the ruling hegemony – a long march through the institutions, as it was later described. Thus the superstructure will be gradually transformed, to the point where the new social order, the emergence of which was blocked by the old hegemony, is able to come forth under its own impulsion. This process, called 'passive revolution', can be accomplished only by the conjunction of two forces: that exerted from above by the communist intellectuals, who steadily replace the hegemony of the bourgeoisie, and that exerted from below by the 'masses', who bear within themselves the seeds of the new social order that has grown from their labour.

The revolutionary transformation occurs only when those forces act in harmony, as an 'historical bloc'. The role of the Party is to produce that harmony, by uniting the intellectuals to the masses as a single disciplined force. The Party is the 'Modern Prince', the single agent of true political change, which can transform society only because it absorbs into its collective action all the smaller actions of the intelligentsia, and combines correct thinking with brute strength. Hence the Party must gradually replace every organization that holds any position within the hegemony of political influence.

Gramsci thought that this kind of systematic infiltration would precipitate the abolition of the state. The communist intellectuals and the masses are, he believed, bound together by an instinctive sympathy. Hence, when they have joined forces, there would no longer be a need for a coercive state. In its place would emerge a new form of government by consensus.[11] Like so many intellectuals of the left, Gramsci does not analyse this ideal government (this 'administration of things', as Engels described it). His argument is therefore powerless to persuade his opponent, who is sceptical precisely of the *results* of communism, and has no doubt about the means for achieving them.

Thus to the realist who asks how, in this society of the future, conflicts are to be accommodated or resolved, Gramsci has no reply. The communist shares with the fascist an overriding contempt for opposition. The purpose of politics is not to live with opposition, but to remove it – to achieve the condition in which opposition no longer exists (the 'historical bloc'). The question of opposition is, however, the single

---

[11] See, for example, the letter to Tania (2 May 1932) in *Letters from Prison*, ed. and tr. Lynne Lawner, pp. 234–5.

most important issue in politics. Conflicts between individuals lead, by free association, to conflicts between groups, to rivalries and factions that will inevitably express themselves in competition for power. How is that competition to be managed? In particular, how is the Communist Party to respond to opposition to its rule? The Leninist prediction is that there will be no opposition, and in a sense that prediction was verified when the opposition disappeared. What else was the Cheka for?

The question is crucial to a 'Marxist humanist' who seeks, like Gramsci, for a politics adapted to human nature. Gramsci assumes that the masses will be united behind the intellectuals. At the same time he is aware of the many millions (who for some reason are not to be included in the 'masses') who had provided fascism with the kind of mass support that communism has seldom if ever achieved. It is indeed the very historical *reality* of fascism that undermines the communist dream – the dream of a society without conflict and opposition, not because the first is resolved and the second accommodated, but because the 'conditions' of conflict have been removed. Marxists assume these conditions to be social, changeable, dependent on 'antagonistic production relations'. But if the conditions of conflict lie, as they evidently do lie, in human nature, then to hope for their removal is to entertain an inhuman hope and to be moved towards inhuman action.

Revolution, according to Gramsci, is not an ineluctable force that sweeps us away, but an *action*, undertaken by heroic individuals. Moreover it is an action that can be pursued without dirtying your hands in the factory. You can calmly proceed to whatever comfortable office has been provided, there to work for the downfall of the bourgeois hegemony, while enjoying its fruits. Such a philosophy is extremely useful to the intellectual – whose views and patience would be severely challenged outside the university – and it is the natural philosophy of student revolution. Add the charmed dichotomy of communism versus fascism – the dichotomy illustrated by Gramsci's own heroic life – and the picture is complete. An enemy is identified, a 'struggle' defined, and a theory provided to show that you can fight with the heroes merely by staying at your desk.

But all this – pleasing though it may be to the person in search of 'painless praxis' – raises considerable doubts as to Gramsci's Marxist credentials. For is he not simply recommending a new class society, with the Party as collective 'philosopher king' and with the intellectuals enjoying the privileges that were once enjoyed by their 'bourgeois' predecessors? Here and there in the *Prison Notebooks* Gramsci wrestles with this question, arguing first that the intellectuals are not a class, and second that the intellectuals, by virtue of their educative role, will be accepted by the masses, so that there will be no coercion involved.[12]

Neither of those arguments is plausible, and the tortuous reasoning that supports them barely conceals Gramsci's awareness that this is so. For the theory of hegemony implies the rejection of the economic definition of class put forward by Marx. It implies the recognition that collective agents exist which have the power accorded by Marxism to classes, and yet which are formed by a *unity of purpose*, such as we might attribute to an intellectual elite. Moreover the ability of a ruling class to persuade the masses (through its priestly arm) to accept its rule was precisely one of the features of the old 'class society' that Gramsci wished to expose and to undermine.

Why is the new priesthood any different, in this respect, from the old? Why is it better for the masses to be dominated by an intellectual elite, than by a hegemony of honest bourgeois? The theory of 'the Party as prince' makes fully clear that the communist future will involve an immense allocation of power to those appointed to 'administer' things. To argue that the power is not exerted *over* the masses, merely because they are to accept and cooperate with it, is to be the victim of an ideological illusion comparable to the belief in the divine right of kings.

To be fair, such issues are not discussed by Gramsci in the *Notebooks* with the assiduity that would permit him to resolve them. The best that could be said is that he so buries them in literary obscurity as to permit the faithful to assume whatever answer they may currently require. But it is interesting to look back to the original of Gramsci's theory of the Party. Gramsci's early writings show that he had grasped two important truths: first, that there are intellectuals who are active anti-communists; second, that there are many non-intellectuals who are prepared to be led by them, so thwarting the aims of the Communist Party.

He invented a class to which these recalcitrant people could be assigned, and, because they must be rigorously excluded from the irreproachable 'masses', they had to be members of the 'bourgeoisie'. Thus was born the myth of the 'bourgeois' nature of fascism. However, it was also palpably the case that the lowest orders of society were more disposed to follow

---

[12] See, for example, the crucial passage 'The Formation of Intellectuals', in *The Modern Prince and Other Writings*, pp. 118–25.

Gramsci's rival intellectual Mussolini than to follow Gramsci himself. Hence the classification of fascism was revised down a notch: fascism was described as a 'petty bourgeois' movement:

> What is Italian fascism? It is the insurrection of the lowest stratum of the Italian bourgeoisie, the stratum of the layabouts, of the ignorant, of the adventurers to whom the war gave the illusion of being good for something and of necessarily counting for something, who have been carried forward by the state of political and moral decadence...[13]

Gramsci thus initiated a standard communist evasion: a vast popular movement that is anti-communist is never a movement of the 'masses', whereas a *coup d'état* by communist intellectuals is always supported by the 'masses', whatever the strength and nature of the opposition, and however thin on the ground the 'masses' turn out to be. Movements like fascism are movements of the 'petit bourgeois' class. The same theory is repeated when leftist historians describe Hitler's rise to power, since clearly the working class could not have supported so appalling a result.

James Joll writes that Gramsci believed that the fascist regime had no class base (and hence was not genuinely 'revolutionary').[14] On the contrary, Gramsci believed that, precisely because it had come to power, fascism must have such a base. He invented a name for this alien class, which, despite including a majority of Italians, was to be regarded as quite distinct from the 'masses', a mere oppositional 'fraction' that, in the outcome of the final 'struggle', would be duly liquidated. And he studied the organization of the party that had led it to power, guided by an intellectual.

In this way he learned the lesson of the fascists, the lesson of 'corporatism', which is the true original of his theory of 'hegemony'. Society, he realized, is composed of a thousand small institutions, a thousand associations, a thousand patterns of communication and response. To reach into every one of these and to impose upon them – while safeguarding the hegemonic power that they contain – the iron discipline of party leadership: this is the secret of politics. This is what had led the fascists to power and what had formed, for the first time since the birth of the modern Italian state, the unity about a common purpose

---

[13] *L'Ordine Nuovo*, 11 March 1921.
[14] James Joll, *Gramsci*, London, 1977, p. 58.

that gave form and coherence to the mass of followers, and also power and principle to the vanguard party that governed them.

In short, the theory of the *Prison Notebooks* is the true theory of fascism: of the power that had pre-empted Gramsci's ambition, by realizing it in other hands. When, in an early article,[15] Gramsci described the proletariat as making up an ideal unity, a *fascio*, he anticipated in his hopes precisely the form of social order that was later to be achieved by his rival. The philosophy of praxis – so like the 'philosophical dynamism' of Mussolini and, like that philosophy, influenced through and through by Georges Sorel's apologies for violence – retains its charm for the intellectual precisely because it promises both power over the masses and a mystic identity with them. But that is the promise of fascism, and if the left needs constantly to identify the fascist as the single enemy we need look no further for an explanation. For what better way to conceal one's intentions than to describe them as the intentions of the enemy?

Gramsci's importance for us today lies in his resolute attempt to lift the work of revolution out of the streets and factories into the realm of high culture. He redesigned the left-wing programme as a cultural revolution, one that could be conducted without violence and whose site would be the universities, theatres, lecture halls and schools where the intellectuals find their primary audience. The work of revolution was henceforth to involve an attack on the old curriculum and the works of art, literature and criticism that belonged to it. It was to be a work of intellectual subversion, exposing the power networks, the structures of domination, that lie concealed within the high culture of our civilization, in order to liberate the voices that have been oppressed by it. And such has been the new curriculum in the humanities ever since.

This programme accelerated changes that were beginning to occur in British institutions of higher education. The Birmingham Centre for Contemporary Cultural Studies, founded in 1964 by Richard Hoggart, was home to a Gramscian movement, the aim of which was to rewrite the curriculum so that the voices of the oppressed, the excluded and the marginalized would at last be audible. Perhaps the most important thinker in this movement, and one who had a far-reaching influence on the teaching of literature in schools and universities throughout the United Kingdom, was the Welsh writer and critic Raymond Williams (1921–88), and it is worth examining his writings, since Williams encapsulates a

---

[15] Quoted in Joll, op. cit., p. 33.

crucial moment of transition from the Old Left of the post-war years, to the New Left of the 1960s and 70s.

Although he joined the Communist Party while a Cambridge undergraduate at the outset of the Second World War, and although he described himself as a 'cultural materialist', Williams was, like Gramsci, far too deeply attached to a national experience and a national culture to accept the internationalist futurism of the Party. He allowed his Party membership to lapse, joined the war effort (at the time forbidden by the Party on account of the Nazi–Soviet pact), and served as an anti-tank captain in the Guards armoured division, before returning to Cambridge in 1945 to resume his studies. He pursued a distinguished academic career at Cambridge while maintaining a lifelong connection with the Workers' Educational Association, and with the cultural institutions associated with the Labour Movement. He ended his life as a Welsh nationalist and a member of Plaid Cymru. In all his work it was the historical experience of the Welsh working-class communities that he had known as a child that principally inspired him.

British socialism – and especially the socialism of the Welsh mining communities – is imbued with a sense of the past, and the remembered experience of shared hardship. In the sentiments of the British socialist, all political action, all social inspiration, take their meaning from their antecedents, and the more firmly rooted these antecedents are, in a historic experience of community, the more claim do they have on our support. We are products of our national history, and to the extent that we find in the past the traces of a spirit that presently moves us, to that extent are we rightly moved, and to that extent are we heartened by our community with the men and women who have gone before.

That sentiment is to be found in all Raymond Williams's writings, adapted to the Gramscian programme of cultural revolution, and linked to the studies of class conflict that we find in Hobsbawm, Thompson, Samuel and Hill. Williams's socialism was haunted by 'ancestral voices', which speak from the pages of *Piers Plowman* and *Everyman*, from the speeches of Protestant radicals and non-conformist divines, and from the great age of Parliament, in which free, dissenting Englishmen seemingly abolished the constraints of hereditary power.

That last extraordinary period of our history has been a major preoccupation of the British left and is constantly returned to by the historians and cultural critics of the Labour movement. The most heartfelt nostalgia of British socialists, and their most romantic sense of loss, are attached to the Interregnum and the events that led up to it. Without the politicized description of this period undertaken by such historians as Tawney and Christopher Hill, British socialism would be a far less confident and indeed far less smiling presence in our national culture. It was established in the minds of those who gathered around the Workers' Educational Association and the Centre for Contemporary Cultural Studies that British socialism has been vindicated by its history, and is nothing but the latest expression of the free-born Englishman's right to the land and culture that are his.

In discussing Sartre and Foucault (Chapter 4) I tried to show the important place of iconography in French left-wing thinking, much of which is devoted to the detailed delineation of the 'bourgeois' enemy. British socialism is also iconographic; but its efforts have been devoted to the portrait of a friend. This friend appears as the idealized John Hamden of Tawney, as the heroic dissenter of Christopher Hill, and as the industrial 'working class' portrayed in the work of Thompson, Hoggart and Williams. There is naturally something endearing in this outlook, which looks for friends before declaring enemies, and which has endowed our left-wing movements with their local colouring. British socialism is as far from the 'internationalist' attitude of Marx (himself an uprooted product of a divided Germany) as is British conservatism. It is a movement that conservatives meet on home territory, fired by a love for home and territory that they share. And all this is contained in the crucial word 'culture'.

For this reason classical Marxism could never be more than a subsidiary influence on British left-wing thinking. Of far greater influence has been the unique tradition of social and literary criticism, which can justly claim to be one of the most important intellectual achievements of the English spirit. It would be wrong to think that this tradition has any natural bias towards socialism. It began with the conservative thought of Burke, Coleridge and Wordsworth, and showed – in the works of Carlyle and Arnold – an anti-egalitarian tendency that it has preserved to this day. Its greatest representative in the post-war period, F. R. Leavis, was claimed equally by socialists and conservatives as one of their number. And interwoven with the melancholy reflections of such defenders of high culture we find the left-leaning thought of Ruskin and Morris, of the pre-Raphaelite brotherhood, of Cobbett, Shaw and the Fabians. It is a further testimony to the rootedness of English socialism that, in the central emphasis and spiritual tendency of this critical tradition, socialist and conservative thinkers have been bound together in mutual influence.

Raymond Williams's roots were firmly in the soil of British socialism, and his best writings exhibit the attachment to place and people that has been the leading inspiration of modern English literature. In such works as *Culture and Society, 1780–1950* (1958), *The Long Revolution* (1961) and *The Country and the City* (1973), he brought a vision of the English working class directly into relation with a theory of social democracy, to give a fresh and personal perspective on the past and present of the labour movement. This perspective finds more concrete expression in two intensely nostalgic novels, *Border Country* and *Second Generation*. Finally, in later studies such as *Keywords* (1976) and *Marxism and Literature* (1977), Williams clothed his outlook in fashionable abstractions, mostly borrowed from the wardrobe of the French and German New Left. Throughout this corpus we find a relentless preoccupation with the working class, its hopes, fears and sufferings, and with the 'long revolution' that supposedly leads from class and privilege to equality and democracy.

Ruskin, Arnold and Morris observed the Industrial Revolution with grief and dismay. In all their thoughts can be discerned the same anxiety: what of civilization will remain when the countryside is empty and the towns brimming with needy and unsettled people, and when the rhythms of rural life have been annihilated by the relentless march of industrial production? Each writer sought for a prophylactic against social decay, and each proposed education and religion as vital ingredients in his suggested remedy. Williams, who shares their sense of tragedy, takes no comfort in religious traditions and indeed hardly mentions this all-important social fact. Instead, he seeks to retrace the territory explored by his nineteenth-century predecessors and to redescribe it in entirely secular terms. Like them he believes in education – and here and there he is disposed to sketch an ideal syllabus that will prepare the child for a 'participating democracy'.[16] But he can accept neither the religious reminiscence nor the anti-modern social doctrine of Ruskin and Morris.

Williams's 'long revolution' is therefore conceived entirely in terms of privilege and power, and the overcoming of both by democracy. It would be wrong to say that his faith in democracy is boundless – for if one thing is clear from his suspicion-laden paragraphs, it is that Williams does not have boundless faith in anything. It is simply that 'more democracy' is the

---

[16] *The Long Revolution*, Harmondsworth, Penguin Edition, 1961, pp. 174–5.

only answer that he is prepared to offer. Occasionally he puts it forward with a naïve generality:

> The democratic revolution...is insistently creative, in its appeal to all of us to take power to direct our own lives...The industrial revolution and the revolution in communications are only fully grasped in terms of the progress of democracy, which cannot be limited to simple political change, but insists, finally, on conceptions of an open society and of freely cooperating individuals which are alone capable of releasing the creative potentiality of the changes in working skills and communication...[17]

But such is his pessimistic temper that Williams at once abandons this line of thought. He withdraws behind the curtain of qualifications, hinting at a solution far more intricate and far subtler than any that he overtly reveals:

> The long revolution, which is now at the centre of our history, is not for democracy as a political system alone, nor for the equitable distribution of core products, nor for general access to the means of learning and communication. Such changes, difficult enough in themselves, derive meaning and direction, finally, from new conceptions of man and society which many have worked to describe and interpret. Perhaps these conceptions can only be given in experience. The metaphors of creativity and growth seek to enact them, but the pressure, now, must be towards particulars, for here or nowhere are they confirmed...[18]

In his very British way, Williams fills in some of the moral detail that is absent from Gramsci's theory of hegemony. The major purpose of *Culture and Society* is to document the practices that have either advanced or impeded the 'true democracy' that promises emancipation to the working class. Williams seeks to remove from the study of culture all elitist overtones, every suggestion that culture is a value accessible only to the few. To the extent that culture defines an elite, he believes, to that extent it is not a value. Here, of course, he differs from Gramsci, who wished – whether or not consciously – to replace one educated elite

---

[17] Ibid., pp. 140–1.
[18] Ibid., p. 141.

by another, and to leave the communist intellectuals in charge. Williams doesn't want to put anyone in charge, but to change the whole culture so that it becomes an asset that we share.

The major question raised by Williams's viewpoint is that of 'true democracy'. For Williams this involves a genuine community between people,[19] modelled on the 'solidarity' of a former labouring class, a sense of shared hopes and sufferings, and a need to stand together against abuse and exploitation. He believes that capitalism, class and privilege are enemies of community, and he does not hesitate constantly to recommend the abolition of 'private property in the means of production'.

As the argument develops, however, he extends his blame from capitalism and private property to the entire ethic of Christian civilization. He profits from a chance remark of Rosa Luxemburg's to argue that Christian charity is a 'charity of consumption', while socialist charity is a 'charity of production' – 'of loving relations between men actually working and producing what is ultimately, in whatever proportions, to be shared'.[20]

It is to this point that Williams returns with the greatest insistence: capitalism, with its consumer ethic, its exploitation, its sovereign indifference to place and people, is the great solvent of community. True community requires a 'participating democracy'. And this in turn is possible only if people achieve the 'equality of being' without which the 'struggle for democracy' is nothing.[21] And 'equality of being' requires that we dismantle the apparatus of privilege and class.

That combination of views is the root of native British socialism. It survives in Williams's writings by virtue of an effort of sentimentalization, whereby he hides from himself the basic facts of modern history. For let's face it, 'consumerism', far from being the enemy of democracy, is its economic expression. It arises inevitably from the market economy, being the psychological correlate of the fact that products are made not merely for use but also for exchange. The production of goods for sale is the real condition of the emancipated workers, who are able to turn their labour into money, and therefore into goods other than those that they produce. Without that capacity they remain either dependent upon the labour of others, or else wedded to forms of production that radically

---

[19] *The Long Revolution*, p. 363.
[20] *The Country and the City*, London, 1973, pp. 43–4.
[21] *Culture and Society*, Harmondsworth, Penguin, 1958, p. 322.

restrict their powers. The market itself is an expression of their free choice – of such free choice as they may, in these circumstances, acquire. It is a mechanism of distribution operated entirely by the voluntary transactions of individuals, each of whom secures his own advantage by soliciting the agreement of those with whom he deals. 'Consumer sovereignty' is another name for that day-to-day 'equality of being' which allows each person's choice to influence the outcome of a social process. The result is not very edifying – but the results of democracy seldom are.

I have sketched an argument that a Marxist will dismiss as 'ideology', responding that there is an 'alternative', in which 'true democracy' will coexist with 'social ownership', the absence of a market, and production for use and not for exchange. But how is it to be done? That is, how is it to be done, given what we know of our limited sympathies, finite expectations, competitive motives and mortal fears? We have never been told – and the myth of the 'new socialist man' is merely a way of dodging the issue, as Williams dodges it. Not only have all known socialist and communist systems retained wage-labour, money, exchange and sale; they have usually abolished the available forms of democracy. Moreover, by interfering in the market process, they have created scarcities, together with the associated black-market deals and privileges, which militate precisely against the 'equality of being' that Williams advocates.

Of course, the theoretical issues here are vast, and not to be resolved in a paragraph. But, given the observed facts of history and human nature, it must be concluded that the onus lies with the socialists, to spell out the conditions for the 'true democracy' that they favour. Who, in this democracy, controls what, and how? The market is the only economic institution in which every participant influences every outcome. How is its abolition to be reconciled with participatory government? And if we are to retain the market, how are we to prevent private property in the means of production, which is the natural result of free exchange, when people are allowed to use and sell their labour as they will? The neglect of such questions is not merely intellectually disreputable. Given the intransigence with which Williams seeks to advance his purposes, it is also pernicious. For it permits the easy advocacy of actions whose consequences are in no way understood.

Williams's appeal is in fact more sentimental than intellectual. It is captured in the reference to 'loving relations between men actually working and producing what is ultimately…shared'. Here are the long-suffering, tender-hearted workers of E. P. Thompson, who need only the abolition of capitalism in order to live together in spontaneous brotherhood, sharing the fruits of their labour. But while it is true that there is a comradeship and solidarity among the oppressed, it is the product of their oppression. Released from their bonds, people see each other as rivals, and only when they are bound together by contracts, agreements and conventions – only when subjected to a market economy in the widest sense – can they be brought again into peaceable association. That is the true meaning of democracy, which is a principle of unsentimental union between rivals and strangers, who agree to be governed by people whom their opponents play an equal part in electing. Democracy arises when people are prepared to renounce their political desires for the sake of agreement with those who do not share them.

The 'long revolution' that Williams praises was described more cautiously by a thinker to whom he only once refers: Alexis de Tocqueville. For Tocqueville self-obsession, individualism and social fragmentation were separate aspects of democracy's 'inevitable' advance. In *Democracy in America* (1835) he argued that the 'principle of equality', far from being an invention of the labour movement (which hardly existed when Tocqueville wrote, and certainly not in America), has been the ruling principle of European development since the Middle Ages.

Tocqueville's prescient analysis of 'equality of being' ought perhaps to have given pause. For he argues that the condition of social impermanence and cultural mediocrity, which for Williams is the consequence of privilege and power, is in fact the result of the democratic process. It is the erosion of privilege, the loss of diverse classes and estates, the destruction of hereditary entitlement, which, for Tocqueville, cause people to break free from community. Those changes render piety and allegiance redundant and awaken the desire to found society on contract, self-interest and consent. We may not agree with that conclusion. But we should recognize that the argument discharges the onus that Williams is too intellectually timorous, or too emotionally committed, to take up.

This reluctance to look beyond his preconceived conclusions is the principal fault in Williams's later writings. Like many who have invested too much love in an imagined friend, he recharges his emotion through hatred of an imagined enemy. The lower class fades from view, and the upper class emerges as the principal object of his attentions. In *The Country and the City* a seething resentment forms premise and conclusion of the argument, carrying the reader through one of the most one-dimensional surveys of English literature ever to have been received as academically respectable. It is perhaps a sense of the hopelessness of his own nostalgia that causes Williams in this book to turn with such vindictiveness on the nostalgia of others, and in particular on that quintessentially English nostalgia – fundamental to our socialist tradition – that finds the ideal of social harmony in a rural past.

Williams is of course right to see a simplifying Arcadianism in this attitude. But he is equally wrong to see nothing else. So fired is he by antipathy to privilege, patronage and leisure, that no writer who is disposed to recognize that the upper class contains members of the human species can escape his condemnation. Crabbe, whose major crime is to have been private chaplain to a duke, must therefore be whipped for his 'static' social vision, which condemns the rich, but rests with condemnation. Jane Austen is castigated for her 'monetary' vision, and for a morality that confines her to the inside of a country house, neither seeing nor feeling the misery that lies at her gate. So the book proceeds, through writers who have sought to paint human society as it is while recognizing that the human exists on many social levels and in many styles, and is in every style imperfect.

Williams represents his hatred of the upper class as a version of his distaste for capitalism. But even if he can hide it from himself, he cannot hide from his reader the fact that capitalism does not hold his attention long enough to inspire even the beginnings of an analysis, and that his hostility is directed indiscriminately at the 'haves' on behalf of the 'have nots', whatever the prevailing social order and whatever the source of the complaint. By the end of the book the iconographical intention is directed not to the friend but to the enemy – or rather, to a sentimentalized friend, made attractive only by the egregious wickedness of the enemy:

> The men and women who came from the country to the cities did not need to be told what they had lost, any more than they needed to be told what they might struggle to gain in their new world...But then it matters very much whether an experience of the country...was ranged for or against them, as they struggled to readjust. A selection of the experience – the view of the landlord or the resident, the 'pastoral' or the 'traditional' descriptions – was in fact made and used, as an abstract idea, against their children, and their children's children: against democracy, against education, against the labour movement.

So he dismisses the tradition of English pastoral literature, adding:

I have watched it [= roughly the complex attitude just reviled] settle into what is now a convention – in literary education especially – [and] I have felt it as an outrage, in a continuing crisis and on a persistent border. The song of the land, the song of rural labour, the song of delight in the many forms of life with which we share our physical world, is too important and too moving to be tamely given up, in an embittered betrayal, to the confident enemies of all significant and actual independence and renewal.[22]

The quotations typify Williams's later style: cliché-ridden, vague and sloganizing. With the loss of confidence in the romantic socialism of *The Long Revolution* and *Border Country*, slogans acquire an increasing prominence in Williams's writing. Unable or unwilling to analyse his loves and hatreds, he rests his commitment instead on certain 'keywords', to which the magic of socialism clings, and which can be used to create the illusion of theory in its absence.

One such word is 'revolution', which was as dear to Williams as to Althusser, though applied far more widely, and indeed to every transformation of which he approved. *Modern Tragedy* extols the 'living alternative' of our time, which consists in 'the recognition of revolution as a whole action of living men',[23] and the language is characteristic. Williams does not *argue* for revolution, nor does he describe it; rather he takes the *word* 'revolution' and cushions it in winsome abstractions: it is a 'whole action' of 'living men'. (It could hardly be a part action of ghosts.) Hence, 'most urgently, in our own time, we need to return to the idea of revolution, in its ordinary sense of the crisis of a society, to its necessary context as part of a whole action, within which alone it can be understood'.[24]

Such breathless prose must again be understood as iconographic. Revolution is made pleasing through associated ideas: the aim is to discourage thought, and to elicit fantasy. Revolution is to become an essentially alluring, rather than a critical, idea. '[S]ince 1917,' he writes, choosing the crucial date, 'we have been living in a world of successful social revolutions'.[25] And more significantly:

---

[22] *The Country and the City*, p. 325.
[23] *Modern Tragedy*, London, 1958, p. 65.
[24] Ibid., p. 66.
[25] Ibid., p. 73.

I am told by friends in the Soviet Union that the decisive battle of the revolution has been won in nearly half the world, and that the communist future is evident. I listen to this with respect, but I think that they have quite as much still to do as we have, and that a feeling that the revolution is over can be quite as disabling as the feeling that in any case it is pointless...[26]

Like his friends in the Soviet Union, Williams had cultivated the art of doublethink. He was able to make his attachment to icons rather than ideas into something simultaneously academically respectable and ideologically correct.

Keywords – 'the record of an inquiry into a vocabulary' – provides the clue to Williams's later thought. The volume, which is neither a dictionary nor a glossary but a work of ideological self-exposure, is an attack on another bastion of the ruling class, the *Oxford English Dictionary* (*OED*), whose alleged 'neutrality' is merely the expression of a 'bourgeois humanism', of the values of a class that feels no need to justify its dominion. Hidden here and there among his tendentious dictionary entries is Williams's final contribution to the culture wars: an attack on his own discipline of literary criticism as 'ideological'

not only in the sense that it assumes the position of the *consumer*, but also in the sense that it masks this position by a succession of abstractions of its real terms of response (as *judgment, taste, cultivation, discrimination, sensibility; disinterested, qualified, rigorous* and so on). This then actively prevents that understanding of response which does not assume the habit (or right or duty) of judgment.[27]

The implication is that Dr Johnson, F. R. Leavis, T. S. Eliot and all the other great 'consumers' of literature rely for their authority on the questionable assumption that literary response and literary judgement are one and the same. The word 'consumer' here works as a magic counter, drawing us by association into the socialist camp. Having rejected 'consumerism' we supposedly recognize without argument that there is another way of understanding literature, on the level of 'specificity' characteristic of 'practice'.

---

[26] *The Long Revolution*, p. 376.
[27] *Keywords*, London, 1976, p. 76.

Williams thereby invokes Gramsci's idea that revolutionary praxis involves seizing the culture. And he imagines he can seize the culture merely by defining words in another way, so disposing in a few lines not only of the entire tradition of English literary criticism but also of the aesthetic philosophy that has its roots in Kant, and which holds that aesthetic experience and aesthetic judgement are inextricable. Williams conveys no sense that anybody might have *argued* for the view that he rejects. On the contrary, he presents it as though it were simply an unconscious assumption of the language of criticism, adopted as part of the class-consciousness of the bourgeois enemy.

The word-magic of Williams's later work arises, I believe, from a desire at all costs to maintain the level of emotional commitment, and to distract attention from any argument or perception that would show it to be self-deceived. This posture, which led him to the 'etymological' stance of *Keywords*, led also to the attempt to shelter his lamp within the box-like abstractions of the New Left. To burn in secret is still to burn, and the vehement passions of *The Country and the City* continue to glow in the dark:

> 'Art' as a categorically separate dimension, or body of objects; 'the aesthetic' as an isolable extra-social phenomenon: each has been broken up by a return to the variability, the relativity, and the multiplicity of actual social practice. We can then see more clearly the ideological function of the specializing abstractions of 'art' and 'the aesthetic'.

The jargon here is that of a writer who has imprisoned his thought in language over which he exerts no intellectual control. While we can all guess what follows from this – that the categories of 'art' and 'the aesthetic' belong integrally to capitalist modes of production, and that they come into prominence with the manufacture of commodities for exchange – it follows with the logic of ritual, and not with the logic of argument. Only the emotional tension of the prose reminds us of the writer, shaking his fist on a dwindling horizon, as the boat of history sails out to sea.

There is indeed an argument to show that the category of the aesthetic belongs to bourgeois ideology and has ceased to be functional in the world in which we live. But it was left to Williams's most distinguished pupil, the critic Terry Eagleton, to put the argument together. In *The Ideology of the Aesthetic* Eagleton passes all art and literature through the grievance mangle, so as to squeeze out the juice of domination.[28] By the time of Eagleton's argument – which I have tried to answer elsewhere[29] – the left intellectuals had moved on from the Workers' Educational Association to the *New Left Review*, and it is in the pages of this publication that the culture wars were most seriously fought.

The *Review* was founded in 1960, when the *New Reasoner* and the *Universities and Left Review* merged, bringing together the major figures of the older intellectual left. Its first editor-in-chief was Stuart Hall, Richard Hoggart's successor as Director of the Birmingham Centre for Contemporary Cultural Studies. Hall was in fact more Old Left than New, and expressed the aims of the *Review*, in his first editorial, in language reminiscent of Raymond Williams:

> The task of socialism is to meet people where they *are*, where they are touched, bitten, moved, frustrated, nauseated – to develop discontent and, at the same time, to give the socialist movement some *direct* sense of the times and ways in which we live.

Hall, born in Jamaica, wrote as Williams did, constantly looking over his shoulder at a disappearing working class. His was the tone of voice that I knew from the socialist household in which I was raised. And if this tone had been retained, the *New Left Review* would have dwindled on the horizon, just as Williams did.

However, in 1962 Hall was replaced as editor by the far more radical Perry Anderson, who edited the journal until 1983, and has remained to this day on its editorial board. Anderson was, at the time, a conscious follower of Gramsci, with a dismissive and in many ways patrician attitude towards the established culture of England, its tradition of social and literary criticism included. Educated at Eton and Oxford, erudite, energetic and committed, with a talent for squeezing history into the Marxist template, Anderson might have pursued a successful career as an academic historian. However, he identified completely with the oppositional mentality of the *New Left Review*, and used it as a platform for a cultural revolution of his own. The review was to be cosmopolitan, sophisticated and disdainful of all establishments, the left establishment included.

---

[28] Terry Eagleton, *The Ideology of the Aesthetic*, Oxford, OUP, 1990.
[29] See Roger Scruton, *Beauty: A Short Introduction*, Oxford, OUP, 2009.

In recent years Anderson has emerged as a sober, melancholy and penetrating critic of the times in which we live. In the *London Review of Books* and other publications he has presented circumspect and far-reaching analytical commentary on a world in which 'neo-liberalism' has replaced 'capitalism' as the all-pervading corruption.

In the 1960s, however, he was fired by an iconoclastic passion that swept all hesitations aside, being determined to make the *NLR* into the English equivalent of Sartre's *Les Temps modernes*. He introduced Althusser, Mandel, Adorno, Debray, Lacan and a score of others to the socialist reader, publishing their writings either in the *Review* or under the imprint of New Left Books – which, under its new name of Verso, remains the primary outlet for real leftist thought. He was therefore a major force behind the 'alternative curriculum' in the humanities and the social sciences. By Marxizing the history of mankind, and issuing biting polemics against leading intellectual figures, he attempted to disestablish the culture of Old England, and to replace it with an elite culture of his own.

Anderson recognized that the left will be prepared to argue seriously only with those who would naturally describe themselves as a part of it. Charlatanry and irrationality are small defects on the left: what matters is the overriding allegiance to Gramsci's 'historical bloc', which unites the intellectual and the proletariat in opposition to 'things by law established'. It does not matter very much that questions are begged, arguments distorted or language abused – all these are of minor significance in a writer with a true opposition mentality. Indeed, it was precisely by filling the pages of the *New Left Review* with the works of charlatans that Anderson guaranteed its popularity among those hostile to the official 'structures' of education, for whom the traditional emphasis on intellectual competence was in any case an instrument of bourgeois domination.

The *New Left Review* therefore provided the ideal power base for the radical mentality of the 1960s: anti-academic, yet with enormous intellectual pretensions; cultivated, yet impatient with the prevailing culture; dogmatic, and yet far-reaching and imaginative in its choice of enemies. Its writers included the revolutionary old guard – Hill, Williams, Hobsbawm and Deutscher – as well as the rising stars of the new cultural hegemony – Tom Nairn, Alexander Cockburn, Juliet Mitchell, Terry Eagleton and Anderson himself. Articles and interviews from Castro and Mao stood beside the feeble outpourings of Michael Foot and Eric Heffer, while – such was the extraordinary temper of the 1960s – respectable figures like Conor Cruise O'Brien and Richard Hoggart jostled with such mavericks as Werner Fassbinder and Régis Debray.

The review came into its own in 1968, when Perry Anderson published the assault on the old British culture that made his name. In a lengthy article entitled 'Components of the National Culture'[30] he surveyed the entire 'official' culture of post-war Britain and condemned it as a culture of reaction, devoted to shoring up the ruins of a shattered social order and implacably hostile to the emerging culture of the revolutionary elite.

Anderson's diagnosis of Britain's cultural decline is simple:

> The culture of British bourgeois society is organised about an absent centre – a total theory of itself, that should have been either a classical sociology or a national Marxism. The trajectory of English social structure – above all, the non-emergence of a powerful revolutionary movement of the working class – is the explanation of this arrested development.

That thesis was taken up by others – notably by Terry Eagleton. But notice the consequence: a healthy culture can be guaranteed only by a 'total theory of itself'. How that applies to the healthy cultures of preceding ages is uncertain. But that it does not apply to our own is surely evident. Our culture has been *stifled* by theories of itself. Never before have there been so many theories, so assiduously plied, by those who can make no real contribution to the thing that they study. And why should our 'totalizing theory' be Marxism? Did that save the culture of Russia, Poland, China or Vietnam?

Anderson's article is less concerned, however, with the positive suggestion embodied in his diagnosis than with the intriguing symptoms of decline. Thanks to our lack of a Marxist theory 'a white emigration rolled across the flat expanse of English intellectual life, capturing sector after sector, until this traditionally insular culture became dominated by expatriates, of heterogeneous calibre'. The red émigrés (Brecht, Lukács, Horkheimer, Marcuse) went to less fubsy places (Russia, for example): what we received were the worst of the bourgeois lackeys who, displaced first by Nazism, and then by 'the victory of communism in Eastern Europe', fled to Britain in search of the reactionary order that they craved. Our enfeebled culture was at once overrun by them – philosophy by

---

[30] 'Components of the National Culture', *New Left Review* 50 (1968).

Wittgenstein, anthropology by Malinowski, history by Namier, 'social theory' by Popper, political theory by Berlin, aesthetics by Gombrich, psychology by Eysenck and psychoanalysis by Melanie Klein.

The thesis is supported by the most feeble reasoning. British philosophy owes as much to Russell and Austin as to Wittgenstein; British historiography as much to Toynbee, Tawney and Trevor Roper as to Namier; British psychoanalysis as much to Bowlby and Winnicott as to Klein; and so on. But such is Anderson's commitment to his foregone conclusion that his identification of the enemy, and his dismissal of the arid culture that this enemy has sought to impose on us, sweeps away all objections. He pauses only to consider the difficult case of literary criticism – the defence of culture itself – in the person of Leavis. Anderson is prepared to admit that Leavis was not a 'white émigré' (though isn't the name a bit suspicious when one thinks about it?). However, 'lacking any sociological formation, registering a decline but unable to provide a theory of it, Leavis was ultimately trapped in the cultural nexus he hated'.

This dismissal is significant. For it is one of the strengths of British culture that it has produced, not sociological theories of itself, but social and cultural *criticism*. To dismiss Leavis is to dismiss Burke, Coleridge, Arnold, Hazlitt, Ruskin and Eliot, all of whom were illuminating critical presences in the national culture. To point this out, however, serves no purpose for Anderson. Such facts contain the seeds of too much hesitation, of too many intellectual scruples, to be put to his polemical purpose.

There is another way of viewing Anderson's factitious list of 'white émigrés'. Namier, Wittgenstein, Gombrich, Popper, Klein, Berlin etc. were all wholly or partly Jewish. This too might have been taken as a reason for dismissing them as 'non-British', and the culture promoted by them as a pollution of what would otherwise have been our native socialism. To have discovered a cultural conspiracy, led by white émigré Jewish plutocrats, poisoners of our national culture with their polluted intellectual heritage, is to have come a long way down a familiar and disreputable path. Not a fair criticism, perhaps, but Anderson's contempt for evidence and his careless need for a fight clearly take him into dangerous waters. And the analogy is borne out by his venomous style:

> The chloroforming effect of such cultural configuration, its silent and constant underpinning of the social status quo, are deadly. British culture, as it is now constituted, is a deeply damaging and stifling force, operating against the growth of any revolutionary Left.

In subsequent writings the venom, and the desire to caricature its target, become less evident, and the revolutionary struggle is more gladly postponed to those who come after us. For Anderson has history on his side, and time on his hands. In the 1970s, therefore, he set out to undermine the ruling culture by expropriating its resources in order to construct a Marxist version of universal history. In two influential and impressive volumes – *Lineages of the Absolutist State* (1974), and *Passages from Antiquity to Feudalism* (1974) – he provided for the New Left a much-needed guidebook to the past.

The range of Anderson's historical knowledge in those two books is extraordinary: no earthly society and no period seems to escape his attention, and while his sources are largely secondary one cannot fail to be impressed by the fact that they include French, Italian, German and Russian authorities, many of whom remained untranslated. There is, indeed, much to be learned from these works, both about the subject-matter of world history, and about the application of Marxist theory to explaining it. Anderson attempts to do for the Marxist vision of history what Spengler and Toynbee did for the 'bourgeois' competitor: to provide a single morphology into which all historical development might fit.

Whether he is successful depends on what we think a Marxist account of history should be. To date self-styled 'Marxist' historiography has addressed itself almost exclusively to the task of identifying and describing the 'revolutionary' periods, in which power is violently transferred from one faction within society to another. Moreover, not every way of identifying these periods is genuinely Marxist – i.e. genuinely committed to the materialist theory of revolutions – and it is significant that so-called Marxist historians of revolution seldom show any real attachment to that theory.

Consider Christopher Hill, whose analysis of the English seventeenth-century 'revolution' is concerned almost entirely with the *ideology* of the protagonists and only fleetingly with the material conflicts that are expressed in it.[31] And in truth the turmoil of the seventeenth century cannot be explained in terms of the clash between forces and relations of production. The conflicts were what they seemed: ideological, political and personal, as well as economic. Even the idea of 'class antagonism' is, in this case, extremely artificial, the opposing groups being, from every Marxist standpoint, factions within a *single* class.

---

[31] See especially *The Century of Revolution, 1603–1714*, London, 1961.

Anderson sets out to rectify this weakness in Marxist historiography –
this almost 'bourgeois' preoccupation with ideology, institutions and law.
He therefore adopts a Marxist terminology pregnant with the desired
interpretation. The lower classes are 'the producers', the upper classes
'the exploiters'; the economic order is a 'mode of production'; religion,
law and politics are 'superstructures'; economic activity is 'the extraction
of surplus value'; and so on. This implies a massive commitment to
Marx's theory of history, including all that is contentious in it, such as
the theory of exploitation and surplus value, and the distinction between
superstructure and base. So how does the resulting history read?

In the closing pages of *Lineages of the Absolutist State* we read that:

Capitalism is the first mode of production in history in which the
means whereby the surplus is pumped out of the direct producer is
'purely' economic in form – the wage contract: the equal exchange
between free agents which reproduces, hourly and daily, inequality
and oppression. All other previous modes of exploitation operate
through *extra-economic* sanctions – kin, customary, religious, legal or
political ... The 'superstructures' of kinship, religion, law or the state
which necessarily enter into the constitutive structure of the mode of
production in pre-capitalist modes of production cannot be defined
except via their political, legal and ideological superstructures.

In other words, only capitalism is really susceptible of description and
explanation in Marxist terms. In pre-capitalist systems the superstructure
belongs to the base or, to put the point more honestly, the distinction
between base and superstructure collapses, and with it the Marxist
theory of history. 'Bourgeois' historiography, as exemplified in Maitland's
powerful *Constitutional History of England*,[32] is no different, when applied
to pre-capitalist society, from Marxist historiography.

If that is so, however, the grand design of Marxist historiography
is destroyed. It is no longer possible to see capitalism as the *outcome*
of the pre-capitalist formations, since the 'laws of motion' that explain
the one do not explain the other. It is equally impossible to argue that
capitalism will itself develop into some 'post-capitalist' formation or to
predict what that formation will be – for the laws of motion of capitalist

---

[32] F. W. Maitland, *The Constitutional History of England*, Cambridge, CUP, 1909.

society remain peculiar to it and applicable only to the narrow sphere of the 'wage contract'.

No member of the New Left would be worried by those criticisms. The credentials of Anderson's paragraph derive entirely from the Marxist vocabulary and the oppositional tone of voice. Those two features are connected. The reference to 'class societies', 'immediate producers', the extraction of 'surplus labour', 'exploitation' and the rest are united by a compelling *sentiment* – the sentiment revealed in the assertion that capitalism 'reproduces, hourly and daily, inequality and oppression'. The bathos of 'hourly and daily' recalls Thompson and Williams. It serves to distract attention from the fact that this conclusion is not proved by the argument, but merely invited by the style. The causality suggested by the term 'reproduces' could not conceivably be established on the basis of the meagre scraps of theory that Anderson offers. But the Marxist vocabulary is enough, since it dresses the premise of Anderson's argument in the sentiment of his conclusion. As I argued in Chapter 1, the first concern of revolutionary movements on the left has been to capture the language, to change reality by changing the way we describe and therefore the way we perceive it. Revolution begins from an *act of falsification*, exemplified equally in the French and the Russian Revolutions, as in the cultural revolutions of the contemporary campus.

The overall thesis of *Lineages of the Absolutist State* – that the 'absolutist' state is the product of capitalism and the political superstructure that capitalism requires – is about as plausible as Wittfogel's explanation of oriental despotism as the politics of irrigation.[33] Nevertheless, despite the strange conclusion that modern America is more absolutist, and more oppressive, than the France of Louis XIV, writers on the New Left were instinctively drawn to Anderson's interpretation. For it identifies capitalism as a form of *political* oppression, and thereby provides a catalyst to action. As with Gramsci's theory of hegemony, it identifies capitalism as something *done*, and therefore something that might be undone, by undoing the capitalist culture.

In *Passages from Antiquity to Feudalism*, Anderson addresses one of the lasting problem areas for Marxist historiography, that of the transition from ancient to feudal economies. The book is a *tour de force* of condensed erudition and detail. Where possible Anderson reproduces

---

[33] Karl A. Wittfogel, *Oriental Despotism: A Comparative Study of Total Power*, New Haven, 1957.

the explanations already offered by other Marxists. But the paucity of such ready-laundered information causes him to draw heavily on 'bourgeois' sources. The result – give or take a few asides – is bourgeois history. The development of the ancient world is described in terms of laws and institutions, and what should have been the 'revolutionary' transition from ancient slavery to medieval serfdom is represented as it was: a process of steady emancipation, interrupted by warring factions and the clash of civilizations.

Anderson recognizes that Roman law survived the transition, as did many other political, religious and social institutions: facts that are strictly incompatible with the Marxist theory. He acknowledges too that the Christian Church influenced and transformed the culture of the Empire without seriously modifying its 'material base': a fact that is again incompatible with the theory of Marx. He recognizes the great civilizing achievement of Carolingian society and the 'new synthesis' through which it preserved the legal and political reality of Europe. And in all these ways he repeats the 'bourgeois' view of European history, as a steady development of institutions, interrupted, as all things are, by the greed, violence and religious zeal of troublemakers and by the cycles of popular unrest. Anderson even recognizes that feudalism was a *judicial* rather than an economic system and that its essence resided in the hierarchy of institutions through which sovereignty was 'mediated' to the subject. Nothing could be further from Marx than that, except perhaps the one final concession to the truth, namely, that many 'feudal' relations are in essence really 'capitalist'.[34]

Anderson makes some attempt to retain the Marxist theory, by the usual device of Ptolemaic epicycles. He admits that:

Contrary to widely received beliefs among Marxists, the characteristic 'figure' of a crisis in a mode of production is not one in which vigorous (economic) forces of production burst triumphantly through retrograde (social) relations of production, and promptly establish a higher productivity and society on their ruins...[35]

---

[34] See the argument of Alan MacFarlane *The Origins of English Individualism: Family, Property and Transition*, London, 1978, and the discussion of medieval property law and the effect of equitable remedies in Arthur R. Hogue, *Origins of the Common Law*, Bloomington Indiana, University of Indiana Press, 1966.
[35] *Passages from Antiquity to Feudalism*, pp. 152–3.

But far from recognizing in that observation the death of the Marxist theory of history, he re-establishes the status quo. Relations of production 'must themselves first be radically changed and re-ordered *before* new forces of production can be created and combined for a globally new mode of production'.[36] This amendment, however, precisely reverses the causality postulated by Marx. It is open to us to join the bourgeois historians and argue that the 'production relations' might themselves be 'determined from above' by the laws and institutions that guide and encumber them. Such would be the most reasonable conclusion from the facts that Anderson himself adduces. In which case we can no longer distinguish base from superstructure in the way the Marxist theory requires. It is precisely the passage from antiquity to feudalism that shows the invalidity of the distinction. It also renders the language of Marxism – 'production relations', 'productive forces', 'producers' and so on – both otiose and scientifically pernicious in its implication that a discredited explanation may yet (by some Ptolemaic contortion) be saved.

As I have argued, revolutions begin by encasing reality in Newspeak, and thereafter are haunted by the fear that reality will break out of its case and become visible as it truly is. To rewrite bourgeois history in Marxese, as Anderson has done, is like rewriting a Haydn sonata movement with a continuous drum-roll on the dominant, so that all is infected by a premonition of catastrophe and nothing quite resolves. The intellectual labour of the New Left has been not to prove the Marxist theory but to describe the world *as though* it were true, so that every existing fact seems to resonate with the distant voice of the oppressed. This is perhaps what Anderson has in mind, when he writes that 'language, far from always following material changes, may sometimes anticipate them'.[37] For language forms our thoughts, our thoughts inform our actions, and our actions transform the world. If this is 'idealism', then so much the better for idealism.

At this point, however, Anderson hesitates. For we now confront the problem of agency. The language of the New Left is a language of accusation and defiance. But these postures make sense only if their targets are conceived as agents, answerable for the changes that they cause. E. P. Thompson, to his credit, cheerfully accepted this consequence, and argued that if there is such a thing as 'class struggle' it is because classes

---

[36] Ibid., p. 204.
[37] Ibid., p. 127.

are *protagonists* in history, motivated by a shared identity, responsibility and collective life. The English working class was made, in Thompson's vision, precisely by its own consciousness of itself, as the class 'in itself', and the class 'for itself' became one and the same. As I earlier argued, the consequences of this are radically anti-Marxist, both theoretically and, so to speak, sentimentally. It is not surprising, therefore, if Thompson's attitude prompts a ballistic response from Anderson.

In one of those remarkable polemics, whereby people on the left display their conviction that serious disputes are all internal to their camp, he addresses himself to the problem of agency, and takes Thompson as his target. He issues the Party line in *Pravda* style:

> The problem of *social order* is irresoluble so long as the answer to it is sought at the level of intention (or valuation), however complex or entangled the skein of volition, however class-defined the struggle of wills, however alienated the final resultant from all the imputed actors. It is, and must be, the dominant *mode of production* that confers fundamental unity on a social formation, allocating their objective positions to the classes within it, and distributing the agents within each class. The result is, typically, an objective process of class struggle.[38]

And yet he is clearly not happy with this line, which, by negating agency, makes both the class and its champions into 'objects' and 'class struggle' into something merely 'objective'.

Caught in this dilemma Anderson experiences many a lapse into bourgeois truthfulness, confessing, for example, that 'the Russian Revolution is…the inaugural incarnation of a new kind of history, founded on an unprecedented form of agency' – in other words that the Revolution was something not suffered but *done*. (The current Russian school history books therefore describe it not as a revolution but as a *coup d'état*, by way of distancing Putin the benign leader from Lenin the mass murderer.) And yet Anderson cannot accept the general consequence, which is that modern history is more a pattern of collective choice than material transformation.

Anderson rescues himself from this dilemma with the help of Althusserian opacity. Thompson's 'conceptual error', he argues,

---

[38] *Arguments within English Marxism*, London, 1980, p. 55.

is to amalgamate those actions which are indeed conscious volitions at a personal or local level, but whose social incidence is profoundly *in*voluntary (relations of marriage-age, say, to population growth), with *those actions which are conscious volitions at the level of their own social incidence*, under the single rubric of agency.[39]

It is apparent from that sentence just how useful to the New Left has been Althusser's device of emphatic meaninglessness – or rather *emphatic meaninglessness*. Thompson is castigated above all for having seen that Althusser is a fraud.

It is pointless to take issue with Anderson. The very quality of his prose in this ideological confrontation shows the extent to which Marxist Newspeak had become, for him, not an instrument of thought but a defence against it. The outrage committed by Thompson was precisely that he had not sunk to such a level of intellectual dishonesty that the difference between science and alchemy no longer mattered to him. Thompson was even prepared to insist 'upon the obvious point, which modern Marxists have overlooked, that there is a difference between arbitrary power and the rule of law.'[40] The remark provokes a storm of protest from Anderson, who attacks with every sophistry at his command, arguing in the end that 'a tyranny can perfectly well rule by law: its own laws.'[41]

In fact the communist tyrannies could not rule by law, not even their *own* law, from which the secret police and the Party were de facto exempt. If Thompson proved occasionally so disturbing to the New Left, it is partly because of his ability to clear away the ideological junk that had been piled against the doors where such facts might enter. Behind Anderson's polemic there advances a desperate attempt to save 'socialist truth' from the malicious encroachments of reality.

In the end, however, the fortified language of the New Left did not guarantee its emotional survival. It proved necessary throughout Anderson's reign at the *NLR* to maintain the discredited myths of Marxist history – for example, the myth that the English working class was *betrayed* by its self-consciousness, which led it to choose the parliamentary, and not the revolutionary, 'road to socialism'.[42] It was necessary to accept

---

[39] Ibid., p. 21.
[40] E. P. Thompson, *Whigs and Hunters: The Origins of the Black Act*, London, 1975, p. 266.
[41] *Arguments within English Marxism*, p. 198.
[42] Ibid., p. 46.

Trotsky's mendacious theory of the 'revolution betrayed', since, 'as every serious Marxist study of the Revolution has shown, it was the cruel inner environment of pervasive scarcity, allied with the external emergency of imperialist military encirclement, that produced the bureaucratization and state in the USSR'.[43] The choice of language is revealing: not to come up with the right conclusion is simply to show that one is not, after all, a serious Marxist. Besides, later revolutions have benefited from the changed balance of forces brought about through Stalinization, and so we can rest assured that the process was, in the long run, all for the good. And as for those bourgeois historians who have amassed what they regard as conclusive evidence that the 'scarcity' mentioned by Anderson was deliberately engineered by Lenin and the Bolsheviks, their arguments are simply unmentionable. If, from time to time, a defector from the New Left says something uncomfortable, the full apparatus of Stalinist Newspeak can be called upon to bury him:

> ...the Leninism that Althusser sought to recall was trampled under foot by the bureaucratic manipulation of the masses and diplomatic collusion with imperialism of the Chinese Party onto which he has naively projected it. In the West the harvest of Maoism in turn yielded an abundant crop of transfugees to the right. Glucksmann and Foucault, formerly hailed by Althusser, vie today in cold war zeal with Kołakowski, once saluted by Thompson. It is difficult to think of any adherent of socialist humanism who has sunk to quite such depths as literati like Sollers, recent champions of materialist anti-humanism...[44]

Subsequently, in *In the Tracks of Historical Materialism* (London, 1984), Anderson turned against the continental fashions with which he had once filled the *NLR*. 'Structuralism' and 'post-structuralism' were both dismissed as hostile to the enduring search for a viable Marxist philosophy. Paris was denounced as 'the capital of reaction', the entire Trotskyite alternative being tainted by the French 'exorbitation of language' as well as the myths and illusions that grow from its own one-sidedness. Even Habermas – respected for his dogged reiteration of leftist commitments – fails in the end to provide the bridge to the true agent of emancipation:

---

[43] Ibid., p. 121. For a crushing refutation of this statement see Mikhail Heller and Aleksander Nehrlich, *Utopia in Power*, New York, Simon & Schuster, 1986.
[44] Ibid., p. 110.

the revolutionary working class. And so on. What is remarkable in all this is not the change of focus or the change of enemy; it is rather what remained unchanged, and which was in truth the greatest illusion of all: the myth of the revolutionary working class, which not only desires 'emancipation', but desires it by way of an alliance with people like Anderson.

Hence, because it was built on the Gramscian theory of the 'historical bloc', the 'cultural revolution' finally expired in Britain. The crucial part of that bloc, the revolutionary working class, went AWOL somewhere around 1970. The culture wars thereafter shifted to America, a country that has never had a revolutionary proletariat, and where there is only the culture to capture. Culture remained the principal site of the battle between the left and the surrounding 'capitalist' order; but the battle was fought by people who saw it only in cultural terms, and without reference to the proletarian partner. The American cultural warriors did not, like Thompson and Anderson, reject the structuralist and post-structuralist alternatives that had been made in Paris, but embraced them as the key to reshaping the entire curriculum. Two figures in particular were influential in this: Richard Rorty and Edward Said. While renouncing any attempt to unite with a revolutionary working class they focused instead on depriving the American cultural inheritance of the belief in its own legitimacy.

Richard Rorty (1931–2007) defined himself as a 'pragmatist', one who renounces the distinction between the true and the useful. In Rorty's words:

> Pragmatists view truth as...what is good for *us* to believe... They see the gap between truth and justification not as something to be bridged by isolating a natural and trans-cultural sort of rationality which can be used to criticise certain cultures and praise others, but simply as the gap between the actual good and the possible better... For pragmatists, the desire for objectivity is not the desire to escape the limitations of one's community, but simply the desire for as much intersubjective agreement as possible, the desire to extend the reference of 'us' as far as we can.[45]

Pragmatism enables us to dismiss the idea of a 'trans-cultural... rationality'. There is no point to the old ideas of objectivity and universal truth; all that matters is the fact that *we* agree.

---

[45] *Objectivity, Relativism and Truth*, Cambridge, CUP, 1991, pp. 22–3.

But who are we? And what do we agree about? Turn to Rorty's essays, and you will soon find out. 'We' are all feminists, liberals, advocates of today's radical causes and the open curriculum; 'we' do not believe in God, or in any inherited religion; nor do the old ideas of authority, order and self-discipline carry weight for us. 'We' make up our minds as to the meaning of texts, by creating through our words the consensus that includes us. There is no constraint on us, beyond the community to which we have chosen to belong. And because there is no objective truth but only our own self-engendered consensus, our position is unassailable from any point of view outside it. Pragmatists not only decide what to think; they protect themselves from whoever doesn't think the same.

Rorty's argument reminds us that the traditional high culture of America was not a 'bourgeois' creation, but an expression of the Enlightenment, a deposit laid down by the extraordinary attempt to transcribe popular sovereignty into an enduring rule of law. In its own eyes the Enlightenment involved the celebration of universal values and a common human nature. The art of the Enlightenment ranged over other places, other times and other cultures, in a heroic attempt to vindicate a vision of man as free and self-created. That vision inspired the old curriculum, and it has been the first concern of the postmodern university in America to put it in question.

That explains the popularity of the other relativist guru to whom I referred – Edward Said (1935–2003). Thirty years ago Said published his seminal book *Orientalism*, in which he castigated the Western scholars who had studied and commented upon the society, art and literature of the East. He accused the orientalists of a denigrating and patronizing attitude towards Eastern civilizations. Under Western eyes the East has appeared, according to Said, as a world of wan indolence and vaporous intoxication, without the energy or industry enshrined in Western values, and therefore cut off from the sources of material and intellectual success. It has been portrayed as the 'Other', the opaque reflecting glass in which the Western colonial intruder can see nothing save his own shining face.

Said illustrated his thesis with highly selective quotations, concerning a very narrow range of East–West encounters. And while pouring as much scorn and venom as he could on Western portrayals of the Orient, he did not trouble himself to examine any Eastern portrayals of the Occident, or to make any comparative judgements whatsoever, when it came to assessing who had been unfair to whom.

Said's targets were not merely living scholars like Bernard Lewis who knew the Muslim world and its culture far better than he did. He was attacking a tradition of scholarship that can fairly claim to be one of the real moral achievements of Western civilization. The orientalist scholars of the Enlightenment created or inspired works that have entered the Western patrimony, from Galland's seminal translation of the *Thousand and One Nights* of 1717, through Goethe's *West-Östlicher Diwan* to FitzGerald's *Rubaiyat of Omar Khayyam*. Of course this tradition was also an appropriation – a remaking of Islamic material from a Western perspective. But why not acknowledge this as a tribute, rather than a snub? You cannot appropriate the work of others, if you regard them as fundamentally 'Other'.

In fact Eastern cultures owe a debt to their Western students. At the moment in the eighteenth century when 'Abd al-Wahhab was founding his particularly obnoxious form of Islam in the Arabian peninsula, burning the books and cutting off the heads that disagreed with him, Sir William Jones was collecting and translating all that he could find of Persian and Arabic poetry, and preparing to sail to Calcutta, where he was to serve as a judge and to pioneer the study of Indian languages and culture. Wahhabism arrived in India at the same time as Sir William, and began at once to radicalize the Muslims, initiating the cultural suicide that the good judge was doing his best to prevent.

If the orientalists had a fault it was not their patronizing or colonialist attitudes but, on the contrary, their lamentable tendency to 'go native' in the manner of Sir Richard Burton and T. E. Lawrence, allowing their love of Islamic culture to displace their perception of the people, to the point where they failed, like Lawrence, to recognize that the people and the culture no longer had much in common. Nevertheless their work remains a striking tribute to the universalism of Western civilization, and has now been vindicated by Robert Irwin, in a book that shows Said's *Orientalism* to be a scandal of pseudo-scholarship comparable to the works of Aleister Crowley or Madame Blavatsky.[46] Irwin exposes the mistakes, oversights and downright lies contained in Said's book and, if it was not obvious before, it is certainly obvious now, that the principal reason for Said's popularity in our universities is that he provided ammunition against the West.

---

[46] Robert Irwin, *For Lust of Knowing: The Orientalists and their Enemies*, London, Allen Lane, 2005.

This is, however, a depressing conclusion to draw. For it suggests that the culture wars have ended in America in a near-universal victory for the left. Many of those appointed as the guardians of Western culture will seize on any argument, however flawed, and any scholarship, however phony, in order to denigrate their cultural inheritance. We have entered a period of cultural suicide, comparable to that undergone by Islam after the ossification of the Ottoman Empire. Encouraged by Said, students learn first to despise, and eventually to forget, the outlook that led those noble orientalists to undertake a task that only someone steeped in Western culture would dream of – the task of rescuing a culture other than their own.

Of course Said is vehement in dismissing that attempt and the culture that inspired it. While exhorting us to judge other cultures in their own terms, he asks us to judge Western culture from a point of view outside – to set it against alternatives, and to judge it adversely, as ethnocentric and even racist. However, the criticisms offered of the old American culture are really endorsements of its claim to favour. It is thanks to the Enlightenment, and its universal view of human values, that racial and sexual equality have such a common-sense appeal to Americans. It is the universalist vision of man that makes Americans demand so much of their art and literature. It is the very attempt to embrace other cultures that makes Western art a hostage to Said's cavilling strictures – an attempt that has no parallel in the traditional art of Arabia, India or Africa. And it is only a very narrow view of our artistic tradition that does not discover in it a multicultural approach that is far more imaginative than anything that is now taught under that name. Our culture invokes a historical community of sentiment, while celebrating universal human values. It is rooted in the Christian experience, but draws from that source a wealth of human feeling that it spreads impartially over imagined worlds. From *Orlando Furioso* to Byron's *Don Juan*, from Monteverdi's *Poppeia* to Longfellow's *Hiawatha*, from *The Winter's Tale* to *Madama Butterfly* and *Das Lied von der Erde*, our culture has continuously ventured into spiritual territory that has no place on the Christian map.

The Enlightenment, which set before us an ideal of objective truth, also cleared away the mist of religious doctrine. The moral conscience, cut off from religious observance, began to see itself from outside. At the same time, the belief in a universal human nature, so powerfully defended by Shaftesbury, Hutcheson and Hume, kept scepticism at bay. The suggestion that, in tracing the course of human sympathy,

Shaftesbury and Hume were merely describing an aspect of 'Western' culture, would have been regarded by their contemporaries as absurd. The 'moral sciences', including the study of art and literature, were seen, in T. S. Eliot's words, as a 'common pursuit of true judgment'. And this common pursuit occupied the great thinkers of the Victorian age who, even when they made the first ventures into sociology and anthropology, believed in the objective validity of their results, and a universal human nature that would be revealed in them.

As a result of the culture wars all that has changed utterly. In place of objectivity we have only 'inter-subjectivity' – in other words, consensus. Truths, meanings, facts and values are now regarded as negotiable. The curious thing, however, is that this woolly-minded subjectivism goes with a vigorous censorship. Those who put consensus in the place of truth quickly find themselves distinguishing the true from the false consensus. And inevitably the consensus is 'on the left'. Just why that should be so is a question that I am trying in this book to answer.

Thus the 'we' of Rorty rigorously excludes all conservatives, traditionalists and reactionaries. Only liberals can belong to it; just as only feminists, radicals, gay activists and anti-authoritarians can take advantage of deconstruction; just as only the opponents of 'power' can make use of Foucault's techniques of moral sabotage, and just as only 'multiculturalists' can avail themselves of Said's critique of Enlightenment values. The inescapable conclusion is that subjectivity, relativity and irrationalism are advocated not in order to let in all opinions, but precisely so as to exclude the opinions of people who believe in old authorities and objective truths. This is the short cut to Gramsci's new cultural hegemony: not to vindicate the new culture against the old, but to show that there are no grounds for either, so that nothing remains save political commitment.

Thus, almost all those who espouse the relativistic 'methods' introduced into the humanities by Foucault, Derrida and Rorty are vehement adherents to a code of political correctness that condemns deviation in absolute and intransigent terms. The relativistic theory exists in order to support an absolutist doctrine. We should not be surprised therefore at the extreme disarray that entered the camp of deconstruction, when it was discovered that one of the leading ecclesiastics, Paul de Man, once had Nazi sympathies. It is manifestly absurd to suggest that a similar disarray would have attended the discovery that Paul de Man had once been a communist – even if he had taken part in some of the great communist crimes. In such a case he would have enjoyed the same compassionate endorsement as was afforded to Lukács, Merleau-Ponty and Sartre. The assault on meaning undertaken by the deconstructionists is not an assault on 'our' meanings, which remain exactly what they always were: radical, egalitarian and transgressive. It is an assault on 'their' meanings – the meanings sequestered in a tradition of artistic thinking, and passed on from generation to generation by the old forms of scholarship.

All that is worth bearing in mind when we consider the current state of the culture wars in Britain and America. Although there are areas like philosophy that have been for many years immune to the prevailing subjectivism, they too are beginning to succumb to it. Teachers who remain wedded to what Rorty calls 'a natural and trans-cultural sort of rationality' – in other words who believe that they can say something permanently and universally true about the human condition – find it increasingly difficult to appeal to students for whom negotiation has taken the place of rational argument. To expound Aristotle's ethics, and to point out that the cardinal virtues defended by Aristotle are as much a part of happiness for modern people as they were for ancient Greeks, is to invite incomprehension. The best the modern student can manage is curiosity: that, he will acknowledge, is how *they* saw the matter. As to how *I* see it, who knows?

From this state of bewildered scepticism the student may take a leap of faith. And the leap is never backwards into the old curriculum, the old canon, the old belief in objective standards and settled ways of life. It is always a leap forward, into the world of free choice and free opinion, in which nothing has authority and nothing is objectively right or wrong. In this postmodern world there is no such thing as adverse judgement – unless it be judgement of the adverse judge. It is a playground world, in which all are equally entitled to their culture, their lifestyle and their opinions.

And that is why, paradoxically, the postmodern curriculum is so censorious – in just the way that liberalism is censorious. When everything is permitted, it is vital to forbid the forbidder. All serious cultures are founded on the distinctions between right and wrong, true and false, good and bad taste, knowledge and ignorance. It was to the perpetuation of those distinctions that the humanities, in the past, were devoted. Hence the assault on the curriculum, and the attempt to impose a standard of 'political correctness' – which means, in effect, a standard of non-exclusion and non-judgement – is also designed to authorize a vehement kind of judgement, against all those authorities that question the orthodoxy on the left.

The subliminal awareness of this paradox explains the popularity of the gurus to whom I referred. The relativist beliefs exist because they sustain a community – the new *ummah* of the rootless. Hence, in Rorty and Said, we find a shared duplicity of purpose: on the one hand to undermine all claims to absolute truth, and on the other hand to uphold the orthodoxies upon which their congregation depends. The very reasoning that sets out to destroy the ideas of objective truth and absolute value imposes political correctness as absolutely binding, and cultural relativism as objectively true. Gramsci's cultural revolution, transferred to the American campus and the *New York Review of Books*, became a corrosive worm in the culture, an instinct for repudiation, but brought nothing into being in place of the things that it destroyed apart from a bleak relativism. The final conclusion of the culture wars was that the old culture means nothing, but only because there is nothing to mean.

8 THE KRAKEN WAKES: BADIOU AND ŽIŽEK

The cultural revolution initiated by Gramsci petered out in the empty relativism that I have just described. Gramsci had hoped to replace the bourgeois culture with a new and objective cultural hegemony. But he was thwarted by the repudiation of the very idea of objectivity, and by the purely negative work of the comfortable professoriat in America. For a while it seemed as though the whole revolutionary programme was at an end. In France the Maoists of 1968 slipped away or joined the anti-communist cause, like Stéphane Courtois; Perry Anderson ceased to edit the *New Left Review*, devoting himself instead to political analysis in the 'bourgeois' press; Williams, Thompson, Deleuze, Rorty and Said were dead, and Habermas was busy burying the leftist message in page upon page of bureaucratic dither. Meanwhile the communist systems of the Russian empire had collapsed and China was on the way to becoming a centre of trans-national capitalism, combining in its mad orgy of consumption some of the worst features of every system of government in living memory.

But it was just at this moment, at the turn of the twenty-first century, that the monster began to stir in the depths. And when it rose from the sea of our complacency, it spoke as Marx and Sartre had spoken, in the language of metaphysics. It pushed aside the tinsel of the consumer culture, to appear in its primordial guise, intruding into the world of phenomena like Erda in *Das Rheingold*, as the voice of Being itself. Only in France could such an event occur; but having occurred it recruited a following all across the intellectual world.

Frege's *Foundations of Arithmetic* and Russell's theory of descriptions lifted the ideas of existence and multiplicity out of the metaphysical underworld into the light of formal logic. Analytical philosophy has inherited from those sources a profound reluctance to consider the question of 'being qua being'. The matters pondered in the poem of the pre-Socratic Parmenides, and discussed in one of Plato's most difficult dialogues, as to whether the One exists, and whether the Many are part of the One, have no clear successor in Anglo-American philosophy.[1] The puzzles over the one-ness of ultimate reality inherited from Islamic philosophy and reaching their astonishing apogee in Spinoza have been put aside as illustrating 'the bewitchment of the intelligence by means of language', as Wittgenstein put it. Being does not become a legitimate field of enquiry just because we write it as be-ing, or be-ness, or divide it into varieties (being-to-hand, being-towards-death, in-advance-of-itself-being and so on) as Heidegger does. We understand being through reflecting on the logic of reference, and on the connection between reference and identity. Such is the background assumption of an impressive tradition of philosophical literature, which includes Strawson's *Individuals*, Wiggins's *Sameness and Substance*, Quine's *Word and Object*, Geach's *Logic Matters*, Kripke's *Naming and Necessity* and many other equally challenging works.

No such assumption has taken root in France. Following Bergson's reflections on time and consciousness, and Kojève's unveiling of Hegel, French philosophy turned to the question of being, be-ing, or be-ness. The appearance of Heidegger's *Being and Time* was received by Sartre with a sense of shock, and the existence of this work, with its strange and compelling language suggesting that the author was for the first time reporting a close encounter with Being, changed the course of French philosophy. Thereafter French philosophers have been afflicted with what one might call 'be-ness envy', a sense of having missed out on the real capacity of philosophical thought, and a determination to capture Being and put it to uses of their own, and in particular to set it to the work of Revolution. Hence Sartre's great treatise, *Being and Nothingness*. And hence Deleuze's *Difference and Repetition*, the plan of which, as I suggested in Chapter 6, is to replace being by difference, and time by repetition, so as to subvert the entire metaphysical underpinning (as Deleuze conceived it) of our 'Western' forms of thought.

The same causality can be witnessed in the title of the book that Alain Badiou describes (in the preface to the English edition) as a 'great' work of philosophy: *Being and Event*. But there are other influences at work in this impressive and mysterious production, including two beliefs that were in the air in 1968, and from which Badiou, for all his

---

[1] Though Russell, in his *History of Western Philosophy*, credits Parmenides with opening up the topic of negative existential statements.

sophistication, has never deviated. The first is that Jacques Lacan was not the crazy charlatan I described in Chapter 6 but a major contributor to the self-understanding of our era. My residual faith in human nature leads me to think that this belief will dwindle in time. For now, however, we have to accept that it is shared by many of the most influential figures in French culture, not to speak of literature professors all across America.

In particular it is shared by those, Badiou among them, who attended Lacan's seminars and who witnessed his astonishing ability to wipe away whole segments of reality with spells. 'There is no subject'; 'there is no big Other'; 'there is no sexual relation'; 'you do not ex-sist'; 'the pursuit of truth hides castration': such mantras resound down the years since those fatal seminars like ancestral curses whose malignant aura can never be shaken off. One particular spell fascinates Badiou, since it seems to connect with his approach to the question of being via the ancient puzzle of the One: '*il y a de l'Un*', or sometimes, even less grammatically, '*il y a d'Un*', which we might translate as 'there is something of One', or 'there is a bunch of One', or even 'there is One, up to a point'.

The other belief that has guided the direction of Badiou's philosophy throughout his life is the belief that there are decisive events that erupt into the scheme of things and usher in the future. The true intellectual must attach himself to such an event and remain 'faithful' to it through all disappointments. Badiou was a student of Althusser, and committed to the great proletarian revolution that would release humanity from its chains. But he is also a Maoist, who missed out on the events of 1968, and has been trying to make up for it ever since, by running small cells of revolutionary activists dedicated to the overthrow of the system.[2] In an essay first published in 1977 he wrote that 'there is only one great philosopher of our time: Mao Zedong'.[3] And he has remained convinced that Mao's Cultural Revolution is the paradigm that the contemporary intellectual must follow. He has reluctantly conceded over the years that it got out of hand, but remains 'faithful' all the same to its inner meaning. 'Fidelity' to the Event is what

---

[2] An amusing, though shocking, account of Badiou's revolutionary activism has been put together by Eric Conan: 'Badiou, la star de la philo, est-il un salaud?' *Marianne* 671 (27 February 2010), p. 18. Conan answers that rhetorical question in the affirmative, and it is very hard to disagree.
[3] Alain Badiou, *The Adventure of French Philosophy*, ed. and tr. Bruno Bosteels, London, Verso, 2012, Ch. 2.

Badiou has set out to justify, not as an ethical choice, but as a metaphysical necessity, a truth implanted in the nature of being itself.

But how on earth can that be so? How can being itself be recruited to the work of revolution? The answer is contained in another Lacanian device – that of the 'matheme', which is, as Lacan put it, 'the index of an absolute signification'.[4] By clothing the big questions in mathematical language, Badiou hopes to remove all elements of contingency and wishful thinking from his revolutionary programme, and to present it as founded in 'ontology' – the pure science of being. Since Badiou, unlike Lacan, has learned enough mathematics to deal without absurdity in mathematical symbols, the result has been credited, by an awe-struck readership, with an entirely new kind of authority. Here at last is the text that accomplishes Marx's dream, of presenting revolutionary politics as a precise science. And here too is the proof of the idea, so fundamental to Marxism in its Leninist interpretation and reiterated constantly by Mao and Althusser, that history moves on the back of contradictions, and that these contradictions are inherent in reality – or would be inherent, were it not for the fact, as Lacan declared, that reality is never really Real.

The position is spelled out in *L'être et l'événement* and its sequel, *Logiques des mondes*. Those two works take set theory as their starting point, and there is nothing unusual in that: analytical philosophy began, after all, in the same way. The paradoxes dwelt upon by Badiou – in particular those that emerge from Cantor's theory of transfinite cardinals and from Gödel's incompleteness proof – have therefore long been subjects of discussion in analytical philosophy. What is new is Badiou's rebranding of set theory as ontology, the pure science of being, and his attempt to rewrite philosophy in 'mathemes', fragments of uprooted mathematics that endow wild speculation with the magical aura of proof. The result is an extraordinary hotchpotch of sense and nonsense, of misapplied jargon and inspired analogy.

One such analogy centres on Paul Cohen's proof of the independence of the continuum hypothesis, which has exerted a strange, almost hallucinatory, influence over Badiou's thinking. The continuum hypothesis arose from Cantor's proof that there are numbers with a higher cardinality than Aleph-0, which is the cardinality of the infinite series of natural numbers. Cantor suggested that there must be a successor to Aleph-0, the first in an infinite series of such successors. He hypothesized

[4] *Écrits*, op. cit., p. 816, English edn, p. 314.

that the cardinality of this successor, Aleph-1, would be that of the power set of Aleph-0 – i.e. 2 to the power of Aleph-0, which is the cardinality of the set of real numbers.[5] And he suggested that there is an ordered series of transfinite cardinals in something like the way that there is an ordered series of natural numbers. Cantor hoped to show that any axioms sufficient to generate the basic laws of arithmetic would also show the continuum hypothesis to be true. But he never found the proof, and others were similarly frustrated in their search for it. Then, in 1963, Paul Cohen showed that the continuum hypothesis is independent of the axioms of Zermelo-Frankel set theory. Hence, given that the axioms of Z-F are sufficient to generate arithmetic, the continuum hypothesis is not an arithmetical theorem. Cohen's own view was that the hypothesis is false.[6]

The continuum hypothesis looks plausible, Cohen argued, because mathematicians are used to creating models with constructive sets – the set of Fs, for some given predicate 'F' in the language of the model. But the axiom of extensionality, which is a cornerstone of Zermelo-Frankel set theory, tells us that sets are identified by their members, and not by the properties that those members share, so that if set A has the same members as set B, A is identical with B, whether or not the two sets gather their members under a single predicate within the model. Hence there could be sets that are not definable within the model, but only by collecting their members in some other way – in terms of a property definable in the wider universe of set theory. These 'generic' sets could be put to work in mathematical proofs, even if the language of the model contains no predicate under which to assemble them.

To prove the independence of the continuum hypothesis we must find a model – a set of sets – for which the axioms of Z-F set theory are satisfied (i.e. are true in the model) while the continuum hypothesis is not (i.e. is false in the model). So long as we deal only in constructive sets we cannot prove this. But by a procedure of 'forcing', whereby generic sets are pressed into the model, we can produce a model that satisfies the axioms of set theory, even though the continuum hypothesis is false in that model.

---

[5] The proof that the cardinality of the real numbers is 2 to the power of Aleph-0 is neatly set out for the lay reader in Lillian R. Lieber, *Infinity: Beyond the Beyond the Beyond*, Philadelphia, Paul Dry Books, 2007, Ch. 9.

[6] Fortunately Cohen's beautifully succinct lectures on the question exist in typescript, and have been published as *Set Theory and the Continuum Hypothesis*, New York, Dover Books, 2008.

The proof is technical and belongs to a family of proofs (Gödel's incompleteness proof among them) that are 'metamathematical' in character. It does not set out either to prove or to disprove the continuum hypothesis, but to show rather that the hypothesis is not provable from a given set of axioms and therefore not a theorem in any mathematical system that takes those axioms as its starting point. For Badiou this is already of great significance, since he sees his philosophy as itself a kind of metamathematics – or a metaontology, as he calls it, whose aim is to give an overview of how the world must be, if mathematics is to describe it.

More importantly, however, Cohen's proof inspires a leap of the imagination from abstract mathematics into concrete history. The words 'generic' and 'forcing' lodge in Badiou's brain, and become key terms in his account of the human condition. According to Badiou there are four ways in which we pursue, create and remain faithful to the important (i.e. revolutionary) events: love, art, science and politics. And he dubs these four things *procédures génériques*, without explaining quite what 'generic' means in these contexts, but always with one eye on the mathemes that might hide and protect his ultimate purpose, which is to claim mathematical authority for his particular brand of Utopia.[7]

He tells us that a generic multitude is unnameable, and that this production of the unnameable group, of the liberated multitude that cannot be confined in any category, is the ultimate goal of all truth-directed activity.[8] Moreover, the revolutionary Event comes about by 'forcing': a situation becomes revolutionary when new things are 'forced' into it, things that are not nameable in the language of the situation.[9] At various points he mentions Cohen's proof itself as an Event, comparable to the French Revolution, Schoenberg's overthrow of tonality, Mao's Cultural Revolution, 1968 in Paris, etc. All such events generate '*vérités soustraites au savoir*' – truths subtracted from the existing bodies of knowledge.

All that is both imaginative and, for its intended audience, exciting. But what, in reality, does it amount to? The prose slips promiscuously from mathematics to the empirical world and back again; the crucial terms, lifted from technical contexts that are only partially or allusively expounded, are given no clear meaning in their extended use, and

[7] *L'être et l'événement*, p. 23.
[8] The choice of the word 'unnameable' is strongly influenced by Beckett's late novella, *L'innommable*, which is one of the few of Beckett's works that are better in French than in English.
[9] *L'être et l'événement*, p. 373.

the reader has the inescapable impression that Badiou is not applying mathematics but hiding behind it. The impression is only enhanced by his frequent invocation of those chthonic mysteries of the pre-Socratics, which tell us that the One is, or is not, or that all is flux, or maybe not. No proof is clearly stated or examined, all remains at the level of first steps, and the jargon of set theory is waved like a magician's wand, to give authority to bursts of all but unintelligible metaphysics. Here is an example, in which Cantor's discussion of the infinite is mixed up with reminiscences of Plato's *Parmenides*:

> That it be in the place of this non-being that Cantor pinpoints the absolute, or God, allows us to isolate the decision in which 'ontologies' of Presence, non-mathematical 'ontologies', ground themselves: the decision to declare that beyond the multiple, even in the metaphor of its inconsistent grandeur, the one is.
>
> What set theory enacts, on the contrary, under the effect of the paradoxes – in which it registers its particular non-being as obstacle (which, by that token, is *the* non-being) – is that the one is not.[10]

In this way Badiou is able to allude, not only to the ultimate political agenda, but also to the deepest questions of metaphysics, which rumble beneath his prose like Alph the sacred river, running forever to its sunless sea. Set theory, we discover, is not only the clue to revolutionary politics, but also the answer to Parmenides, the final proof that the One *is not*. Of course, *il y a de l'Un*; for we can make sets, and when we make sets we count a multitude as one. So Lacan was right. The One is not, but there is One, sort of and up to a point, because we can count things as one. Counting as one is the primary human intervention in the great multiplicity that surrounds us. However, as Cantor showed, this multiplicity is in itself not just uncountable but, when taken as a whole, inconsistent: or rather, it 'in-consists'.

Why should Badiou take set theory as authority for such vast claims? The answer is that he sees set theory as ontology, the science that tells us what ultimately exists. But – and here is the stunning part – set theory does not presuppose the existence of anything. It deals only in sets, and all the sets required by arithmetic – all the numbers – can be constructed from φ, the empty set, the set of all things that are not identical with themselves.

---

[10] *Being and Event*, translation, p. 42.

(Thus for 0 put φ, for 1 the set whose only member is φ, for 2 the set whose members are φ and the set whose only member is φ, and so on.) This well-known method of constructing arithmetic from no ontological assumptions is taken by Badiou in the opposite sense, as showing that the ultimate reality is φ – *le vide*, or the Void as his translators put it. Since we can construct mathematics from no ontological assumptions, it would be natural to conclude that it is not mathematics but physics, say, which tells us what ultimately exists. But no, that is not Badiou's conclusion. Since mathematics is ontology, he argues, we can conclude that the world consists in multiplicity and the void. Moreover, the multiplicity is, for reasons shown by Cantor, essentially inconsistent.

If you play with those ideas long enough you come up with some striking Lacanisms. For instance ontology is a 'presentation of a presentation'; and 'if the multiple is presented, the one is not'.[11] φ is the 'multiple of nothing', and the null set axiom names the void as multiple. 'The multiple is inconsistent – in other words it "in-consists". 'It is true that inconsistency is nothing; false that inconsistency is not.'[12] Hence:

> *Le vide est le nom de l'être – l'inconsistance – selon une situation, en tant que la présentation nous y donne un accès imprésentable, donc l'inaccès à cet accès, dans le mode de ce qui n'est pas-un, ni composable d'uns, et donc n'est qualifiable dans la situation que comme l'errance de rien.*[13]

This 'wandering of nothing', which aptly describes Badiou's prose-style, also recalls Lacan's devastating announcement that 'Nothing exists except in so far as it does not exist.'[14]

One of the difficulties presented by *L'être et l'événement* and its successor, *Logiques des mondes*, is that the mathemes are very tightly woven into an argument that in fact has little or nothing to do with them. When linguists write of phonemes and morphemes they mean something precise: the smallest independently functional parts of spoken or written words. This is

---

[11] *L'être et l'événement*, p. 36.
[12] Ibid., p. 67.
[13] Ibid., p. 69. Hard to translate, but how about: 'The void is the name of being – inconsistency – according to a situation, in so far as presentations gives us access to the unpresentable, and therefore inaccess to this access, in the manner of that which is not-one, nor composable from ones, and which is therefore qualifiable in the situation only as the wandering of nothing.'
[14] *Écrits*, p. 392.

not what Lacan or Badiou mean by mathemes, nor does either of them say what else he means. The problem is compounded in French by the spelling – *mathème* conjures the *poème* as though these were two postures towards a single mystery. And indeed, at a certain point, this is how Badiou treats them, arguing that Plato's approach to being is precisely that of replacing the poem (as in the poem of Parmenides) by the matheme, thereby setting an example for all future philosophers, Badiou included.[15]

That kind of hocus-pocus seems not to irritate Badiou's followers however, maybe because it puts association in the place of argument, and so enables argument to go just where you want. The mathemes also function as a kind of Newspeak. They suck the being from whatever they latch upon, leaving only the withered forms of destroyed reality, as they rise on vulture wings towards their next assignment. At one point Badiou, having picked up the music of Dutilleux and dropped it writhing to the ground, refers to the 'terror of the matheme'.[16] Maybe that is what he has in mind.

Badiou's enterprise comes up against a difficulty that it requires some ingenuity to negotiate, namely, the discovery that set theory is not the only way of deriving mathematics from minimal axioms. There is also category theory, first introduced by Eilenberg and Mac Lane in 1945, in which mathematical operations are treated purely syntactically, as 'structure-preserving transformations'. In category theory there are only signs and their transformations, and no field of entities to which they refer.[17]

Category theory is particularly associated with the name of Alexander Grothendieck, a German-French recluse, who pursued a revolutionary career on the edge of the 1968 events before disappearing into the Void, and who is, for that, if for no other reason, an important person in Badiou's pantheon. But the implication of category theory is not that mathematics is founded on the 'void' and the procedure of 'counting as one' (i.e. the procedure of assembling into a set), but that mathematics *has* no ontological foundations – it can be constructed in whatever way you like, provided that certain basic syntactical transformations are consistently followed. Badiou's attempt to treat mathematics as though it simply *is* ontology therefore involves a kind of systematic misperception

---

[15] *L'être et l'événement*, p. 144.
[16] *Logiques des Mondes*, Paris, Éditions du Seuil, 2006, p. 98.
[17] See Jean-Pierre Marquis, *From a Geometrical Point of View: A Study of the History and Philosophy of Category Theory*, Springer Science & Business Media, 2008.

of its character. In a celebrated article, 'What Numbers Could Not Be', published in 1965, Paul Benacerraf gave good philosophical reasons for thinking that mathematics is not about sets. Nor, in a crucial sense, is it about anything else. Any elements can be chosen as its domain, just so long as they permit the construction of numerical proofs.[18]

Badiou deals with the problem in characteristic fashion. In *Mathematics of the Transcendental*, he presents the first steps in category theory, setting out the moves more or less as you would find them in an introductory textbook. But in lieu of an explanation, he turns the mathematics into mathemes, inserting fragments of nonsense – nonsemes, as we might call them – between the symbols. The reader is meant to receive the impression that any difficulty that might have been presented by category theory has been overcome, and that this too has been added to Badiou's philosophical armoury. Here is an example:

> But are they [the true and the false] really two? We should be wary: in the categorial universe, difference is cunning and identity evasive. The true and the false are after all two arrows, two monomorphisms. Moreover, these elementary monomorphisms have the same source (I) and the same target (C). Can they not be, 'these' arrows, two names for the same act? We should then have a kind of rational scepticism, where truth-values superimpose (as in the thought of Nietzsche) their nominal duality upon an identical principle of power.[19]

You can puzzle for hours over the meaning of such passages, but I am confident that they will not prove to be translatable into any idiom but their own. For they juxtapose ideas that have no connection with each other, and which have been lifted clear of the contexts that give them their sense. And that, precisely, *is* their sense: like the mathemes of Lacan and the rhizomes – the ingrowing toe-nails – of Deleuze, they teach a new way of thinking, which is guaranteed to turn any subject in the required direction, regardless of whether they cast any light on it.

It is of course entirely possible that I have failed to understand what Badiou is getting at, in his crypto-mathematical works. But something in the style suggests to me that there is less to them than meets the eye.

---

[18] Paul Benacerraf, 'What Numbers Could Not Be', *Philosophical Review* (1965).
[19] Alain Badiou, *Mathematics of the Transcendental*, ed., tr. and with an introduction by A. J. Bartlett and Alex Ling, London, 2014, p. 79.

The mathemes are not there to offer the kind of indubitable support that only mathematics can offer, but to create the impression of rigour in its absence. They are used to lend authority to sentences like this: 'if the thought of being does not open to any truth – because a truth is not, but comes forth from the standpoint of an undecidable supplementation – there is still a *being of the truth*, which is *not* the truth; precisely, it is the latter's being'.[20] Nonsemes and mathemes stand next to each other in detached and mutually irrelevant jumbles. They lack the crucial valency that ties sentence to sentence in a truth-directed argument or formula to formula in a valid proof, and they can accumulate forever without getting to the point of saying or revealing what they mean. They form the conclusions of Badiou's argument, and are usually thrown at the reader like a trump card, with some such word as 'precisely' or 'exactly' emphasizing to the doubters that their game is up.

Badiou's way of writing is not altogether exceptional. Since the origins of philosophy in the pre-Socratics the topic of being has generated endless impenetrable texts that fascinate without being obviously meaningful. The One of Parmenides, the Being-qua-Being of Aristotle and Aquinas, the *haecceitas* of Duns Scotus, the *Istigkeit* of Jakob Boehme, the Being and Becoming of Hegel – right down to the Being-towards-death and ahead-of-itself-Being of Heidegger – all is clouded in mystery and it is the same mystery that wraps the idea of God. Whether Kant freed us from this enchantment when he showed that existence is not a predicate, or whether Frege completed the job with his theory of the existential quantifier, we shall never be sure. For the clouds swirl back after every defeat, and the clearing is revealed only for the shortest periods, to eyes dazzled by the brightness. We should not blame Badiou for swelling the cloud with mathemes and nonsemes, when it is in any case so full of memes and dreams. However he has a special purpose of his own, which is connected not with Being but with Event, the second term of his title. Philosophical truth, as he envisages it, is not about Being. It is focused on the Event, and it is through the theory of the Event that Badiou tries to rescue the revolutionary consciousness that got him thinking in the first place.

The idea is this. In all the multiplicity by which we are surrounded and in which we are involved, we are confronted by happenings that are a source of 'truth' for us, and which we then 'subtract' from the flux of quotidian knowledge. When we grasp these things, and remain faithful

---

[20] Ibid., p. 355.

to them through all opposition and disappointment, we become part of a 'truth process'. A 'truth process' is one of those happenings to which Badiou assigns the honorific title of 'Event'. It is an interruption in the flow of things, a singularity that overthrows the preceding conception of what is possible, since it is literally impossible within the language of the existing situation.

Badiou's paradigm here is revolution, and in particular the French Revolution of 1789. Revolutions, Badiou believes, generate their own 'truths', of which they themselves are a part. They exist only if they also know themselves to be revolutions. Given a matheme or two this comes out as the claim that a revolution is a set of which the revolution itself is a member.[21] And that is forbidden by the foundation axiom – the axiom introduced into Zermelo-Frankel set theory precisely to avoid Russell's paradox of self-membership. In other words revolutions are ruled out by the 'language of the situation', by the prevailing forms of 'knowledge' (*savoirs*).[22] With the eruption of the event, Badiou puts it, the situation 'confesses to its void'.[23] The 'truth process' intervenes to create a new condition, which is 'unnameable' since it cuts across all existing knowledge. It is a 'generic' process, intent on collecting singularities without reducing them to a shared classification. The revolution envisages a classless multitude. From such a generic process there emerges 'the multiple being of a truth'.

All that is an exuberant mixture of wishful thinking, political excitement and pseudo-mathematics. But it gives Badiou a vehicle for his general theory of the Event. An Event is known to be impossible until it happens, but then demands total fidelity to the 'truth process' that it initiates, the process that ushers in the future. Badiou uses the word 'truth' as it was used by Christ, when he described himself as 'the way, the truth (*hē alētheia*) and the life' (John 14.6). It is not the ordinary semantic idea of correspondence with the facts, but the exalted idea of faith in, and truth to, a cause, or a way of being – Heidegger's 'authenticity', or Sartre's '*bonne foi*'. Somehow the 'truth process' offers a way of redemption to the person who commits to it, as well as an opening through which the future can enter the world.

---

[21] See *L'être et l'événement*, pp. 208, 212.
[22] As noted in my discussion of Foucault in Chapter 4, 'savoir' admits of a plural, 'knowledge' does not. The use of 'knowledges' by Badiou's translators is one sign that they are not really concerned by the truth of what he says, but only by the exhilarating effect of it.
[23] *L'être et l'événement.*, p. 212.

Another Lacanism intrudes at this point. Lacan wiped away the subject as a noun. But he provided a verb to replace it. Through a process of 'subjectivation' I can begin to ex-sist – in other words to exist objectively, as a self-knowing person. This particular way of expressing the old Hegelian concept of *Entäusserung* has exerted a profound influence over Badiou. Subjectivation becomes an 'intervention' through which the Event emerges. Badiou introduces the idea with a pseudo-definition: 'I call "subjectivation" the emergence of an operator consequent upon an intervention that bestows a name (*une nomination intervenante*)'[24] – in other words subjectivation means intervening in events by *naming* them for what they are, in the way that St Just and Robespierre *named* the French Revolution and so made it theirs. Always subjectivation takes the form of a Two – i.e. a joining of the self-realizing subject to a larger world. (Badiou's examples: Lenin and the Party, Cantor and 'ontology', St Paul and the Church, lover and beloved…) Subjectivation is the thing by which 'a truth is possible'. 'It turns the event towards the situation for which it is Event.'[25] It is also the process whereby a subject comes to be, involving the 'becoming irreplaceable' of the individual.[26]

It gradually becomes clear, through the haze of mathemes and nonsemes, that Badiou is rewriting – or rather over-writing – the Sartrean philosophy of commitment. He is telling us that we become free subjects through intervening in the course of things, so as to commit ourselves to the great Event. What then is Badiou's message? One can, to use Wittgenstein's metaphor, 'divide through' by the mathemes, so as to discover the real argument beneath them – the very same argument that is presented in Badiou's *Ethics*, in *L'hypothèse communiste*, and in *St Paul*. The argument involves stepping away from logic entirely, no longer using 'truth' as the semantic value of a well-formed formula, forgetting about ontology, and using the jargon of 'forcing', 'construction' and 'generic sets' purely as metaphors. The purpose is to advocate a religious leap of faith – a leap into the unknown, or the 'unnameable'. And the goal is the old communist dream, of an absolute, unmediated (and so 'generic') equality.

---

[24] *L'être et l'événement*, p. 430.

[25] Ibid., p. 435.

[26] *Ethics: An Essay on the Understanding of Evil*, tr. P. Hallward, London, Verso, 2001, p. 43.

We must, Badiou argues, distinguish the 'ordinary' realm of established interests and approved knowledge from an 'exceptional' realm of singular innovations or *truths*.[27] The ordinary realm is, as Althusser argued, 'structured in dominance'. In other words, it consists of the familiar system of inequalities, built in the interests of 'capitalism' and the bourgeoisie. It is only by a radical break that we can discard the structures of dominance. However the break is 'unnameable' within the existing system. Hence we cannot *prove* this break (the Event) but only affirm it, through our 'resilient fidelity' to its consequences. Badiou adds that subjects 'become immortal' through the affirmation of a truth, as did the Jacobins and the Bolsheviks, as did such lovers as Héloïse and Abelard and as did St Paul – of whom more later. Not that they live forever, but that they act *as if* this is so, so that their *significance* lives forever. Moreover it is only in this way, by commitment to a 'truth process', that a subject emerges and becomes an irreplaceable individual.[28] Fidelity to a truth process is the primary form of 'subjectivation'.

This elevation of revolution to the status of a personal redemption is exactly what it seems: a self-directed ego trip, whose benefits are clear only for the person who embarks on it. In all his discussions of the French, Russian and Maoist revolutions Badiou pays little or no attention to the vast sufferings that they caused, and regards 'fidelity' to the event as a sufficient justification for carrying on regardless. Fidelity justifies itself, and indeed can be justified in no other way, since the Event abrogates the language with which it could be criticized from any standpoint other than its own. The exultant intellectual, immersed in his 'truth procedure', has no need to cast his eyes around at the corpses, for they belong to the ordinary realm of established interests and *savoirs*. Kick them out of the way, and get on with the job. True redemption comes from accepting 'the possibility of the impossible, which is exposed by every ... sequence of emancipatory politics'.[29]

Of course, various people have pointed out the consequences of this kind of utopian thinking – notably André Glucksmann and the other *nouveaux philosophes*, who thereby show how little they deserve that title. Theirs is 'sophistry at its most devastating'.[30] To dismiss the call to revolution

---

[27] Here and in what follows I am summarizing the argument of *Ethics: An Essay on the Understanding of Evil*.
[28] *Ethics*, p. 43.
[29] Ibid., p. 39.
[30] Ibid., p. 13.

as utopian is comparable to resisting a new paradigm in science,[31] or to refusing, like Stravinsky, to acknowledge that neo-classicism is 'not generic', unlike the dodecaphonic system of Schoenberg.[32] The call of the future must be answered in all those areas where 'generic procedures' are available. In effect, Badiou's vision of revolution is entirely aestheticized. It is you, your purity and authenticity that are at stake, just as they were for the misguided Stravinsky, and it is sufficient that you remain faithful to the 'truth procedure': the body-count can be expressed only in a language that has no application to the Event in any case.[33] It is surprising, in Badiou's eyes, that someone who calls himself a philosopher should not see this.

It is the next two stages in the argument that are most revealing. In all his works, Badiou identifies just four areas which admit of 'generic procedures', and in which the call to fidelity is heard: science (including mathematics), love (by which he means erotic love), art and politics. And it is only through fidelity to such a 'generic procedure' that we achieve the good. Hence only those who can devote themselves to science, love, art or politics can be truly good. The rest are, from the moral point of view, distinctly second-rate. Devote your life to law, business, farming, tailoring, cobbling or nursing, and you cut yourself off from the path of redemption. Badiou has a self-vaunting way of defining his own path through life, as in the preface to his (in my view) uncomprehending book on Wittgenstein:

> ...a philosopher is a political militant, generally hated by the powers that be and their lackeys; an aesthete, introducing the most improbable creations; a lover, whose life is capable of being turned upside down for a man or a woman; a scientist, who frequents the most violently paradoxical applications of the sciences. And it is in this effervescence, this in-disposition, this rebellion, that he produces his cathedral of ideas.[34]

Having carved out a heroic role for himself, it is not surprising that Badiou should dismiss the ethics of the world in which we live – the world of capitalo-parliamentarism[35] – as a form of nihilism, a refusal

---

[31] *L'Être et l'événement*, pp. 436–7.
[32] Ibid. pp. 443–4.
[33] This, I think, is how we should read the extraordinary apology for Mao's Cultural Revolution in *L'hypothèse communiste*, pp. 90–3.
[34] Alain Badiou, *L'antiphilosophie de Wittgenstein*, Caen, Nous, 2009, p. 7.
[35] *L'hypothèse communiste*, p. 32.

to recognize the good, by placing the protection against evil at the centre of moral thinking. That, he suggests, is the real meaning of the philosophy of 'human rights'. This philosophy, embodied in the categorical imperative of Kant, assumes the existence of subjects without those heroic acts of subjectivation by which we, the elect, fling ourselves into the stream of things and thereby redeem them, or if not them, at least ourselves. The philosophy of human rights therefore places a spurious universality in the place where creative individuals should be. More importantly, it has put evil over good in the scheme of values, and lent itself to all those orthodoxies that perpetuate the structures of inequality – market economics, property rights, freedom of contract and trade, the defence of bourgeois privileges against the *sans-papiers* who pose a threat to them. In short it is 'a violently reactionary movement against all that was thought and proposed in the 1960s'.[36]

Not content with attacking the ethic of human rights, Badiou mounts a challenge to what he sees as the principal source of resistance to his kind of revolutionary absolutism, namely the moral philosophy of the Other, as we find this in the writings of Lévinas. According to this philosophy the moral life arises from my recognition of the other, who comes before me with an absolute demand for my respect and protection, and whose recognition I seek through the mutuality of our dealings. This thought (catalysed once again by Kojève, whose lectures Lévinas attended) has its roots in the Torah and in Christ's parable of the Good Samaritan, and was embedded in philosophy by Kant's categorical imperative, and by the Hegelian dialectic. But it is anathema to Badiou, since it suggests another avenue to the belief in human rights, and to the purely negative ethic that tells me to respect the mortality of human beings, and to refrain from all that might hurt them. The Other of Lévinas, he argues, becomes 'a category of pious discourse', a kind of decomposed religion.[37] Moreover, the other is accepted only as a 'good other'; the real meaning of this 'otherism' is 'become like me and I will respect your difference'. It is a way in which the 'good man', the 'white man', maintains his privileges in being, against the radical threats from those who are excluded.[38] (Who said leftists are opposed to racial stereotyping?)

---

[36] *Ethics*, p. 5.
[37] Ibid., p. 22.
[38] Ibid., p. 13.

So is Badiou, like Sartre, putting self before other in his vision of salvation? The answer is yes, and yes again. The only genuine morality, for Badiou, is that of the 'truth process', which is confined to the four practices of science, (erotic) love, politics and art – the practices that define the lifestyle of people like Badiou. Entering such a process I cast aside the concerns of mortality, to become faithful to the Event.[39] Ethics, as presented by the prevailing system, is based on the 'underlying conviction...that the only thing that can really happen to someone is death'.[40] Against this ethics I commit my energies to the 'unnameable', to that which is yet to be, through an act of subjectivation whose end-point is me. I become the true subject, the artist-scientist-lover-revolutionary who has shaken off the claims of those petit-bourgeois others and their self-serving human rights, to become the 'immortal of the situation'.[41] Hence:

> The possibility of the impossible, which is exposed by every loving encounter, every scientific re-foundation, every artistic invention and every sequence of emancipatory politics, is the sole principle – against the ethics of living-well whose real content is the deciding of death – of an ethic of truths.[42]

In embracing the 'possibility of the impossible' I am fully myself and also 'in excess of myself', since the uncertain course of fidelity 'passes through me'.[43] That is the meaning of Lacan's exhortation to *ne pas céder sur son désir*, not to give up on your desire. I am in some deep sense *alone* in this embracing of the Event. The immortal that I am capable of being cannot be spurred in me by communicative sociality, it must be *directly* seized by fidelity.[44] It *happens* to me, and I am singled out by it.

Badiou illustrates this new existentialist ethic with a surprising example: that of St Paul. On the road to Damascus Paul experienced the very thing that Badiou experienced in 1968: a sudden call to embrace the impossible and to remain faithful to it. The impossible was the Event, and the Event, in St Paul's case, was the Resurrection of Christ. Behind this

---

[39] Ibid., p. 15.
[40] Ibid., p. 35.
[41] Ibid., p. 15.
[42] Ibid., p. 39.
[43] Ibid., p. 45.
[44] Ibid., p. 51.

event, like a crowd pressing into being from the future, was the promise of emancipation. Paul summoned through his faith the 'generic' multitude, the unnameable masses to whom the old distinctions no longer apply. Jew and gentile, citizen and slave – all are offered the revelation, and all, like Paul, can cast off the body of this death and become members of the body of Christ, God's own 'generic set'. Such was the Church, in Paul's original understanding.

Badiou devotes a whole book to the example, and frequently refers to it elsewhere. Yet it is evident that it sheds a wholly sceptical light on his wider philosophy. Paul was not engaged in one of those four 'generic procedures' that define the sole permitted lifestyles of the left-wing intellectual. He was neither poet, nor scientist, nor lover nor political revolutionary. He was a religious evangelist, a Roman citizen, and someone who sought to reconcile his new religion with the legal order of which he was a part. Moreover, the Event that he announced, the belief in which was to transform the world, is not an event that actually *occurred* – not, at any rate, in Badiou's view of things. Badiou is an atheist, for whom resurrection of the dead really is impossible, and there is nothing in Badiou's writings to suggest that he believes otherwise. In which case might not the same be true of Badiou's own 'truth procedure'? Could it not be that the revolutionary Event, the outcome of which is a condition of absolute equality, is just as impossible as the evidence of history suggests it to be? Could it not be that the impossible does not after all become possible through my fidelity to it, and that it remains impossible? And if that is so, what is so despicable about those people like André Glucksmann and Alain Finkielkraut who try to point this out?

All those sceptical thoughts are, in my view, as nothing compared with the real objection to Badiou's thought, which is that it is entirely fortified against reality. His dismissal of the doctrine of human rights is based on a few shallow remarks about Kant. The origins of this doctrine in the theory of natural law and the Roman law principle of *alterum non laedere*, its articulation by the English courts of common law and also by Locke, its translation into real and peace-making legality in the American Constitution – these gain no mention. The idea of law, and all the jurisprudence through which our legal systems have sought to define and uphold the sovereignty of the individual against the power of the state, fail to attract a moment's notice from the position at which Badiou stands. Of course the concept of right can be used in fast and loose ways, as we have seen in the judgments of the European Court of Human Rights. But this is of no significance for Badiou, who with characteristic insolence dismisses unexamined both the concept and the ordinary lives that have been built on it. Such things are unworthy of serious attention from the exalted stance of the true intellectual.

Likewise, Badiou's account of the French Revolution as a truth procedure, justified by St Just's and Robespierre's 'fidelity' to the goal of popular sovereignty, ignores every adverse historical fact, and sweeps away all the devastating evidence of history with a few swipes at François Furet.[45] His account of Maoism and its effect is of an embarrassing naivety, and expresses a kind of dismissive contempt towards the many Chinese people who had the impertinence to cherish their traditional culture at a time when the French intellectuals had, in their ignorance, waved that culture to extinction. Badiou remains locked in his intellectual fortress, the mathemes and nonsemes trained on the enemy, with no quarter given to those whose only weapon is the Real.

Hence when it comes to defining evil Badiou follows the path of the later Sartre. Evil is the province of the false intellectual, the one who is not faithful to a truth procedure, because either he betrays it, or is deluded by a simulacrum, or tries to impose it without the qualifications that it contains. Putting it in this abstract way enables Badiou to hold on to his heroes – St Just, Lenin, Mao – while dismissing others, like Hitler, who in so many ways resembled them but who are not (or at any rate, not standardly) placed on the left. The theory of the 'Event' and the intellectual's fidelity to it, if it justifies Lenin and Mao, ought also to justify Hitler. In long tortuous passages Badiou wrestles with this difficulty, arguing that the Nazi revolution was not a real Event but a 'simulacrum'. He presents a deft sequence of nonsemes with which to persuade himself of this:

Fidelity to a simulacrum, unlike fidelity to an event, regulates its break with the situation not by the universality of the void, but by the closed particularity of an abstract set (the 'Germans' or the 'Aryans') ... The void, 'avoided' (*chassé*) by the simulacrous promotion of an 'event-substance', here returns, with its universality, as what must be accomplished in

---

[45] Naturally René Sedillot's *Le coût de la Révolution Française*, Paris, 1987, gains no mention, and as for all the damning Anglo-American scholarship from Richard Cobb, Simon Schama, and others, it might as well not exist, so far as Badiou is concerned. See my essay 'Man's Second Disobedience', in *The Philosopher on Dover Beach*, Manchester, 1989, for a survey of some of the literature.

order that this substance can be. This is to say that what is addressed 'to everyone' (and 'everyone', here, is necessarily that which does not belong to the German communitarian substance – for this substance is not an 'everyone' but, rather, some 'few' who dominate 'everyone') is death...[46]

From which Badiou concludes that 'fidelity to the simulacrum...has as its content war and massacre. These are not here means to an end: they make up the very real of such a fidelity.'

The nonsemes divert attention from the real problem. It is true that Hitler's revolution favoured certain classes of people and condemned others. But so too did the revolutions in China and Russia: what else did all that rhetoric about the bourgeoisie and the proletariat stand for? Rephrasing the problem in terms of 'the closed particularity of an abstract set' won't make it go away, even for those who pick up the allusion to Cohen's proof. Nor is there much relief to be found in the implied contrast between Nazi war and massacre (described as ends in themselves) and the wars and massacres conducted by the communists (described as means to an end). In the context, and on the scale that these things displayed, it is impossible to take the distinction seriously. Someone who can write as Badiou writes has clearly lost all sense of crime. As with Hobsbawm, Sartre, Lukács and Adorno, crime for Badiou isn't crime, if the goal is utopia.

The apologetic is of course longer than the fragments I have excerpted. But it shows the remarkable state of mind from which Badiou's nonsemes flow. He is in the grip of a complete commitment to something unreal, which is dressed up as a 'truth procedure', an 'event', a 'generic multitude', 'the unnameable' – terms that do nothing to conceal the underlying nothingness – and an equal commitment to sweeping away any reality that conflicts with it. If this were merely an intellectual exercise, a kind of fantasy mathematics, it would matter less. But like Sartre Badiou is loud in defence of revolutions wherever they occur, and dismisses the political process in his country as the 'capitalo-parliamentarism' that always favours the bourgeoisie (*les salauds*, as Sartre called them). His goal is to induce a distrust of parliamentary democracy and the rule of law – two great benefits that have conferred on him a life of secure retirement after his years as a professor at the École Normale Supérieure. And in an extraordinary intervention in the politics of his country, he attacked

---

[46] *Ethics*, p. 74.

the *barbarie sarkozyenne*, comparing Sarkozy's government unfavourably with that of Stalin.[47]

All the evidence that violent revolutions conducted by exultant elites lead to genocide, impoverishment and the loss of liberty counts for nothing in Badiou's eyes, since it is evidence from the empirical world. The true Event – the Event to which one must be faithful in the midst of all merely empirical failure – takes place elsewhere, in a transcendental realm that is also a 'becoming real'. It is a 'truth event', which does not mean that it happens – on the contrary, truth is defined precisely *against* mere realities. The mathemes surround this truth like guards of honour around the throne, sworn to secure it against all the threats from the 'knowledge' of those who base their reactionary worldviews on mere observation.

Badiou's most influential disciple, Slavoj Žižek, who grew up in the comparatively mild regime of communist Yugoslavia, feels the same need as Badiou to discount the deliverances of his senses, and to found his undaunted confidence in revolution on principles so abstract and arcane that no empirical disproof could possibly dislodge them. He has adapted to his own uses Badiou's philosophy of the Event,[48] and joined with Badiou in expressing a public commitment to 'the communist hypothesis'. He sees nothing amiss with the mathemes and nonsemes that gather around the throne, and adds nonsemes of his own whenever challenged. However, he also looks to other and earlier sources for the proof that revolution, which is empirically impossible, is nevertheless, and *for that very reason*, transcendentally necessary. The result is an unstoppable flow of words, images, arguments and references, proceeding from question to question and speculation to speculation while avoiding all the real obstacles that mere reason can lay in their way.

To be fair, Žižek, who qualified as a 'dissident' during the declining years of communism in his native Slovenia, offers proof of one feature in which the communist system had the edge on its Western rivals: he is seriously educated. He writes perceptively of art, literature, cinema and music, and when he is considering the events of the day – be it presidential elections in America or Islamist extremism in the Middle East – he always has something interesting and challenging to say. He has learned Marxism, not as a flamboyant pursuit of an emancipated leisure

---

[47] *De quoi Sarkozy est-il le nom?* Paris, Lignes, 2007.
[48] See, for example, Slavoj Žižek, *Event: Philosophy in Transit*, New York, Penguin, 2014.

class, but as an attempt to discover the truth about our world. He has studied Hegel in depth, and in what are surely his two most sustained pieces of writing – *The Sublime Object of Ideology* (1989), and Part I of *The Ticklish Subject* (1999) – he shows how to apply this study to the confused times in which we live. He has responded to the poetry of Hegel as well as to the metaphysics, and he has retained the Hegelian longing for a total perspective, in which being and nothingness, affirmation and negation are brought into relation and reconciled.

If he had stayed in Slovenia, and if Slovenia had stayed communist, Žižek would not have been the nuisance he has since become. Indeed, if there were no greater reason to regret the collapse of communism in Eastern Europe, the release of Žižek on to the world of Western scholarship would perhaps already be a sufficient one. By seizing on Jacques Lacan's psychoanalytic vision as the transcendental ground for his new socialist philosophy, Žižek raises the level of excitement beyond anything achieved by his predecessors. And his slick, all-inclusive style offers constant hints of persuasive argument. Unlike Badiou Žižek can be read with ease for pages at a time, with a full sense that he is sharing matters that could form an understanding between himself and his reader. At the same time he passes quickly over outrageous statements that seem, at first, to be slips of the pen, but which the reader discovers in time to be the true content of his message.

As an indication of Žižek's style here are some of the topics touched on in three consecutive pages chosen more or less at random from his engaging book *In Defence of Lost Causes*: the Turin shroud, the Koran and the scientific worldview, the Tao of physics, secular humanism, Lacan's theory of fatherhood, truth in politics, capitalism and science, Hegel on art and religion, postmodernity and the end of the grand narratives, Lacan's concept of the Real, psychoanalysis and modernity, modernization and culture, the superego and its relation to fundamentalism, solipsism and cyberspace, masturbation, Hegel and objective spirit, Richard Rorty's pragmatism, and is there or is there not a big Other?

The machine-gun rattle of topics and concepts makes it easy for Žižek to slip in his little pellets of poison, which the reader, nodding in time to the rhythm of the prose, might easily swallow unnoticed. Thus, we are not 'to reject terror *in toto* but to re-invent it';[49] we must recognize that the problem with Hitler, and with Stalin too, is that they 'were not

---

[49] P. 7.

violent enough';[50] we should accept Mao's 'cosmic perspective', and read the Cultural Revolution as a positive Event.[51] Rather than criticizing Stalinism as immoral, we should praise it for its humanity, since it rescued the Soviet experiment from 'biopolitics'; besides, Stalinism is not immoral but too *moral*, since it relied on the figure of the big Other, which, as all Lacanians know, is the primordial mistake of the moralist.[52] We must also recognize that the 'dictatorship of the proletariat', is 'the only true choice today'.[53]

Žižek's defence of terror and violence, his call for a new Party organized on Leninist principles,[54] his celebration of Mao's Cultural Revolution, the thousands of deaths notwithstanding and indeed lauded as part of the meaning of a politics of action – all this might have served to discredit Žižek among more moderate left-wing readers, were it not for the fact that it is never possible to be sure that he is serious. Maybe he is laughing, not only at himself and his readers, but at an academic establishment that can seriously include Žižek alongside Kant and Hegel on the philosophy curriculum, with a *Journal of Žižek Studies* now in its fourth year of publication. Maybe he is cheering us all on in a holiday from thinking, scoffing at the idiots who imagine there is anything else to be done with thinking than to escape from it:

Here, however, one should avoid the fatal trap of conceiving the subject as the act, the gesture, which intervenes afterwards in order to fill in the ontological gap, and insist on the irreducible vicious cycle of subjectivity: 'the wound is healed only by the spear which smote it', that is, the subject 'is' the very gap filled in by the gesture of subjectivization (which, in Laclau, establishes a new hegemony; which, in Rancière, gives voice to the 'part no part'; which, in Badiou, assumes fidelity to the Truth-Event; etc.). In short, the Lacanian answer to the question asked (and answered in a negative way) by such different philosophers as Althusser, Derrida and Badiou – 'Can the gap, the opening, the Void which precedes the gesture of subjectivization, still be called "subject"?' – is an emphatic 'Yes!' – the subject is both at the

---

[50] Pp. 151, 152.
[51] P. 175.
[52] P. 224.
[53] 'Robespierre, or, the "Divine Violence" of Terror', in Maximilien de Robespierre, *Virtue and Terror*, London and New York, Verso, 2007, p. xxvii.
[54] *Revolution at the Gates*, London and New York, Verso, 2004, p. 297.

same time, the ontological gap (the 'night of the world', the madness of radical self-withdrawal) as well as the gesture of subjectivization which, by means of a short circuit between the Universal and the Particular, heals the wound of this gap (in Lacanese: the gesture of the Master which establishes a 'new harmony'). *'Subjectivity' is a name for this irreducible circularity, for a power which does not fight an external resisting force (say, the inertia of the given substantial order), but an obstacle that is absolutely inherent, which ultimately 'is' the subject itself.* In other words the subject's very endeavor to fill in the gap retroactively sustains and generates this gap.[55]

Notice the sudden intrusion into the logorrhea of a long italicized sentence, no more clear than any others, as though Žižek had paused to draw a conclusion before passing exultantly to the next half-formed conception.

The passage is part of a contribution to the Lacanian theory (if theory it is) of 'subjectivation', which we have already seen at work in the philosophy of Badiou. But its main import is to bring home to the reader that, whatever might be said by the other purveyors of fashionable nonsense, Žižek has said it too, and that all truths, all insights, all useful nonsemes, are tributaries flowing into the unstaunchable flood of his all-comprehending negativity. The prose is an invitation: you the reader should plunge in too, so as to be washed clean of the taint of reasoned argument and to enjoy at last the true refreshing waters of the mind, which flow from topic to topic and from place to place unimpeded by realities, and always flowing to the left.

Žižek publishes at the rate of two or three books a year. He writes at an ironical distance from himself, aware that acceptance is obtainable in no other way. But he is also concerned to undermine the superficial plausibilities of the consumerist society which has replaced the old order of communist Yugoslavia, and to discover the deep *spiritual* cause of its ailments. When he is not writing allusively, jumping like a grasshopper from topic to topic, he is trying to unmask what he sees as the self-deceptions of the global capitalist order. Like Badiou, he fails to provide a clear alternative. But, in the absence of a clear alternative, an unclear alternative, even a purely imaginary alternative, will do, whatever the

---

[55] *The Ticklish Subject: The Absent Centre of Political Ontology*, London and New York, Verso, 1999, pp. 158–9.

consequences. As he puts it, using Badiou's language: 'Better a disaster of fidelity to the Event than a non-being of indifference towards the Event.'[56]

In order to support this notion he leans on two intellectual sources, the philosophy of Hegel, and the ideas of Lacan as expounded by Jacques-Alain Miller, Lacan's son-in-law, whose seminar Žižek attended during time spent in Paris in 1981, and who also became Žižek's analyst. To summarize Žižek's position is not easy: he slips between philosophical and psychoanalytical ways of arguing, and is spell-bound by Lacan's gnomic utterances. He is a lover of paradox, and believes strongly in what Hegel called 'the labour of the negative' though taking the idea, as always, one stage further towards the brick wall of paradox.

Hegel argued that concepts become determinate through negation, whereby we establish the limits beyond which they do *not* apply.[57] In a similar way, he suggested, we come to self-knowledge through a series of negatives. We learn to distinguish the world from our will by encountering a limit, a barrier, which is the frontier presented by the will that opposes us – the will of the other. Hence, for Hegel, the negation of our will makes us conscious of that will as *ours*.

For Žižek things are far more drastic, since he follows Lacan in taking negation to its extreme point – not simply as a way of setting limits to a concept, but as a way of *ruling it out*. We become self-conscious by an act of total negation: by learning that there is no subject. Instead of the subject, there is the act of *subjectivation*, which is a defence against the subject – a way in which I prevent myself from becoming a substance, an identity, a centre of being.[58] The subject does not exist before 'subjectivation'. But through subjectivation I read myself back into the condition that preceded my self-awareness. I am what I become, and I become what I am by filling the void of my past.

As in Hegel, this 'coming to be' of the self is made possible only by relation with the other. Hegel gave a beautiful and compelling description of the process, which I summarized in Chapter 4, and occasionally Žižek refers approvingly to it, and to Marx's version in his early theories. But he is far more interested in the mutilation of Hegel's view at the hands of Lacan, for whom, as we have seen, the other assumes a new and mysterious importance. For Žižek, as for Lacan, there is the 'little other',

---

[56] *Lost Causes*, p. 7.
[57] See Žižek, *Tarrying with the Negative*, Durham, NC, Duke University Press, 1993.
[58] *Lost Causes*, p. 343.

which appears as the object of fantasy, and also of desire, and the big Other, the mother imago who dominates the growing child, the authority who brings order, the 'consistent, closed totality' to which we aspire but which always eludes us since 'there is no big Other'.[59] As with the subject, so with the object – it doesn't exist, and non-existence is its way of existing. This is the aspect of Lacan that Žižek finds most exciting – the magic wand that conjures visions, and promptly waves them to nothingness.

The mystical vision of the Other dominates Žižek's thinking, and is used to take short cuts to many of his surprising conclusions. It is because Stalinism relies on the figure of the big Other that it is too moral – a nice excuse which nobody is in a position to refute, since no procedure exists, in Lacan or Žižek, for establishing either the existence or the non-existence of this ill-described nonentity. Democracy is no solution, because although it implies a 'barred big Other', as Jacques-Alain Miller has apparently shown, there is another big Other, the 'procedural big Other' of electoral rules, which have to be obeyed whatever the result.[60]

But perhaps the real danger is populism, in which the big Other returns in the guise of the People. Or is it okay to invoke the People, if you do it in the spirit of Robespierre, whose invocation of Virtue 'redeems the virtual content of terror from its actualization'?[61] There is no knowing, but who cares? Certainly not Žižek, who takes refuge behind the skirts of big Other whenever the little others come with their irritating questions. In this way he can defend himself from the anti-totalitarians whose thoughts are 'a worthless sophistic exercise, a pseudo-theorization of the lowest opportunist survivalist fears and instincts…'[62] – language which has all the authenticity of those Newspeak denunciations that composed the editorials of *Pravda*, *Rudé Pravo* and the Slovenian *Delo* in the days of Žižek's youth.

From Lacan Žižek also takes the idea that mental processes fall into three distinct categories: fantasy, symbol and the reaching for the Real. Desire comes through fantasy, which proposes both the object=a (the *objet petit a*), and the first subjectivation: the mirror stage in which desire (and its lack) enter the infant psyche. I am trying, here, to make sense of something that is always *alluded to*, but never fully explained. Here, for what it is worth (namely, zero) is the explanation given by one of Žižek's disciples:

---

[59] See 'From Symptom to *Sinthome*', in *The Sublime Object of Ideology*. London, Verso, 1989.
[60] See *Lost Causes*, p. 264.
[61] Ibid., p. 164.
[62] Ibid., p. 7.

There is an ontological void at the core of our subjectivity and it is this incompleteness that *objet petit a* masks and compensates for, but only seemingly so – the impression of completeness in one's identity that *objet petit a* provides is delusory. It is a fantasy object that fills out the fissure in our sense of being, arising from the way our libidinal investment gives it a sublimity that it does not and cannot possess...[63]

Such statements are in no way to be confounded with Hegel's great argument concerning the interdependence of self and other in the unfolding of human community. For Hegel's argument proceeds by *a priori* steps whose validity does not depend upon observation but on the logic of our concepts. He is telling us what it *is* to be a person among persons, and at the same time allowing for all the ways in which one person can differ from another. Not so Lacan and Žižek, whose assertions could not conceivably be valid *a priori*, but which are never provided with the evidence that might support them. We are told that we people our world with little others, and that we do this through fantasy. But we are not given the evidence for this assertion, still less a clear account of what it means.

So what does fantasy amount to? It is connected with that key term of Lacanian analysis – a term that incidentally entered and dominated French literary theory under the influence of Roland Barthes – namely *jouissance*, which is Lacan's substitute for the Freudian 'pleasure principle'. Fantasies enter our lives and persist because they bring enjoyment, and they are revealed in *symptoms*, those irrational-seeming fragments of behaviour through which the psyche protects its achieved terrain of enjoyment from the threatening realities of the world beyond – from the unvisitable world of the Real. This thought gives rise to a spectacular emendation to Freud's idea of the superego, expressed in terms that unite Kant with the Marquis de Sade:

It is a commonplace of Lacanian theory to emphasize how [the] Kantian moral imperative conceals an obscene superego injunction: 'Enjoy!' – the voice of the Other impelling us to follow our duty for the sake of duty is a traumatic irruption of an appeal to impossible *jouissance*, disrupting the homeostasis of the pleasure principle and its

---

[63] Seán Sheehan, *Žižek: A Guide for the Perplexed*, London, Continuum, 2012, p. 21.

prolongation, the reality principle. This is why Lacan conceives Sade as the truth of Kant...[64]

Having pushed the nonsense machine this far, so as to identify Kant and Sade, and thereby to dismiss as a kind of obscenity the Enlightenment morality by which Western society has tried for two centuries to anchor itself, Žižek is able to offer a new theory of ideology, and one that renews the Marxist critique of capitalism.

Ideology, in the classical Marxist analysis, is to be understood in functional terms. It is the system of illusions through which power achieves legitimacy. Marxism offers a scientific diagnosis of ideology, reducing it to a symptom, showing how things *really* are behind the fetishes. By doing so it 'opens our eyes' to the truth: we see exploitation and injustice where previously we had seen contract and free exchange. The illusory screen of commodities, in which relations between people appear as the law-like motion of things, crumbles before us, and reveals the human reality, stark, unadorned and changeable. In short by tearing away the veil of ideology we prepare the way for revolution.

But in that case, Žižek reasonably asks, why has the revolution not come? Why is it that capitalism, achieving this consciousness of itself, continues to assert its ever-growing dominion, sucking more and more of human life into the maelstrom of commodity consumption? Žižek's answer is that ideology is renewed through fantasy. We cling to the world of commodities as the scene of our deeper *jouissance*, and we shun the reality beyond, the Real that refuses to be known. We come to understand ideology, not as serving the capitalist economy, but as serving itself – it is enjoyable for its own sake, in the way that art and music are. We enter the condition that has been described by Gilles Lipovetsky and Jean Serroy as 'the aestheticisation of the world'.[65]

Ideology becomes a toy in our hands – we both accept it and laugh at it, knowing that everything has its price in our world of illusions, but that nothing of value will ever appear there. This at least is how I read remarks like this one, which is about as clear as Žižek gets on the topic:

---

[64] *The Sublime Object of Ideology*, p. 81.
[65] Gilles Lipovetsky and Jean Serroy, *L'esthétisation du monde: vivre à l'âge du capitalisme artiste*, Paris, 2013. This book, written subsequent to Žižek's best-known work, contains a wealth of fascinating material concerning the world of coveted things – a world that is simultaneously enchanted and disenchanted, since all the glittering illusions are known to be illusions, and yet no reality can possibly intervene to discredit them.

Why must this inversion of the relation of aim and means remain hidden, why is its revelation self-defeating? Because it would reveal the enjoyment which is at work in ideology, in the ideological renunciation itself. In other words, it would reveal that ideology serves only its own purpose, that it does not serve anything – which is precisely the Lacanian definition of *jouissance*.[66]

It is at this point, however, that clarity is imperative. Is Žižek telling us that the world of commodities and markets is with us to stay, and that we must learn to make the best of it? What does it mean that he has arrived at his position by deploying those strange Lacanian categories which appear throughout his prose in lieu of foundations, but which are themselves entirely foundationless? Is there a real argument here, one that might be persuasive to a person who has not had the benefit of brainwashing by Jacques-Alain Miller? Almost always, at the critical juncture, when a clear argument is needed, Žižek takes refuge behind a rhetorical question, into which he packs all the mysterious incantations of the Lacanian liturgy:

Is not the paradoxical topology of the movement of capital, the fundamental blockage which resolves and reproduces itself through frenetic activity, *excessive* power as the very form of appearance of a fundamental *impotence* – this immediate passage, this coincidence of limit and excess, of lack and surplus – precisely that of the Lacanian *objet petit a*, of the leftover which embodies the fundamental, constitutive lack?[67]

The syntactical pressure exerted by such rhetorical questions is directed towards the response 'of course, I should have known that already'. The goal is to *escape the real question*, which is that of the meaning and foundation of the terms. I give another and spectacular example, since it is directly relevant to the theme:

Is not the ultimate domain of psychoanalysis the connection between the symbolic Law and desire? Is not the multitude of perverse satisfactions the very form in which the connection

[66] *The Sublime Object of Ideology*, p. 84.
[67] Ibid., p. 53.

between Law and desire is realized? Is not the Lacanian division of the subject the division that concerns precisely the subject's relationship to the symbolic Law? Furthermore, is not the ultimate confirmation of this Lacan's 'Kant avec Sade', which directly posits the Sadeian universe of morbid perversion as the 'truth' of the most radical assertion of the moral weight of symbolic Law in human history (Kantian ethics)?[68]

If you answered 'no' to any of those questions, the response would be '*No? What on earth do you mean, no?*' For the *real* question is 'What on earth do *you* mean?'

But this brings me to the heart of Žižek's leftism. The Real, touched by Lacan's magic wand, vanishes. It is the primary absence, the 'truth' that is also castration. The wand waves away reality, and thereby gives fresh life to the dream. It is in the world of dreams, therefore, that morality and politics are now to be implanted. What matters is not the discredited world of merely empirical events (which are not *real* Events, as Badiou has shown), but the goings-on in the dream world, the world of the exalted intellectuals, for whom ideas and enthusiasms cancel mere realities.

Thus, in a singularly repulsive essay on 'Revolutionary Terror', Žižek praises the 'humanist terror' of Robespierre and St Just (as opposed to the 'anti-humanist, or rather inhuman' terror of the Nazis), not because it was in any way kind to its victims, but because it expressed the enthusiasm, the 'utopian explosions of political imagination' of its perpetrators.[69] No matter that the terror led to the imprisonment of half a million innocent people, and the deaths of as many more. The statistics are irrelevant, waved away by Lacan's wand, reduced to the square root of minus one – a purely imaginary number. What is relevant is the way in which, through speeches that Žižek would recognize to be self-vaunting bombast did his critical faculties not desert him in the face of a revolutionary hero, Robespierre 'redeemed the virtual content of terror from its actualisation'.[70]

In this way, for Žižek, thought cancels reality, when the thought is 'on the left'. It matters less what you do than what you think you are

[68] *The Ticklish Subject*, p. 152.
[69] *In Defense of Lost Causes*, p. 175. See also the introduction to *Virtue and Terror*, op. cit.
[70] Ibid., p. 164. There is, in this phrase, an oblique reference to Deleuze, whose 'redemption of the virtual' is sometimes singled out for praise, on the grounds that the virtual is another kind of real. Should we enter this fog?

doing, provided what you think you are doing has the ultimate goal of emancipation – of *égaliberté*, as Althusser's disciple Étienne Balibar expresses it.[71] The goal is not equality or liberty conceived in the qualified sense that you or I would understand those terms. It is absolute equality (with a bit of liberty thrown in if you are lucky), which can by its nature be achieved only by an act of total destruction. To pursue this goal might also be to acknowledge its impossibility – is that not what all such 'total' projects amount to? No matter. It is precisely the impossibility of utopia that fastens us to it: nothing can sully the absolute purity of that which will never be tested.

We should not be surprised, therefore, when Žižek writes that 'the thin difference between the Stalinist gulag and the Nazi annihilation camp was also, at that moment, the difference between civilization and barbarism.'[72] His only interest is in the state of mind of the perpetrators: were they moved, in however oblique a manner, by utopian enthusiasms, or were they moved, on the contrary, by some discredited attachment? If you step back from Žižek's words, and ask yourself just where the line between civilization and barbarism lay, at the time when the rival sets of death camps were competing over their body-counts, you would surely put communist Russia and Nazi Germany on one side of the line, and a few other places, Britain and America for instance, on the other. To Žižek that would be an outrage, a betrayal, a pathetic refusal to see what is really at stake. For what matters is what people *say*, not what they do, and what they say is redeemed by their theories, however stupidly or carelessly pursued, and with whatever disregard for real people. We rescue the virtual from the actual through our words, and the deeds have nothing to do with it.

Reading Žižek I am reminded of a visit I once made to the cemetery of Devichye Pole in Moscow, in the days of Gorbachev. My guide, a dissident intellectual not unlike Žižek in appearance and manner, took me to the grave of Khrushchev, on which stood a monument designed by the sculptor Ernst Neizvestny, who had been singled out for particular denunciation by Khrushchev when, following a visit to an exhibition of modernist art, the latter had decided to attack the entire artistic community. My guide regarded this particular tantrum of Khrushchev's

---

[71] Étienne Balibar, *La proposition de l'égaliberté*, Paris, Presses Universitaires de France, 2010.
[72] *Lost Causes*, p. 262.

far more seriously than his destruction of 25,000 churches, and found nothing wrong in his burial here, in what was once consecrated ground.

The monument shows Khrushchev's head, mounted on two intersecting trunks of stone, one black, one white, symbolizing the contradictions in the leader's character. After all, my guide insisted, it was he who denounced Stalin and showed himself thereby to be the friend of the intellectuals, just as it was he who denounced artistic modernism, and so declared himself to be the enemy of the intellectuals. It was brought painfully home to me that the Russian people have counted for nothing in the intellectual history of Russian communism, either in the minds of its champions or in the minds of its critics, for whom the entire modern period has been a kind of dialogue – conducted at the top of the voice and with every available weapon – between the Party and the intelligentsia. The millions of serfs have gone silently to the grave simply in order to illustrate some intellectual conclusion and to give to the arguments of power the decisive proof of another's helpless suffering.

This discounting of reality reminds us of the crucial fact: that the goal of a supreme emancipation, which will also be the reign of total equality, is a matter of faith, not prediction. It expresses a religious need that cannot be discarded, and which will survive all the evidence adduced towards its refutation. For a while, in the wake of 1989, it looked as if the communist agenda had been defeated, and that the evidence pointed to the decisive rejection of the ideas that had enslaved the people of Eastern Europe since the War. But the nonsense machine was wheeled on to obliterate the shoots of rational argument, to cover everything in a mist of uncertainty, and to revive the idea – already present and poisonous in Lukács – that the real revolution has yet to come, and that it will be a revolution in thought, an inner liberation, against which rational argument (which is mere 'bourgeois ideology') has no defence. In this way the reign of nonsense buried the question of revolution so deeply beneath the possibility of rational enquiry that it could no longer be directly stated.

At the same time, the alchemists never ceased to propose revolution as the goal, the thing that was finally to be conjured from the darkness that their spells created. What exactly were they hoping for? Let us step back into the world of rational analysis, so as to notice that there are at least two kinds of revolution, and that it is important, when we make an idol of this word, to ask ourselves which of the two we mean by it. There is the kind exemplified by the English Glorious Revolution of 1688 and the

American Revolution of 1783, in which essentially law-abiding people attempt to define and protect their rights against usurpation. And there is the kind exemplified by the French Revolution of 1789, and the Russian Revolution of 1917, in which one elite seizes power from another, and then establishes itself by a reign of terror.

The difference between those two things is enormous and of vast significance to us, looking at the course of modern history. But from Althusser to Žižek the alchemists dismiss the distinction with a sneer. For Badiou the English and American Revolutions were not true Events, but at best 'simulacra'. They did not scintillate in the imagination of exultant intellectuals, but merely pressed themselves into being through the needs of real people. Instead of examining what such revolutions achieved, whether it might not have been sufficient and in any case the best that can be hoped for, thinkers like Althusser, Badiou and Žižek prefer to bury themselves in scholastic disputes with their fellow leftists, shifting blocks of formidable Newspeak around the sanctuary where the idol has been hidden, and sprinkling the battlements with nonsemes.

Those who imagined, in 1989, that never again would an intellectual be caught defending the Leninist Party, or advocating the methods of Josef Stalin, had reckoned without the overwhelming power of nonsense. In the urgent need to believe, to find a central mystery that is the true meaning of things and to which one's life can be dedicated, nonsense is much to be preferred to sense. For it builds a way of life around something that *cannot be questioned*. No reasoned assault is possible against that which denies the possibility of a reasoned assault. And thus it is that utopia stepped again, unchallenged, into the place vacated by theology, to erect its own *mysterium tremendum et fascinans* in the centre of intellectual life. A new generation rediscovered the authentic voice of the proletariat, which speaks the language of the nonsense machine. And despite all the disappointments, they were reassured that 'the dictatorship of the proletariat' remains an option – indeed the only option. The proof of this is there in Žižek's prose; you have his word for it.

In the persons of Badiou and Žižek we find astonishing evidence of the fact that the 'communist hypothesis', as Badiou describes it, will never go away. Notwithstanding Marx's attempt to present it as the conclusion of a science, the 'hypothesis' cannot be put to the test and refuted. For it is not a prediction, nor in any real sense a hypothesis. It is a statement of faith in the unknowable, the unnameable, in the 'wandering of nothing'. Badiou and Žižek unhesitatingly add their weight to every cause that is directed, in whatever way, against the established order of the Western democracies. They even set themselves against parliamentary democracy, and have no qualms in advocating terror (suitably aestheticized) as part of their glamorous detachment. But they recognize no obligation either to examine or even to propose an alternative.

Their few empty invocations of equality advance no further than the clichés of the French Revolution, and are soon reissued as mathemes by way of shielding them from argument. But when it comes to real politics they write as though negation is enough. Whether it be the Palestinian intifada, the IRA, the Venezuelan Chavistas, the French *sans-papiers*, or the Occupy movement – whatever the radical cause, it is the attack on the 'System' that matters. The alternative is 'unnameable in the language of the system'. Didn't Paul Cohen prove the point?

As in 1789, as in 1917, as in the Long March of Mao, the Great Leap Forward and the Cultural Revolution, the work of destruction feeds on itself. The Event is 'the void at the heart of the actual'. Fidelity to the Event means commitment to nothing. The windbaggery of Žižek and the nonsemes of Badiou serve one purpose, which is to turn attention away from the actual world, from real people and from ordinary moral and political reasoning. They exist in order to promote a single and absolute cause, the cause that admits of no criticism and no compromise, and which offers redemption to all who espouse it. And what is that cause? The answer is there on every page of these fatuous writings: Nothing.

9 WHAT IS RIGHT?

F undamental to the left's way of thinking is the linear order implied in its name. People who describe themselves as 'on the left' believe that political opinions and movements can be assembled from left to right, and that, to the extent that you are not on the left, to that extent you are on the right. At the same time, by a relentless campaign of intimidation, left-wing thinkers have sought to make it unacceptable to be on the right. As a rule they give no definition of what the 'right' consists in, nor do they explain why national socialists, fascists and economic liberals should all be included in the category. Nevertheless, they are clear about one thing. Once identified as right-wing you are beyond the pale of argument; your views are irrelevant, your character discredited, your presence in the world a mistake. You are not an opponent to be argued with, but a disease to be shunned. This has been my experience, as it has been the experience of all the dissidents I have known. If books by authors on the right are noticed by left-wing reviewers (and in the academic world left-wing reviewers are the norm) it is only in order to trash them.

All that, you might think, puts an enormous onus on left-wing thinkers to define their alternative. But looking back across the bleak landscape that I have travelled in this book I witness only negatives. Occasional lip service is paid to a future state of 'emancipation', 'equality' or 'social justice'. But those terms are seldom lifted out of the realm of abstractions, or subjected to serious examination. They are not, as a rule, used to describe an imagined social order that their advocates are prepared to justify. Instead they are given a purely negative application. They are used to condemn every mediating institution, every imperfect association, every flawed attempt that human beings might have made, to live together without violence and with due respect for law. It is as though the abstract ideal has been chosen precisely so that nothing actual could embody it.

I therefore search the writings of Hobsbawm, Thompson, Badiou, Lukács and Adorno in vain for a description of how the 'equality of being' advocated in their fraught manifestoes is to be achieved. Who controls what and how in the realm of pure equality, and what is done to ensure that the ambitious, the attractive, the energetic and the intelligent do not upset whatever pattern it is that their wise masters might impose on them? Everything remains on the level of the hunting, fishing and literary criticism promised in *The German Ideology*. And when, in the writings of Adorno, I discover that the alternative to the capitalist system is utopia I congratulate the writer for his honesty, since that is another way of saying that there is no alternative. Of course you can rewrite utopia as an 'ideal speech-situation', a *groupe en fusion*, a *procédure générique*, or even a *fascio* – but those descriptions are descriptions of nothing. They propose a society from which all that makes society possible – law, property, custom, hierarchy, family, negotiation, government, institutions – has been removed.

In a moment of doubt about the socialist record Eric Hobsbawm once wrote: 'If the left have to think more seriously about the new society, that does not make it any the less desirable or necessary or the case against the present one any less compelling.'[1] There, in a nutshell, is the sum of the New Left's commitment. We know nothing of the socialist future, save only that it is both necessary and desirable. Our concern is with the 'compelling' case against the present, which leads us to destroy what we lack the knowledge to replace.

A blind faith drags radical leftists from 'struggle' to 'struggle', reassuring them that everything done in the name of equality is well done and that all destruction of existing power will lead towards the goal. They desire to leap from the tainted world that surrounds them into the pure but unknowable realm of total emancipation. This leap into the Kingdom of Ends is a leap of thought, which can never be mirrored in reality. 'Revolutionary praxis' therefore confines itself to the work of destruction, having neither the power nor the desire to imagine, in concrete terms, the end towards which it labours. We should not be surprised therefore if the pursuit of an unmediated equality has, in recent times, produced a world of real enslavement, whose brutal arrangements were incongruously described in the language of emancipation: 'liberation', 'democracy', 'equality', 'progress' and 'peace' – words which, in the world that I remember, were never uttered by a citizen of a socialist state without a pained, sardonic smile.

[1] E. J. Hobsbawm, 'Should Poor People Organise?' in *Worlds of Labour*, London, 1984.

Exactly the same result can be discerned in the 'culture wars', which, under Gramsci's influence, offered an armchair version of the revolutionary struggle. Here too the 'labour of the negative' succeeded in wiping away the face of our inherited culture, pulling down the monuments and blocking all the avenues to consolation. But nothing came in place of that culture, save the soft relativism of Rorty or the mendacious enmity of Said. The final result of the culture wars has been an enforced political correctness, by which the blasted landscape of art, history and literature is policed for the residual signs of racist, sexist, imperialist or colonialist ways of thinking.

At this point I face a challenge from the intelligent reader, who will say that, in my assault on the negativity of the intellectual left, I too have been merely negative. It may be reasonable to criticize the left for offering only unrealities; but what is the *real* alternative? In this chapter I shall sketch an answer to that challenge. It won't be a complete answer. But it might serve as a fitting introduction to ideas that I have developed at greater length elsewhere.[2]

Thinkers of the left often begin their critique of our social and political systems with an assault on the language, as part of a far-reaching strategy to put power and domination at the top of the political agenda, while debunking the ways in which human relations are mediated by the search for agreement. Leftist Newspeak is a powerful tool, not only because it wipes away the face of our social world, but also because it describes a supposed reality that underlies the genial appearance and also explains that appearance away as a deception. Marx's 'material forces', 'antagonistic production relations' and 'ideological superstructure'; Foucault's ruling 'episteme' and 'structures of domination'; the 'forcing', 'generic sets' and 'truth procedures' of Badiou, the big Other of Lacan and Žižek, the 'reification' and 'commodity fetishism' of Lukács – all those mystifying technicalities have the purpose of confiscating reality from our ordinary human understanding. The effect is to put the social world beyond the reach of politics. We are being invited to believe that there can be no resolution of our conflicts short of total transformation, total revolution or, as Joseph Conrad's Professor expresses it, in *The Secret Agent*, 'the destruction of all that is'.

---

[2] See *A Political Philosophy: The Case for Conservatism*, London, Continuum, 2008; *Culture Counts*, New York, Encounter Books, 2009; and *How to be a Conservative*, London, Bloomsbury, 2014.

The greatest task on the right, therefore, is to rescue the language of politics: to put within our grasp what has been forcibly removed from it by jargon. It is only when we have found again the language that is natural to us that we can answer the great accusations that are constantly thrown at our world from the left. And it is only when we have found that language that we can move on from the one-dimensional left/right, with us/against us, progressive/reactionary dichotomies that have so often made rational discussion impossible.

Two accusations against our political inheritance have lodged in the brains that I have examined in this book: first, that 'capitalist' society is founded on power and domination; second, that 'capitalism' means 'commodification', the reduction of people to things, and the fetishizing of things as agents. Different thinkers have expressed the two complaints in different ways. But always they are there, and the first step in offering the real alternative to the left is to answer them.

'Capitalism' is in most of its uses a term of Newspeak. It suggests a comprehensive theory to explain our society, and a strategy to replace it. But there is no such theory, and no such strategy. We know this from a very simple observation, namely that, after all social transformations, however fundamental, after all adaptations, achieved with whatever effort and at whatever cost, the term 'capitalism' still surfaces as a description of the result. This is even true of the state that resulted from the communist revolution in Russia, described as 'state capitalism' by thinkers of the Frankfurt school. The growth of the welfare state, the expansion of home-ownership, the increased social mobility, the evolution of cooperatives, self-employment and shareholding – none of the ways in which society has moved on since Marx or adapted to the needs of its members has loosened the grip of this potent word, which, because it applies to everything, says nothing.

So let us replace the word with a true description. People in our societies own things, their labour included, and can trade those things freely with others. They can buy, sell, accumulate, save, share and give. They can enjoy all that their freely exercised labour can secure for them and even, if they choose, do nothing and still survive. You can take away the freedom to buy and sell; you can compel people to work on terms that they would not freely accept; you can confiscate property or forbid this or that form of it. But if those are the alternatives to 'capitalism' there is, now, no real alternative save slavery.

The old socialist complaint creeps in behind the Newspeak: where there is private property there is also power – the power of the one who owns over the one who needs, of group over group, of class over class. Always in the wake of the attack on 'capitalism' comes the yearning for a 'powerless' world. But this yearning, which finds its most eloquent expression in the writings of Foucault, is incoherent. The condition of society is essentially one of domination, in which people are bound to each other by their attachments, and distinguished by rivalries and competition. There is no society that transcends those human realities, nor should we wish for one, since it is from those things that our worldly satisfactions are composed. But where there is attachment there is power; and where there is rivalry there is the need for government. As Kenneth Minogue once put it: 'the worm of domination lies at the heart of what it is to be human, and the conclusion faces us that the attempt to overthrow domination, as that idea is metaphysically understood in ideology, is the attempt to destroy humanity'.[3] Our concern as political beings should be, not to abolish the powers that bind society together, but to mitigate their exercise. We should not aim for a world without power, but for a world where power is consented to, and where conflicts are resolved according to a shared conception of justice.

Thinkers of the Left have been impatient with the 'natural justice' that lies dormant within our social intercourse and whose workings I described in Chapter 3. Either they discard it, like the Marxists, as a figment of 'bourgeois ideology', or else they divert it from its natural course, replacing it with a conception of 'social justice' that disregards historic rights, duties and deserts in order to 'treat everyone as an equal', while assuming that this is the way to *respect* rights rather than to override them. This second stance – illustrated in the work of Dworkin – is anti-revolutionary in its methods but revolutionary in its aims. American liberals are as convinced of the evil of domination as are the Parisian *gauchistes*, but distinguished by their recognition that institutions are, in the end, necessary to their purpose, and that ideology is no substitute for the patient work of law.

The New Left has not, in general, shared that laudable respect for institutions. Its denunciations of power have therefore been accompanied by no description of the institutions of the future. The goal has been for a society *without* institutions: a society in which people spontaneously group together in life-affirming globules, from which the dead shell of law and custom has fallen away. In pursuit of this world without power

---

[3] Kenneth Minogue, *Alien Powers: The Pure Theory of Ideology*, London, 1985, p. 226.

left-wing writers find themselves plagued not only by real institutions but also by hidden devils. Power is everywhere about them and within, implanted by the alien ideas of a dominating order. As Foucault writes:

> A stupid despot may constrain his slaves with iron chains; but a true politician binds them even more strongly by the chains of their own ideas...the link is all the stronger in that we do not know what it is made of.[4]

But the attempt to achieve a social order without domination inevitably leads to a new kind of domination, more sinister by far than the one deposed. The seeds of the new structure of power are present in the organization necessary for the violent overthrow of the old, for, as Andrew Marvell said of Cromwell:

> ...those arts that did gain
> A power must it maintain.

A study of the logic of 'revolutionary *praxis*' confirms the celebrated observation of Roberto Michels, that an 'iron law of oligarchy' constrains all revolutionary parties towards the opposite of their emancipatory goal.[5] It is a century since Michels – himself a radical socialist – expressed those thoughts, and no socialist has ever bothered to answer him, even though history has confirmed his conclusion at every point.

But what of the other complaint against our world – the complaint against 'commodification', 'reification', 'consumerism', 'instrumentalization', 'fetishism'? The labels are many, but the thing complained of is one. Newspeak veils the reality, and prevents us from perceiving this. Here too we must find the language with which the evil might be accurately described, and which will not only identify the problem, but also tell us that the problem is *ours*, not to be solved through politics, but to be managed, if at all, through a *change of life*.

The legitimate protests that are made against the 'consumer' culture urge us to distinguish two ways of living. Kant told us that we are persons, to be treated as ends and not as means. Hegel invoked our 'realization' as free subjects in a world of objects. Aristotle argued that

---

[4] *Surveiller et punir*, Paris, 1975.
[5] Roberto Michels, *Political Parties*, tr. C. and E. Paul, London, 1915.

we must discipline our appetites so that virtue triumphs over vice. Oscar Wilde distinguished things with a value from things with a price. Ends/means; subject/object; virtue/vice; value/price – all these are ways of working around a single distinction, between free beings and the temptations that threaten them. To respect humanity is to raise the human subject above the world of objects, into a realm of responsible choice. And from that realm, as we learn from the founding myth of our culture, a person may 'fall' into the world of mere things, so as to become a thing himself.

When all our aims are appetites, then all that we pursue is ephemeral and replaceable. Markets exist precisely for that reason, namely, that the objects of appetite are exchangeable. They can be traded and priced. But the things that really matter to us cannot be traded. Sex, for example, and the love that derives from it, are not marketable. To put them on sale is to void them of their human essence – and this has been known and warned against from the beginning of time, else why do we refer to the 'oldest profession'? And of course the more abundant the objects of appetite the more they capture our attention, the easier it is to obtain them and the more thickly do they overlay and obscure the realm of intrinsic values.

In every area of human interest the distinction shows itself, between things with a value and things with a price. Things with a value reward the search for them in ways that we cannot foretell, since they fulfil what we are and not what we merely want. We are sorely tempted beings, and we turn from fulfilment under the delusion that this or that bauble might provide a convenient substitute. The Old Testament warns against idolatry, which is the habit of investing mere things with a soul; modern psychology warns against addiction, in which the 'dopamine fix' expels the long-term projects of the heart; the Aristotelians tell us that happiness resides in virtue, in which reason triumphs over immediate desire; Adorno tells us that real art engages what we truly are, and that the popular fetish wraps us in the warm nothingness of clichés. We should look at all those things from the perspective of our own self-knowledge, and recognize that our happiness depends on wanting the right things, not the things that happen to capture our attention or to inspire our lust. Overcoming temptation is a spiritual task. No political system, no economic order, no dictatorship from above could possibly replace the moral discipline that we each must undergo if we are to live in a world of abundance without putting everything that is most dear to us – love, morality, beauty, God himself – on sale.

This does not mean that things have not changed for the worse. But if the problem is abundance, then are we to retreat from it, to a world in which we are once again in need? If the problem is the malleability of appetite, how are we to control it, and by what decrees? The fact is that we know the solution, and it is not a political one. We must *change our lives*. And to do this we need spiritual authority, the ability to make sacrifices, and the refusal to be degraded into the *machines désirantes* of Deleuze and Guattari. This changed way of life does not come from politics. It comes from religion and culture, and in particular from the God-imbued culture that the thinkers discussed in Chapter 7 wished to replace with a purely political way of seeing things.

That is, of course, only the first step towards an answer to all the many thinkers who have focused on idolatry, sensuality and materialism as the evils of our time – without using those words, however, since they are the natural words of the existing culture. I don't deny that people are more lost in addictive pleasures now than once they were, that businesses are ever more devoted to the manufacture of destructive appetites, that kitsch and cliché have silted up the channels of communication as they were never silted up before. But those on the left who have noticed those facts – Adorno pre-eminently – have offered no solution save Utopia, for the very reason that the solution, if it exists, is not political. Of course, we can censor advertising and the media; we can regulate the distribution of commodities; we can, up to a point, direct public subsidies to the kind of art and music that refuses to be kitsch. But this won't involve rejecting the 'capitalist' system, nor will it be effective if people have no spiritual resources that will help them to stand against their fallen nature. Without those resources all the complaints from the left are so many futile lamentations, exhortations to a revolution against original sin.

But that returns me to the real question. What is the alternative, and how do we frame a politics that respects and applies it? Three ideas, it seems to me, are fundamental to any substantial answer to the arguments I have examined in this book: civil society, institutions and personality. I will discuss each in turn.

The distinction between state and civil society was made in different ways by Burke and Hegel. Both were responding to the French Revolution, and to the confiscation of the French social inheritance that the Revolution initiated. It has been the universal experience of the twentieth century that the socialist state absorbs and extinguishes free associations, replacing them with top-down bureaucracies of its own. In the radical leftist vision all powers within civil society are ascribed, explicitly or implicitly, to the state, or to the 'class' that controls it. They belong to the ruling 'hegemony' (Gramsci) or to the 'ideological state apparatus' (Althusser). For the leftist every association, every institution, every 'little platoon' is 'always already' political. Hence, when the state steps in to abolish private schools, to nationalize industries, to confiscate church property, to replace the local rescue squad or to criminalize some 'incorrect' activity such as hunting foxes or smoking in pubs, this in no way seems like an abuse of authority. The state is in charge of social life, and in such cases it merely replaces one form of society with another and better one.

At the same time there is, in the leftist vision, scant knowledge of, let alone sympathy for, the little platoon. I noted the absence from Habermas's dreary reports of all that German art, literature and music have told us about the beauty of associations: as though Germans had never got together except when organized by bureaucrats. The *groupe en fusion* of Sartre is a 'general will' without a home, an unmediated cadre of activists, which is neither peaceful nor purposeless, but always on the march towards its next field of battle.[6] Badiou praises St Paul's 'fidelity' to his church, but the Church itself, as a place of worship, meeting and prayer, has no place in Badiou's philosophy. Williams and Thompson wax lyrical about the solidarity of the urban working class; but where, in their writings, do we encounter the chapels, brass bands, glees and study groups, the choirs, fairs and cricket clubs, the local schools and mechanics institutes, the dances, theatres and holiday clubs, and the rich social life that my father knew in the slums of Ancoats, that I knew too from my home town of Marlow on Thames and that is familiar in any case to all of us from Arnold Bennett and Thomas Hardy? In its 'totalizing' vision the left fails to distinguish civil society from the state, and fails to understand that the ends of life arise from our free associations and not from the coercive discipline of an egalitarian elite, whether or not inspired by Althusser and Gramsci.

Thanks to the law of trusts we in the Anglosphere can establish institutions and clubs without the permission of the state. Elsewhere official approval is needed, and without the rubber-stamp of the

---

[6] See the criticisms of the later work of Sartre in Raymond Aron, *D'une Sainte Famille à une autre*, Paris, 1975.

bureaucrat citizens can found neither a church nor a school, nor in any other way intrude on the sacred territory that the state wishes to control. Even in Britain and America that territory is closely guarded. It was only after a long fight by the Amish that the American Supreme Court conceded the right to home schooling and in Britain all meetings must now conform to the vigilant demands of Health and Safety and to rules of non-discrimination that make Scouts, Guides and Youth Clubs uncertain areas for those still attached to their Christian ethos. Nevertheless, institutions survive and grow, and it is through their mediating presence that politics is softened, and people are protected from the worst kinds of dictatorship.

Consider the institutions of the law. In Britain these are not, and have never been, a branch of government. The legal system is answerable to government without being controlled by it, and the judgments of the courts can be neither overruled nor dictated by the political process. Judges and barristers belong to the 'Inns of Court', private societies established around the ancient church of the Knights Templar in London. Membership of an Inn brings with it both professional standing and social warmth. My own Inn, the Inner Temple, maintains a beautiful choir and an ancient church famous for its dignified services. We have a drama club, moots and visiting speakers, gala dinners and concerts. And through this collegiate society the law gains a human face and a shared devotion to its long-lasting values.

Similar things can be said of colleges and schools, of clubs, regiments, orchestras, choirs and sporting leagues – all of which offer, along with the benefit of membership, a distinctive ethos of their own. By joining these things you not only put yourself under the conventions, traditions and obligations of the group; you acquire a sense of your own worth as a member, and a bond of association that gives meaning to your acts. Such institutions stand between the citizen and the state, offering discipline and order without the punitive sanctions through which the state exerts its sovereignty. They are what civilization consists in, and their absence from the socialist states of modern times is entirely explicable, since free association makes it impossible to achieve the 'equality of being' towards which socialists aspire. To put the matter simply: association means discrimination, and discrimination means hierarchy.

My alternative political philosophy, therefore, would advocate not only a distinction between civil society and the state, but also traditions of institution building outside the control of the state. Social life should be founded in free association and protected by autonomous bodies, under whose auspices people can flourish according to their social nature, acquiring the manners and aspirations that endow their lives with meaning. That 'right-wing' vision of politics will not be devoted to the structures of government only, or to the social stratifications and class divisions that are obsessively referred to on the left. It will be largely devoted to the building and governance of institutions, and to the thousand ways in which people enrich their lives through corporations, traditions and spheres of accountability. It will refer to politics too – to the structure of representative institutions, to the division of powers, and to the delegation of authority to civil bodies and local government (all matters that seem to have had no interest for the writers whom I have considered in this book). But it will acknowledge that institution building is as much a precondition of politics as a result of it, and it will look back with respect on the long traditions of collegiate, ecclesiastical and recreational association that have shaped the European forms of peaceful order.

This brings me to the topic of personality. By this term I mean all that pertains to the agency and accountability of individual human beings, and also of the institutions that include them. Throughout this book I have had to deal with attitudes to class and class conflict that are downstream from the Marxist theory, according to which classes are not agents but by-products of the economic order. Despite Marx's warnings to the contrary, left-wing thinkers are constantly tempted to identify classes as agents, which can be praised and blamed for what they do. If that is so, then we might reasonably argue that the bourgeoisie acts as a class in oppressing the proletariat, and that the acts of retribution that are provoked by this are not only justified but deserved. The collective agency of the ruling class is also a collective liability, and if this or that bourgeois is stripped of his rights for the sake of the new society, then this is no more than a just return for the sufferings that his class inflicted.

That pattern of thought leads as logically to the Gulag as the Nazi ideology of race led to Auschwitz. And, like the Nazi ideology, it is riddled with intellectual confusion and moral exorbitance. The New Left, in attributing agency to that which does not possess it, connived at the removal of responsibility from that which does – from the state and the party. The world of communism was a world of impersonal dominion, where all power lay with a party that could never answer for its actions nor ever be accused of them. That state of affairs was no accidental correlate of a ruling philosophy that encouraged the myth of class agency, and which saw every moderating institution, including law itself, as an elaborate conspiracy against the working class.

It was precisely in locating agency in entities that were answerable for nothing that communism created such an agency, and placed it at the summit of power. By identifying itself with a 'class' the Communist Party appropriated both the agency that its theory wrongly attributed to the proletariat and the unanswerability that in fact attaches to every social class. That, I believe, was the source of its criminal momentum. The Party was an agent whose collective decisions were subject to no law and answerable to no human purpose but its own.

The alternative is genuinely personal government, in which collective agents are also corporate persons, answerable for their actions and subject to the law. Roman Law, the *Genossenschaftsrecht* of medieval Germany, the English law of trusts and corporations – all such legal systems recognize that the features of individual human beings whereby we are moved to praise or blame them, to accord to them rights and liabilities, to oppose them and to ally ourselves to them, can be displayed by collective entities. Such systems also recognize that collective agency is a danger, until brought before the law as a composite person, equal to the individual whom it might otherwise oppress.

By the device of corporate personality the 'capitalist' world has ensured that, wherever there is agency, there is also liability. No such maxim held in the world of communism, where the Party, although the supreme agent within the state, was outside the law, and could be neither prosecuted for a crime nor sued in a civil action. That difference between the communist and capitalist worlds has been ignored or downplayed by the left, and notably by Galbraith, Thompson, Hobsbawm, Foucault and Habermas. But it has been far more important than any similarity.

The abolition of true corporate liability in the communist world meant the abolition of effective law, and this too was a direct result of leftist ways of thinking. Convinced of the absolute evil of domination, left-wing thinkers see their task as that of abolishing power. They are therefore impatient with institutions that have the limitation, rather than the abolition of power as their primary object. Such was the posture of Foucault in his early writings. Moreover, because the violent overthrow of the old order requires a greater power than that upon which it rested, left-wing revolutions have always sanctioned the destruction of limiting institutions, the law included.

The case of Foucault shows this clearly. The judiciary is seen merely as part of Althusser's 'ideological state apparatus'. The language offered by Althusser and Gramsci likewise led to a devaluing of law, a refusal to judge law by its own internal criteria, and a spurious invocation of the 'class struggle' as the fundamental fact in any conflict. Judicial independence was no longer seen for what it is – a means of standing back from human disputes in order to resolve them – but as another instrument of domination, another functional device, whereby the power of the old ruling class was preserved by an ideological fiction of justice.

Hence, throughout the period of their ascendancy, thinkers of the New Left were prodigal of excuses for the communist regimes and unable to see the real difference between the rule of the Party and the rule of law. Our European legal systems, patiently constructed upon the established results of Roman Law, Canon Law and the common law of the European nations, embody centuries of minute reflection upon the realities of human rivalry and the procedures for soothing it. Such legal systems have tried to define and to limit the activities of every important social power, and to install in the heart of the social order a principle of answerability that no agent can escape.

The rule of law is no simple achievement, to be weighed against the competing benefits of some rival political scheme. It is the *sine qua non* of political freedom, available only where law is independent of the executive power and able to stand over it in judgment. Without a rule of law opposition has no guarantee of safety, and where opposition is unprotected it also disappears. A government without opposition is without the means to correct its own mistakes or even to notice that it is making them – such, indeed, has been the kind of government introduced by leftist regimes wherever they have come to power by means of a *coup d'état* or a revolution.

Almost all the thinkers I have discussed in this book have adopted the same annihilating approach to their opponents as leftist parties in power. For the opponent is the class enemy. Should he put his head above the parapet in the culture wars he is not to be argued with, for he cannot utter truth: he is the false intellectual of Sartre, the devotee of Badiou's 'simulacrum', the person whose thought, in Žižek's words, is 'a worthless sophistic exercise, a pseudo-theorization of the lowest opportunist survivalist fears and instincts...' Such an enemy is not to be the object of negotiation or compromise. Only after his final elimination from the social order will the truth be perceivable.

In order to drown the still small voice of disagreement communist parties have had recourse to ideology – a set of doctrines, for the most part doctrines of a staggering imbecility, designed to close the avenues of intellectual enquiry. The purpose of this ideology was not that people should believe it. On the contrary, the purpose was to make belief irrelevant, to rid the world of rational discussion in all areas where the Party had staked a claim. The idea of a 'dictatorship of the proletariat' was not supposed to describe a reality; it was supposed to bring enquiry to an end, so that reality could not be perceived.

That feature of ideology has long been apparent.[7] But exactly the same goal of hiding reality behind inviolable screens of words can be found in the mathemes of Lacan and Badiou, in the litanies of Deleuze and Guattari, and in the rhetorical questions of Žižek as he patrols the world in search of those who still possess the risible belief in the Big Other and who have not yet discovered that they don't ex-sist.

The right rests its case in representation and law. It advocates autonomous institutions that mediate between the state and the citizen, and a civil society that grows from below without asking permission of its rulers. It sees government as in every matter accountable: not a thing but a person. Such a government is answerable to other persons: to the individual citizen, to the corporations, and to other governments. It is also answerable to the law. It has rights against individual citizens and also duties towards them: it is tutor and companion to civil society, the butt of our jokes and the occasional recipient of our anger. It stands to us in a human relation, and this relation is upheld and vindicated by the law, before which it comes as one person among others, on equal footing with those who are also subject to its sovereignty.

Such a state can compromise and bargain. It recognizes that it must respect persons not as means only, but as ends in themselves. It tries not to liquidate opposition but to accommodate it, and socialists too have a part to play in this process, provided they recognize that no change, not even change in their favoured direction, is or ought to be 'irreversible'. The immense achievement represented by such a state is neither respected nor noticed by radical left-wingers, who will dismiss it as 'capitalo-parliamentarism', to use Badiou's Newspeak. By demoting

---

[7] See Leszek Kołakowski, *Main Currents of Marxism*, Oxford, 1978; Raymond Aron, *L'Opium des intellectuels*, Paris, 1955; Alain Besançon, *The Intellectual Origins of Leninism*, tr. Sarah Matthews, Oxford, 1981.

law and politics to epiphenomena, and by seeing all states as 'systems' based on structures of economic control, left-wing thinking effectively blanks out the real distinctions between representative government and totalitarian dictatorship. It compares political organisms as an anatomist compares bodies: recognizing the similarity in function and structure but failing to see the person, whose rights, duties, reasons and motives are the true objects of our concern.

The pursuit of equality at all costs, and of a purely noumenal emancipation, is vain and even contradictory. Yet, however devastating the proof that equality can be pursued only at the cost of liberty, and unmediated liberty only at the cost of consensual politics, the leftist position bounces back. Žižek the jack-in-the-box and Badiou the magician are now dancing on the stage, and Deleuze grins wide from his coffin.

Why is this? Why is it that after a century of socialist disasters, and an intellectual legacy that has been time and again exploded, the left-wing position remains, as it were, the default position to which thinking people automatically gravitate when called upon for a comprehensive philosophy? Why are 'right-wingers' marginalized in the educational system, denounced in the media and regarded by our political class as untouchables, fit only to clean up after the orgies of luxurious nonsense indulged in by their moral superiors? Is it as the evolutionary psychologists say, that egalitarian attitudes result from an adaptation, one that sustained those hunter-gatherer bands when sharing the quarry was the primary social bond? Is it as the Kantians say, that we reach the bedrock of practical reason only when we have thought all empirical conditions away, and are left then with nothing but our noumenal selves, for whom equality is the only conceivable condition, since noumena have no distinguishing features? Or is it, as Nietzsche tells us, that resentment is the real default condition of social beings, who know only that the other has what they want, and must be made to suffer for it?

Whatever the explanation, we have seen, in every writer considered in this book, the assumption of an *a priori* correctness. It does not matter that equality cannot be defined or concretely situated. It is *just obvious* that it is the answer, so obvious that we have no need to define the question. At the same time there exists on the left a remarkable fear of heresy, a desire to safeguard orthodoxy and to hound the dissident – witness Althusser's response to Marxist humanism, Anderson's attacks on E. P. Thompson, Badiou's denunciation of those who pursue the 'simulacrum' instead of the true Event, Lukács's haunted search for the malignant 'ism' of the day and Sartre's denunciation of the 'false intellectuals'.

Clearly we are dealing with the religious need, a need planted deep in our 'species being'. There is a longing for membership that no amount of rational thought, no proof of the absolute loneliness of humanity or of the unredeemed nature of our sufferings, can ever eradicate. And that longing is more easily recruited by the abstract god of equality than by any concrete form of social compromise. To defend what is merely real becomes impossible, once faith appears on the horizon with its enticing gift of absolutes. Every reality must then shrivel up, reduced to a fragment of the old 'hegemony', condemned as a fetish and a simulacrum, strangled by rhizomes, scythed from its roots by the square root of minus one. As Žižek reminds us, the Real is an illusion and you, who seek to defend it, don't ex-sist.

Nobody has perceived more clearly than the reformed totalitarian Plato that argument changes its character when the onus is transferred from the one who would introduce a new order of things to the one who would keep things as they are: 'How is one to argue on behalf of the existence of the gods without passion? For we needs must be vexed and indignant with the men who have been, and still are, responsible for laying on us this burden of argument.'[8] Like Plato I have, in this book, tried to pass the burden back to the one who created it. And like Plato, I know that the onus will never be accepted.

---

[8] *Laws*, X, 887.

INDEX OF NAMES

INDEX OF SUBJECTS